The Jews of Biržai

THE LAST SABBATH

MICHAEL R BIEN

M MENSCHENIT

www.menschenit.com

Front Cover Image (top): Pictured here are some former residents or descendants from Biržai. Some witnessed, survived, or were murdered in the summer of 1941. The assigned numbers are matched with their names.

1. Gita Bass	*2. Dr. Avram Levin*	*3. Tame Khait*
4. Dr. Eliyahu Levin	*5. Morris Dishler*	*6. Aaron or Yehudah Bass*
7. Berl–David Magid	*8. Simon Chait*	*9. Leib Khait*
10. Berl–David Magid	*11. Sore Levin*	*12. Sonja Beder*
13. Gita Bass	*14. Rose Khait*	*15. Tauba Bass*
16. Reba Kirsch	*17. Isaac Khait*	*18. Gershon Bilicki*
19. Tauba Bass	*20. Rifka Bass*	*21. Aaron Bass*
22. Itzik Mas	*23. Rabbi drawing by*	*24. Yehudah Bass*
	Robert Kirsch	

Front Cover Image (bottom): A picture of Biržai, circa 1915, reproduced by permission of Tomasz Wiśniewski.

Back Cover Image: The Watch Maker is a charcoal drawing created by Robert Kirsch.

This is a work of narrative non-fiction. Names, characters, places, incidents, and events portrayed in this book are largely factual though there is some slight restructuring of events and creative dialogue to effectively reproduce the daily lives and struggles of the people of Biržai. This is done minimally as extensive research into historical documents and personal interviews were conducted and memoirs are referenced that authenticate the events that occurred in Biržai in the summer of 1941 and sadly culminated in its holocaust on August 8, 1941.

Copies of this book may be purchased through online retailers and independent bookstores or by contacting the author directly.

Front and Back Cover Design – JoAnn Barnes

Library of Congress Cataloging-in-Publication Data has been applied for
Michael R. Bien

ISBN 979-8-9850223-0-8 (Paperback)
ISBN 979-8-9850223-2-2 (Hardback)
ISBN 979-8-9850223-1-5 (e-book)

First Edition: December 2021

10 9 8 7 6 5 4 3 2 1

Published by Menschenit, www.menschenit.com.

This book is dedicated to God, for the life He has given me, the joys He has brought to my life, His spiritual direction, and His guidance to always do the right things.

This book is dedicated to my family for tolerating my total immersion into Biržai and enabling my compulsion to complete this project so I could eulogize an entire community.

For the Jewish citizens of Biržai who, perished in the summer of 1941, and all victims of the Holocaust, who lost their lives in a most horrific fashion.

For the descendants of Biržai and survivors of the Holocaust who gave us life even though they were surrounded by death.

For all the people that I bothered tracking down every possible piece of data in various languages.

In memory of Gillian Kay, the feisty South Afrikaner, and another descendant from Biržai, who was murdered. May her spirit and gust for life inspire us all to live more tolerant lives.

Table of Contents

Foreword

Written By: Abel and Glenda Levitt

W e became actively involved with Lithuania about twenty years ago, where we focused on the town of Plungyan[1]. Abel's father was from Plungyan and many of his relatives, including his grandmother, uncles, aunts, and cousins were all murdered by local Lithuanians, supervised by two Germans in July 1941. We helped establish a Tolerance Center at the Saules Gimnazija in Plungyan and a couple of years later we established an annual art competition at the school, which has now grown to incorporate the inclusion of many additional schools in Lithuania. In 2011, we collected donations and erected a memorial wall with names of victims alongside the mass graves outside Plungyan. This was the first ever memorial in Lithuania where names of Holocaust victims were placed at the actual site of the mass graves.

While we were visiting Lithuania again in 2014, we learned from our friend Ingrida Vilkiene, responsible for Tolerance Centers throughout Lithuania, that we would be traveling to Birzh[2] to meet two special people. Neither of us had ever heard of Biržai and with some reluctance we agreed to go. After meeting with the impressive teachers, Vidmantas Jukonis and his son, Merūnas, they took us to

---

[1] Plungė is a northwestern town in Lithuania, Plungyan in Yiddish.

[2] Biržai (Lithuanian), Birzh (Yiddish), and Birsen (German) are the multiple references of the town.

1

meet Irute Varziene, the then mayor of the town. Having heard of what we had done in Abel's ancestral town of Plungyan, Irute asked us if we would do something similar for Birzh and we agreed to help in some way.

Ten days later, while we were on holiday in Cape Town, South Africa, we went to visit Ben Rabinowitz, a friend and a renowned philanthropist. We approached him about donating to help our projects in Plungyan. Ben immediately and heatedly answered, "Plungyan, I've got nothing to do with Plungyan! Go and ask Plungyaners. My family comes from the shtetl Birzh." We were astounded and intrigued to hear, once again, someone mention the same town we had never heard of until just recently. Ben was astonished to hear that not only had we just been to Birzh, but it was a functioning town. He had heard that it had been destroyed during World War II.

After we returned home to Israel, my sister Rolene and I discussed the fact that regretfully, we didn't know our maternal grandmother's maiden name, nor where she had been born. We only knew she had married in Rakishok. Not long after that discussion, Abel, by sheer coincidence, was at a shiva house and recognized someone whom he thought was related to Glenda's late mother. Abel approached Max Pesach, and a meeting was arranged in Max's hometown in Beersheba, Israel, to examine his family tree. After paging through Max's family tree looking for any linkage to our grandmother, Rolene and I suddenly, found our grandmother's name, Ada Blume, including her maiden name, Peskowitz. To our absolute astonishment, we discovered that she was born in Birzh. We were initially doing this project based on our promise to the Mayor and Ben's connection to Birzh, to help honor the story of the Jews of Birzh in a town we had never heard of, and now we had our own very personal connection to this town.

With the project taking shape, we were off and running and we flew to the United States to meet with and interview Allan Evans, from Queens, New York, to learn from him and make a connection with Jonathan Dorfan, from Palo Alto, California. We returned home to Israel, now with the spark and inspiration on what we needed to do and how to undertake this project. Together, we agreed with Ben Rabinowitz, that the Birzh project would be similar to what we had completed in Plungyan. We would build a memorial wall with names, engage with the students, help to create a Tolerance Center in the high school, honor the Savers of Jews, and we would also conduct a tour for Birzh descendants.

Next, we visited Yad Vashem to examine the list of victims murdered in the forest of Birzh. Sadly, we found the names of a few of our family members that had been murdered on August 8, 1941. Our commitment grew with intensity as I became inextricably bound to the place of my roots and my sorrow.

Word spread quickly of the planned tour to Birzh; inquiries streamed in and connections were made from Israel, South Africa, England, France, Canada, and the United States. We were struck by an email we received from a man named Michael Bien. People responded to our suggestions about interacting with locals, but it was Michael who answered with an intriguing idea. He suggested that we ask every tour participant to write about themselves and their connection to Birzh and then present that information during the tour to foster a sense of community.

We gave this thought-provoking proposition serious thought. We considered the fact that there would be a gathering of approximately fifty people together from all over the world for one or two weeks with nothing in common other than their Birzh ancestry. Michael's initiative resulted in an unforgettable evening in Birzh of shared stories. This evening of fostering connections was marked with warmth, instant bonding, a comradeship, and a feeling of being together with landsleit[3] that has remained ongoing within our group to this date. It was an outstanding evening. Michael absorbed every aspect of our

---

3   Landsleit means fellow Jews in Yiddish, those who come from the same district or town, especially in Eastern Europe.

multi-faceted journey and returned home with a burning desire to express what he experienced into creating a pulsating, living tale of the Jews of Birzh.

Michael is a man who understands the power of the written word.

This book is a follow-up to the 2019 tour and memorial dedication. It is a hugely important vehicle to help remember the names of those murdered. Michael's book is no less necessary than the memorial.

To craft this book, Michael compiled both his tour experiences and his deep research required to cover daily life, jobs and work, religious life, education and schools, dating, marriage, children, culture and leisure activities. This book remembers and describes the daily life of Jews leading to the period that started with the advent of Nazism in the 1930s.

Because of Michael and this book, I made a startling discovery. After receiving the first draft of his book, I sat down with a cup of coffee and immersed myself into the bygone days of Birzh. As Michael's story unfolded, drawing a picture of daily life, I suddenly came across a sentence which took my breath away: "Motel Levitan and his wife, Chaya (nee Pesakhovich), and their baby son, Leiba." I had just discovered more Birzh family. I phoned Rolene with this great news, who said, "So carry on reading, there may be more to discover." Sure enough, she was right; Motel and Chaya are mentioned once again, this time with the lively little Leiba and their new baby Golda. Then came the extraordinarily heart-wrenching revelation in Michael's description of the day of the murder, where he describes in painstaking detail the events that led to 2,400 souls murdered on one day, including some of our family members.

Thank you, Michael, for giving us readers an invaluable gift of putting into words the daily life, the joys, the sadness, the pressures, the tensions, and the terrible end—the story of our ancestors.

The Jews of Biržai draws the reader gently into the pre-World War II life of Birzh Jews—the everyday normalcy, the joys, sorrows, and concerns that were experienced. The reader participates as the story evolves from normalcy to concern, to anxiety, to fear, and finally to the resignation of betrayal, hopelessness, and the horror of an inevitable reality of fate.

In *The Jews of Biržai*, our work in Birzh culminates. This book will help keep alive the feeling we experienced during the ceremony that dedicated the memorial. While only a handful of the relatives of the murdered were able to attend the tour, your book memorializes not only the lives of our relatives, but the life and death of the Birzh shtetl. Yes, there were some difficult parts to read because of the horrors that occurred in the summer of 1941, but there were also many positive and hopeful stories from both the Jewish people who suffered through this time and the righteous who helped and saved some of them. We thank Michael, from the bottom of our hearts, for his passion, commitment, and friendship, and for this book that provides a legacy of the shtetl and the Jewish inhabitants, including our ancestors.

Prologue

L
ike many Americans, I descend from immigrants who came to this country seeking a better life for themselves, their children, grandchildren, and, ultimately, for me and my family. Through my genealogical research, I discovered I am an ethnic mix of German, Lithuanian, and Estonian, and a third-generation American Jew.

While growing up in Philadelphia, I was told very little about my heritage, though I was always interested in learning more about my Eastern European ancestors. What had been shared with me was my distant relatives in Europe were Jewish, like me, and they were raised Orthodox, not like me. When I fell in love and married Teresa, a lovely Irish-Italian, Roman-Catholic woman, I moved a little further away from the traditions of my extended family, but remained curious about who they were as people.

Teresa and I lived in England during our first year of marriage. We returned home to America in the fall of 1994, newlyweds eager to set down roots and build our lives here. Among the first people we visited was my grandmother, Reba Kirsch (nee Chait), whom we called Mom Mom (figure 1). Sitting in her small kitchen in Philadelphia, eating cookies and drinking tea, Teresa peppered Reba with questions about our family history. Traditionally, Reba had been the best source for stories about everyone in our family and quickly filled Teresa in with everything she could remember about everybody. While Teresa heard them for the first time, I sipped my tea and listened with fresh ears, watching both of them enjoy each other's company.

Figure 1. Reba Kirsch in Philadelphia in 1952.
Permission of Phyllis Soufer (nee Kirsch).

At one point, Reba rose quickly from her chair and almost sprinted to the infamous family drawer. You know the drawer I mean; we all have one in our kitchens. She shuffled through it for a minute before returning to the table with a small pile of papers and suddenly...no, not suddenly...more like finally—that pile of papers in her hand is what led me to write this book for the many generations who will follow us, for those who will now know and I pray never forget, the Jews of Biržai.

Reba's papers inspired Teresa and me to begin conducting what wound up to be years of research filled with sprees of letter writing and cold calling, trips to libraries to read microfiche, and hours of asking and answering questions with family members, so we could publish a coffee-table book about our families.

What my grandmother handed to us almost forty years ago is what we now refer to as "genealogical gold." We use that phrase for a couple of reasons. First, it is truly priceless. Literally, and from our perspective, of course, you cannot put a price tag on certain original documents, pictures, and signatures from relatives. Second, the information contained within them solved huge research questions. Finding such papers often happens during the research process; rarely do they kick-start a project, and seldom does such an ah-ha moment get pulled out of a junk drawer and placed into the researcher's lap.

We knew immediately that the gold mined from my grandmother's junk drawer was valuable and important information regarding the family history. So, guess what we did with it? Nothing! Absolutely nothing! Sure, we were intrigued by the aged, yellowed, one-hundred-plus-year-old documents, but we had not yet coined the phrase "genealogical gold" and didn't quite have the same reaction we would thankfully later embrace. As newlyweds, we had other things on our minds. We politely accepted the ancient, handwritten Yiddish letters and postcards, along with a much-worn ketubah[4] (held together by strips of Band-Aids), thanked her, and went on our way.

We soon found a place to live and proceeded to perform what amounted to an ironic symmetry: we transferred Reba's "genealogical gold" from her junk drawer to ours. As the years slid by, we proceeded to have the predictable family of the dog, cat, and two kids that everyone dreams about. The letters were safe. They remained hidden from daylight for decades. Although protected, they couldn't translate themselves. They continued to grow more fragile from age. So, too, were our parents and grandparents, the folks we needed to unlock the family secrets from the old country.

At one point, when my parents were preparing to downsize from their Northeast Philadelphia home to a new community, my mother Phyllis Soufer (nee Kirsch) handed Teresa and me bags of old black and white photos: picnics, bar mitzvahs, weddings, school photos, and the whole gambit that families collect through the years. As we perused the musty-smelling box of old pictures, our inquisitive sons walked into the room. Our five-year-old asked, "Who are these people?" and without knowing it, he got this whole megillah[5]

---

4   Ketubah is the standard marriage contract that Jewish law requires a groom to provide to his bride on their wedding day.

5   Megillah means scroll or volume in Hebrew. Usage translates to a long involved story or account.

off and running. Because the older generations lacked the insight to know their progeny might want to know the answer to that very basic question, they might have written names on the back of the pictures. But no, that would be way too easy. They must have believed we would be up for the challenge to find out.

So, there we were. Fate had nudged an octogenarian grandmother to put in our hands documents over a hundred years old that nobody could read, then prompted a sexagenarian mother to give us one-hundred-plus-year-old pictures nobody could identify, and blessed us with an innocent son who asked a simple question that nobody could answer. Yes. Finding the answers was our mission. And we finally decided to accept it. As you will see from the next set of chapters and stories, we got way more than we bargained for in our research. As they say, "the rest is history," and that will be explained in this book.

Sadly, in 2003, Mom Mom (Reba) passed away just as we started the project. Of all the family members who assisted and contributed to it, she was the most engaged. Neither in her kitchen in 1994, nor on her death bed in 2003, did she know where her immigrant, Yiddish-speaking parents were from. Russia was the standard answer, or "the old country." But, thanks to Google Translate, we were able to translate one Cyrillic letter at a time on a postmark from a 1905 postcard that she had given to us (figure 2). Those letters pointed to a small shtetl in Lithuania called Biržai.

After conducting some basic research on the town we'd just discovered, it immediately became very clear that something really awful happened there in August 1941. Something much more than awful.

Twenty-four hundred people were massacred.
Men: . . . . .720 killed.
Women: . . . . . .780 killed.
And children: . .900 killed.

Figure 2. Postcard from Leib Khait to Isaac Khait from Biržai to Amsterdam in 1906. Reproduced by permission of Phyllis Soufer.

On a hot, humid, ill-fated day, August 08, 1941, 2,400 people were murdered. Massacred. The official records tell the world that 900 children, 780 women, and 720 men were murdered between eleven o'clock in the morning and seven o'clock in the evening on that single day, in that small, once-serene town in northern Lithuania. It was an otherwise unremarkable summer morning when none of the doomed men, women, and children had any expectation that death would come so suddenly, so mercilessly on that day.

The massacre of those innocent, defenseless people was just one incident among many of slaughter and mass executions committed throughout Europe by killing squads of Nazi German soldiers and their local collaborators under the swastika flag of the German Third Reich. It was part of their insane leader's master plan to remove the Jewish people from Europe, and later from the face of the earth, a plan ominously titled the Final Solution.

The research and the link to Biržai made the Holocaust very personal for me and my family. My great-grandfather came to the United States in 1905. He had never mentioned the seven sisters who had remained there, six of whom would be killed later in the Holocaust, a few slaughtered on that fateful day in Biržai.

I have since added multiple names of my family members, and many others who were murdered there, to the Yad Vashem Shoah databases. Through this book, I am striving to personalize and memorialize as many of the 2,400 who had died that day as I can by depicting the rise and genocide of the Jewish population in Biržai, Lithuania, as seen through the eyes of survivors, and based on their memories.

My intention of this book is to remember the fallen by changing your perspectives of them. They will no longer be nondescript murder victims. Instead, they will be real people with real names, lives, families, faces, stories, and hopes and dreams.

Author's note: The use of italics scattered occasionally throughout the book is selected to present historical information and events which are closely related to the specific time or place depicted in the current chapter.

PART I:

A 20-Year Simmer

"One Man's Dream Is Another Man's Nightmare...
It's All About Your Prospective People"

Timothy Pina

CHAPTER 1:

Returning Home

Steady clouds of billowing steam dutifully trailed above the long line of wooden boxcars as the old weather-beaten locomotive pulled its cargo closer to its final destination. The decades-old steam engine had labored bravely to cover its 1,000-mile journey, stopping only twice for the necessary coal and water it required to keep it moving forward. Fortunately, the distance it covered was mostly on flat ground with few mountains and nearly zero twists and turns along the way—moving steadily on the straight line of railroad track stretching monotonously westward from Kazan, Russia to Biržai, Lithuania. The only landmark of any importance on the route was Moscow, Russia's capital city, which lay at the mid-way point between the two towns. Moscow held no interest in either of the small towns, and the people in those small towns thought even less often about Russia's capital city.

The passengers in this long line of boxcars were completing the return part of a roundtrip that originated from Biržai five years earlier. Both journeys were thrust upon the Jews of Biržai by the order of government authorities who decreed their removal from their homes. The families were not consulted prior to either move. They were not asked for their opinion. Cautioned by a long history of anti-Semitism, they said very little, heard even less, and never questioned authority. Life was tenuous for Jewish people living in Europe. It was more so in 1920. With acquired wisdom, they understood things happened

15

when they did. The present was their immediate concern and tomorrow was the extent of their planning for the future. They knew their future was in their own hands only until it suddenly wasn't. The good news this time rested in the knowledge this train would take them home to Lithuania, to a place where they might be safe, and they could all renew their lives as they were in 1915.

✡

Biržai, a small town, barely more than a village at that time, was nestled between two rivers in northeastern Lithuania near the borders of two neighboring countries: Latvia to the north and Russia to the west. Though some of the people in Biržai knew the train was coming, no one knew exactly when it would arrive. That's how the governments worked in Eastern Europe after the First World War. The war, praised at its beginning as 'the war to end all wars,' had devastated the continent. After four years of destruction (1914–1918), all of the countries in Europe, both the victors and the conquered, were crippled: their economies and political and social institutions were in disorder. Political unrest, economic stagnation, extreme unemployment, and starvation were rampant. The most notable example in 1920 was on Biržai's western border where Russia suffered post-war chaos after a bloody revolution in 1917 forced Russia's Tsar Nicholas II to abdicate his crown in March 1917. He and his wife, Alexandra, and their children were held captive and later murdered in July 1918. Political and social upheaval threatened all of the countries across Europe as the train of boxcars continued its steady course to Biržai.

In the thirtieth hour of the journey, the thunderous roar of the locomotive and its train of cars was reduced considerably as the engine slowed from thirty miles an hour to ten, then to five as it began its approach into the train depot. The repetitive clackety-clack noise of the boxcars' wheels on the rusty steel rails grew more noticeable as the engine quieted and the train crawled to a stop alongside the platform, successfully delivering its cargo to the quiet village of Biržai.

Figure 3. A European map that highlights the location of Biržai in northern Lithuania. Reproduced by permission of © OpenStreetMap contributors.

Once the engine and the boxcars halted, a deafening silence remained. There was no sound, not even birds chirping, as the dying clouds of steam descended onto the boxcars. The chalky white clouds drifted eerily past the cars, unveiling locked and windowless, shabby, wooden structures bolted onto wheels. There was no sound coming from inside these cars while the passengers inside waited anxiously for the next instruction to be issued from the train's Russian crewmen.

Without windows, and without sounds coming from within the train, the people on the platform stared at what appeared to be a ghost train. There was no sign of life. The cars were battered and old, a mixture of thirty-two and forty-foot-long units. None of the cars looked safe. They were falling apart; most of them pre-dated the First World War by one or two decades. All of the boxcars were originally built to carry cargo, cattle, wheat, and sometimes military equipment, even soldiers in wartime or for military exercises. They were used all across Russia and its neighboring border countries. Constructed of wood, the difference between the two sizes were the steel beams running from end to end across the tops of the larger cars. The smaller cars had steel frames added in vertical and horizontal alignment to reinforce the wooden walls. All of the cars had wooden floors. The cars were not insulated; they were rife with holes on all sides and leaky roofs, making them frightfully cold in winter and fiercely hot in the summer. If necessary during military campaigns, the larger cars could accommodate fifty soldiers and then only for short distances because there was no latrine, no bunk accommodations, and no windows for circulation.

This was the method of transportation for the Jews of Biržai who were being repatriated to the homes they were exiled from in 1915. The passage was free of charge, but its price was at the expense of degradation, over-crowding, and physical and emotional abuse.

✡

Berl-David Magid was seven years old and he was a veteran of the family's first ride in a boxcar. He was barely a year old when the family was exiled to Kazan. Now, he and his family and carloads of other families were completing a thirty-hour ride without food and water except for the few provisions they managed to keep hidden from the Tartar guards who took anything they could pry loose from the transients. The men, women, and children were loaded into the boxcars in Kazan; loaded like cattle, each car was packed with 100-150 people, two to three times more than capacity. The latrine facilities consisted of buckets in the corner of the cars which were emptied through a single narrow opening located chest-high in the boxcar's side wall while the train was moving.

The smell was vile. Berl covered his nose when he could, even holding his breath for short periods of time because the stench of the latrine buckets and the crush of sweaty bodies upon bodies jammed together without any air circulation was awful and nauseating. But it was impossible for him to do anything else to find an escape from the smells. He couldn't move except to slide down onto the floor and inch his body sideways just to see his mother and father and siblings around him. Fortunately, the majority of the people in each car were family or friends and neighbors so they cooperated with one another to allow some minor movements, taking turns using the buckets, sitting or leaning against the walls, but the rocking motion of the boxcars and the lack of air on the wooden floors made two of those 'luxuries' barely worth the effort. For many adults, the thirty hours were primarily spent standing upright and leaning on each other for support, a mass of bodies rocking back and forth in unison to the rhythm of the wheels against the steel rails—half of them asleep, the other half exhausted but too worried and anxious about the future to sleep. Children and the elderly took turns seated in little air pockets on the floor, but they needed to be rotated to be certain none of them died from asphyxiation or dehydration. Even with such precautions, some passengers did not survive the long train ride home.

While the clouds of steam and smoke from the resting engine slowly dissipated, the station master and a small collection of welcoming neighbors stood on the wooden platform staring left and right at the long line of cars not knowing which way to look, expecting one large sliding door or a small rectangular opening on the sidewall to open. The doors handles were on the left side of the door facing them and the slide rail for the door indicated the door would slide left to right. Still, nothing moved. The station master was the first person to notice the chains and locks on the door handles. He stepped toward the closest car.

"Don't touch that door," bellowed a large beefy man with a caustic Russian accent. He was slowly trudging his way toward the station master. "I'll open it."

Inside the car, standing beneath the small rectangular cutout on the side wall closest to the platform, Berl heard the man's voice and the words, "I'll open it." He and others who heard the words were excited and hopeful this was the last stop. They began to move closer toward the side wall. "We're home at last," was their single thought.

The beefy man pulled a large set of keys dangling from his dirty, baggy work pants and placed a brass key into the lock. He slipped the hook on the top of the lock out of the loop on the door handle, then tugged on the chain until it fell to the ground. Now grunting loudly, he braced his legs, placed his hands and arms on the edge of the door and pushed with all his strength to force the door to slide open.

The door rumbled noisily along a bottom rail attached to the outside of the boxcar until the door was flown wide open. Before a word could be said by anyone, Berl felt his eyes sting from the massive wave of light flooding into the car, momentarily blinding him and everyone around him. It was as if he was staring directly into a blazing sun. Immediately, daylight and clean, crisp, fresh air came rushing over everyone in the car. Once his eyes finally opened, he realized why he could not move. There were bodies all around him ten people deep on the side closest to the wall where the door opened and as many as thirty to fifty people deep on the other three sides around him. Some were sitting. There was no joyous noise.

How long had he, had they, been like this? Inside the boxcar without light, movement, or any reference points, time had no meaning for him, for anyone. But now there were happy sounds. Faint at first, then louder as more car doors were opened and people removed themselves and others from the temporary prison cells. In the rush of exiting the car, Berl was separated from his family. He called out, "Ima,"[6] in a croaking voice; it was the first time he had raised his voice louder than a whisper in almost three days. Frightened after hearing no answer from his mother among the many voices all calling out to find and reconnect with loved ones and family, he repeated, "Ima," once again.

"Over here! I'm over here," shouted his mother.

---

6   Ima or Eama means mother in Hebrew.

He was safe. He was with his mother and family. Safe. Away from Russia. Home in the countryside. Freed from the dilapidated wooden boxcar and the rusty coal-dusted locomotive. Safe from war now that the 'war to end all wars' was over.

✡

After they exited the boxcar, the Magid family walked to the brewery where they were shocked to learn the shtetl and their house were burned to the ground by the Germans during the war. The Magids were now homeless, destitute; they were bezshentses[7] and would live in the brewery until they could rebuild their lives. Moishe and Sheina, husband and wife, were already anxious about the trip home and this news made them more unnerved. But now they were hungry. Just before they began their journey back from Kazan, the Tartars robbed the exiles of all their food, including the baked goods Sheina Magid had prepared for the journey east. Sheina's anxiety was peaking at the moment Berl interrupted her thoughts.

"Ima, I can't wait to get back to our house! When do we get back home?" he asked with childish excitement.

Trying to be brave and reassuring, yet remain honest, she told him what happened to their house and the shtetl during World War I. "Our sweet home is gone, but don't you worry, we will live at the brewery for a little while and we will be fine in no time," she said sweetly in her well-practiced motherly voice.

But Berl's curiosity still wasn't finished. "Ima, what is a shet-all?"

Ever patient, she smiled at her youngest son and explained that shtetl means "little town" in Yiddish, and refers to the small, Jewish market towns in Eastern Europe and Russia during the nineteenth and early twentieth centuries. She went on to tell him the shtetls range in size from several hundred to several thousand residents, that

7   Bezshentes means refugees in Yiddish.

forests and fields often surrounded them, and gentiles (or non-Jews) tended to live outside of the shtetls, while Jews lived within.

This was more than Berl cared to know about shtetls but he listened closely out of respect for his mother.

"The streets," his mother added, "were, for the most part, unpaved, and the houses constructed of wood." Berl's respect for his mother's explanation of a shtetl was not strong enough to hide his fidgeting and growing disinterest in shtetls from his mother's eyes. Otherwise, she would've told him the names of all the public areas in a shtetl such as the synagogues (often wooden), the beit midrash,[8] shtiblekh,[9] the Jewish cemetery, the Christian churches (Russian Orthodox or Roman Catholic, depending on the location), bathhouses, and, of course, the marketplace. But as mothers do, she understood he had heard enough. She stopped, smiled at him, and asked him if she had answered his question.

With such an extensive explanation to ingest, Berl said what most seven-year-old children would say.

"Yes," he replied, and swiftly directed his attention elsewhere.

✡

How was it possible that some human beings would force other human beings to accept this ordeal? But they did. Berl-David Magid, a seven-year-old Lithuanian Jew, his family, and many other Jews of Biržai had survived this odyssey twice—once in 1915 when they were transported from Biržai to Kazan during World War I, and now as they returned to their home in Biržai in 1920. Berl, his father Moishe Magid, mother Sheina Rivka Magid, brothers Naftali and Khatseh-Maneh, and sisters Sore Libe and Zelda endured both journeys. Perl, his youngest sister, was born during their exile in Russia.

---

8   Beit midrash means study house in Hebrew.

9   Shtiblekh means a smaller, residential house of prayer in Yiddish.

Figure 4. Standing from right to left: Zelda Magid, Berl-David Magid, Sore-Libe Magid, Naftali Chaim Magid, and Perl Magid. Seated: Moishe Aba Magid and Sheina-Rivka Magid. Source: Berl-David Magid, *What I Have To Tell: Pages From a Life* (Peretz Publishing, 1992).

So it was the Magid family returned to Biržai destitute and homeless and moved into a brewery. Nevertheless, the parents and the children were delighted they were home and grateful for their freedom.

They struggled to rebuild their lives. Later, they lived in a house in an orchard near an ancient, princely castle. They were safe and free to begin their lives again, unaware of the stormy clouds of war and the spectra of the Holocaust gathering in the distance.

✡

For geographical and genealogical reference, Biržai is an ancient, northern Lithuanian municipality, located on the European continent just south and west of the Latvian and Russian borders. It lies between the Apaščia and Agluona rivers, as well as between two lakes, Lake Širvėna and Lake Kilučiai. The etymology behind the name Biržai reflects the geography of the area, in particular the abundance of birch trees, or beržynas in Lithuanian (a small forest of birch trees is beržynėlis). It was customary for Lithuanian

23

shtetls to have a nickname. Biržai's Yiddish nickname was Birzher groypn zuper which literally translates to "Birzher barley sippers." Grouypn can mean grain for cereal or barley for beer (Biržai has a large beer industry), and zupen means to sip. So, barley sippers could also mean beer drinkers, yielding "Biržai beer drinkers," which makes much more sense in context.

Lithuanian Jews, or Litvaks as they were called, first settled in Biržai in the sixteenth or early seventeenth century. The Magid family was originally from Vabalninkas, a tiny village in the district of Biržai where Moishe Aba Magid, Berl's great-grandfather and the author of a religious book, had a stellar reputation as a scholar. By 1921, a year after the Magids returned with many of the other Jewish families, the Jewish population swelled to approximately 1,200—three quarters of all homes in the area were owned by Jews.

The shtetl in Biržai was slightly different from most at that time. In the shtetl in Biržai, the Jews had their own community. Though they were clustered together in harmony with each other, they were also part of the larger community and lived amicably with their Christian neighbors. Jews and non-Jews alike considered themselves, above everything else, Lithuanians living together in the town of Biržai.

Figure 5. A view of the Biržai Shtetl in 1915 from the Apaščia River. Reproduced by permission of Tomasz Wiśniewski.

Figure 6. The Great Beit Midrash and the Great Synagogue on Karaimų Street. Reproduced by permission of Biržai Region Museum Sėla.

Unfortunately, while the shtetl life provided rich religious education and wisdom, it may have fallen short on providing a global or worldly view for its citizens. They did not study the advanced topics in their schools and were behind the times on western culture. Their focus was on piety, mysticism, culture, and family. These values may seem alien in today's modern world, but they provided a uniqueness and a way of life that worked for hundreds of years. They led a fine Jewish life before they were deported to Russia.

The deportations began in 1915, near the beginning of the First World War when the Russians announced Jews living in Russian-Polish towns in Lithuania, including Biržai, would be forced to leave. No one would openly say why that was necessary. Rumor mills provided many reasons including false accusations and newspaper articles with lies about the Jewish people. One particular incident reportedly happened close to Biržai in a village named Kuziai. There it was rumored that Jewish people had attacked Russian troops. The accusation ultimately gave the Russian authorities their justification for expelling the Jews from all of Lithuania. It was at that time that the Magids, among many other Jewish families, were loaded into crowded freight cars and carried eastward to the Volga area of Russia where they were required to settle.

The lies followed them. The transporters told everyone the Jews were spies, not refugees who were forced to leave their homes. Consequently, they were treated very badly. The trains did not stop at stations; the people were locked in the cars for days. And when they arrived in Kazan, more than a thousand miles away from Biržai, many climbed out of the boxcars sick and infirm, only to find few families in Russia who would accept them. Instead, they struggled to find homes. When the Magids arrived in Kazan, there were approximately 1,500 Jews already there. As more Jews arrived from Lithuania, their numbers swelled to 4,000. Though the Jews had a community, the conditions in Kazan were so harsh that several neighbors from Biržai suffered and died there during the first war. Fortunately, the Russians, who had put restrictions on Jews practicing their faith in other Russian cities, relaxed their laws for Kazan. They allowed Jews to practice their faith on a regular basis. This provided some solace and strengthened their community until the war was over and they were returned to Biržai.

✡

A map of the Biržai shtetl (figure 7) shows the location where the Jews of Biržai primarily lived. The complete listing (table 4) of the streets in the shtetl and the Jewish families that lived there, including their house number and year they lived on the street where that data was available, can be found in the End Notes section the book. Some of the street names have changed:

- Rinkos, formerly J. Janonio
- Zemaites, formerly Apaščios
- Zemoji, formerly Rabino Lintupio

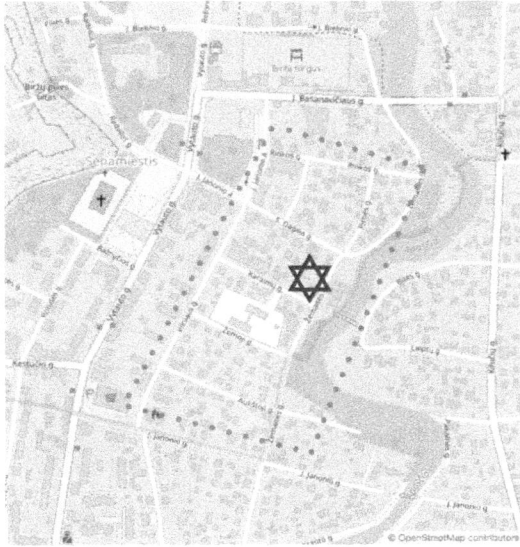

Figure 7. Re-creation of the Biržai Shtetl. The Jewish star represents the location of the synagogues and the ritual bath locations, and the red dotted line is the outline of the ghetto established in July 1941. Illustration by author.

CHAPTER 2:

Renewing Friendships

About 100,000 Lithuanian Jews returned from Russia after the end of the Great War in 1918. This helped form a Jewish community of over 160,000 in independent Lithuania. But not all Jews had to find shelter in a brewery or elsewhere. The Beder family of Biržai were a little more fortunate than the Magid family. They were able to return to their original home on a small farm at 21 Vytauto Street.

Sheina Magid realized her children probably didn't remember much about their first home and their life in the shtetl since they had been gone for years, so she had an idea. Shortly after the deported families were settled in their new homes, she decided to take her children to meet with the Beder family, who were their close friends. She would be able to check in on her friend to see how they were doing since they had returned to their original house and farm. Sheina was looking forward to sharing stories about shtetl life with the children. Khane-Sora Beder[10] (nee Novosedz) was the matriarch. She lived there with her husband, Berel, and her children: Motel-Yosel, Chackelis,[11] and Sonja.

---

10   Sonja's mother is also spelled Chana/Khane-Leye but I've standardized to Khane-Sora.

11   Sonja's brother is also spelled Khaskele/Khatzkele/Chaska but I've standardized to Chackelis.

"It is so great that we were all able to get home and return from Russia," were the first words Khane-Sora Beder said when she saw Sheina.

"Yes, I don't know what was worse—the freight car and the train ride, or being packed in the cattle trucks," Sheina replied.

"I agree. So, tell me, Sheina, how you are doing? Wait. Before you start, do you want some tea?" Sheina nodded her head affirmatively and Khane-Sora turned to go outside to the well to get water. "I'll check on the kids while I am out there."

Once outside, Khane-Sora opened the fence that her family shared with the neighbors adjacent to them at the rear of the house. The well stood here between the two properties and it was shared among the neighbors, something that many families did in small towns. She drew the water from the well and before going back inside, she yelled toward the kids.

"If you kids need to go to the bathroom, this one is where you go." She pointed to a specific outhouse. There were three of them: one for the parents, one strictly for the children, and a third one for strangers. She was pleased with the multiple outhouses and with the arrangement with local farmers who came and took away the waste in the middle of the night, not in the daytime. As she walked back to the house, she thought to herself, "I still don't know what they do with that waste," slowly shaking her head from side to side. Khane-Sora carried the water back into the kitchen, and the two mothers moved forward with catching up.

"So," Sheina began, "tell me all about how Berel and the family business is doing before we bring in the kids."

Before updating Sheina on her husband and their business, Khane-Sora poured the fresh well water into the kettle on the stove, then stoked the fire to be certain it was still hot from earlier in the morning. "Sheina," she began. "My mother is still running her bakery from the house. She uses the oven every day to cook her famous bagels with her special recipe. People come all the way from Latvia to eat her bagels. When they get to be a bit stale, mom gives them to the poor, such a good heart with that woman."

She went on to explain to Sheina that their re-opened general store in town was doing well. Their family business specialized in fish and the customers called her husband "Berel the Fisher," pleased that he was the fisherman who would do the fishing for them.

"In fact," Khane-Sora confessed. "My husband Berel couldn't catch a fish if it hadn't eaten for three days and was swimming in a bucket." The ladies let out a great laugh. "But he is good at keeping those fish from spoiling. We have a little building with blocks of ice where he keeps those fish. That shack of his is not the cleanest, so if you don't mind a little sawdust on your fish, it will at least be very cold." They laughed again, feeling so free and safe to be home again.

Sheina and Khane-Sora went on like this for a while, exchanging stories and sharing good laughs before they herded the kids in for some hot bagels. They decided they would skip the sawdust fish for lunch.

After the kids had some food in their stomachs and had played outside in the fresh air for a while, they were better able to focus on the stories that Khane-Sora began to share with them.

"As you look down our town streets, you will see a mixture of some stone buildings like churches, the police station, government buildings, and the post office, mixed in with older wooden structures which are primarily houses and businesses. The wooden structures are of various sizes and shapes and the roof lines are mostly triangular, but they are made of different materials. Our house, like your house now and the one you had before you went to Russia, are wooden and are built close together. I am told they assembled a great volunteer fire brigade just before we returned. I hear your cousin Simon Chait will be joining some of the other Jewish fire brigade members including Chief Gershon Belicki, photographer Boruch Michelson, and Itzik Mas."

Figure 8. The administration of Biržai volunteer firefighters' association in 1936. L-R (sitting): photographer Boruch Michelson, the chairman and the chief of the team A. Puodžiūnas, Gershon Belicki. L-R (standing): Simon Chait, S. Steponavičius, V. Budrevičius, J. Variakojis, and Itzik Mas. Reproduced by permission of Biržai Region Museum Sėla.

Sheina looked at Khane-Sora and nodded approvingly. "I am so glad that we have this fire brigade, because our ovens get so hot and the wood that makes up our homes is very flammable."

Khane-Sora paused and asked the kids who, very surprisingly, were quiet and paying close attention, "What do you think about that?"

Motel says, "Oh, I know Ima. It is really cold in the winter and because the walls are so thin, I can hear you and Abba[12] making sounds in your room..."

Khane-Sora blushed a fiery red and she put her hands to her face, but before she could react and stop Motel, he continued, "praying every night." Khane-Sora let out a big breath, recovered, and continued with her stories.

"Yes," Khane-Sora smiled warmly at Motel, "It is really cold in the winter. You know the stove we made your fresh bagels in, well

---

12   Abba means father in Hebrew/Yiddish.

it is what provides us the heat for the winter. We also had a really warm material we would take to the shoemaker and he would add on leather and it would keep us warm. And everyone in Biržai had boots for the snow and rain. Have you noticed many of the streets are not paved, but have stones and dirt? Do you know what we used to call those streets growing up?" Khane-Sora paused and then she told them. "We called them 'blote gas' which means mud street. We never left our house without our boots."

Sheina was impressed to see all the children listen so intently to Khane's stories. She also enjoyed the stories for the memories they brought back to her of when she was a child.

Khane-Sora went on. "Our street, Vytauto, is considered to be the main town promenade. It is a very European style that is usually the main street in a city or town. Vytauto Street is just five blocks and walking straight ahead you would come to what was called the 'New Biržai.' We would get dressed up on Saturday or Sunday and walk one way down the promenade, turn around, and then go back. It's funny because people would go that way and return the same way, and you always saw the same people. You never saw any other people. The majority of them were on the same sidewalk. Like where we lived across the street, I don't know why they walked on the other side of the street because we had sidewalks on our side, too. The other side is what they called the 'schloss,' or castle, with a beautiful park. People would say from wherever they came that Biržai is the most beautiful corner in Lithuania. For Pesach,[13] everybody had new clothes and used the promenade to show them off. One year we were parading up and down and Gersh Zundelevitch saw us walking and he came over to see little Raiska in her new clothes. He picked the baby up out of the buggy and grabbed her and kissed her. He owned the Metropole Hotel (figure 9) that had the only gasoline pump in town out in front. He was also a salesman for the Metropolitan Insurance

---

13   Pesach means the Jewish holiday of Passover in Hebrew.

Company and he gave the kids candy for Pesach." Changing subjects quickly, Khane-Sora said with a wide smile, "Do you kids want to go on the promenade and get candy this week?"

Figure 9. The Metropole Hotel with the only gasoline pump in Biržai out in front. Reproduced by permission of Biržai Region Museum Sėla.

"Do we have to get dressed up?" asked Perl. The mothers laughed and shrugged their shoulders and with raised eyebrows, gave the universal parenting signal of "We'll see."

The parents finished telling their stories to the kids and sent them back outside for more play time. At the conclusion of the day, the Magid family returned home, ending an ideal day in the Biržai shtetl they missed for so long.

CHAPTER 3:

Bagels and Castles

"Bagels here, get your fresh bagels. Hot from the stove…make me an offer." This was one of the signs that life was slowly returning to normal in Biržai after the Great War. The merchants were out in droves again. They sold their wares in the market square, which regularly became a sea of people, tables, and goods. Whenever snow fell in the evening, the beauty of the square and the surrounding buildings housing local businesses and apartments were accentuated with glistening snowflakes. Then, shortly after the selling began the next morning, the well-travelled paths of footprints and hoof-prints would make a stark contrast with the remaining areas still covered with pristine white snow.

While the town had a variety of merchants, tailors, and seamstresses, most of the raw goods everyone needed to create what they sold came from Riga, about seventy-five miles away. On Sunday mornings, a caravan of ten to fifteen men in covered wagons would leave for Riga to purchase goods from the wholesale houses. They would return on Friday mornings, in time for Shabbat, then sell their goods to the storekeepers on the following Saturday evening after the sun went down. Many of the storekeepers didn't have the money to pay for their purchases. There was a lot of debt, some of which was paid for by trading tea and cigarettes used as substitutes for money. During the Great War, the scene at marketplace (figure 10) was quiet and serene.

After thousands of Jews were allowed to return home, it was full of frenetic activity especially on the eve of Shabbat. It was always tough to tell if business was better on the Mondays after families devoured everything while celebrating Shabbat, or on Thursdays when they would prepare for the next Shabbat. But always, the marketplace was the best place to be, not just for business transactions or deal negotiations, but for kibitzing among the local folks in Biržai and others from the surrounding communities. People descended upon Biržai from the surrounding villages, arriving by horse and cart, or sleigh, depending on the season. Many of the local residents would also come to buy for their families or sell something to make a living. A little bit of everything could be found here, making marketplace days an important part of the Biržai economic structure.

Figure 10. The Biržai marketplace on Rinkos Square in the 1930s–1940s, close to where the houses and shops of the Jewish people were located. Reproduced by permission of Biržai Region Museum Sėla.

Besides selling products at the marketplace, many Jews made their living processing flax, which was and still is integral to Lithuania's economic well-being. There were also plenty of Jews who were merchants with their own stores, and there were buyers, dealers, tailors, shoemakers, hairdressers, butchers, bakers, photographers, artists, and musicians. There were embroiderers, weavers, knitters, and many others involved in timber and other trades. Many men were employed in the two Jewish-owned flour mills where Jewish families would go to grind their grain or to buy flour. The flour produced in these mills was also packed in sacks and sold all over Lithuania. And, of course, there were plenty of Jews who were professionals: engineers, doctors, dentists, pharmacists, and lawyers.

Then there was Shmuel. Shmuel was a singular character in Biržai. Berl-David Magid recalled the one day when Shmuel saw Berl buy a fresh bagel from a merchant. "Hey Berl," Shmuel called out. "That bagel looks great, did you buy one for me?"

Figure 11. A man selling a bagel at the Biržai marketplace.
Reproduced by permission of Allan Evans.

"Oh, I'm sorry Shmuel, I didn't see you, let me go grab you one," said Berl.

"No, I'm just kidding with you," Shmuel laughed. "It is good to see you. I am so glad you and your family have settled back in from your journey. How long has it been?" Shmuel asked. "Two or three years?"

"It has been more than three years, we got back in 1920. Abba has me now starting to train for my bar mitzvah, Hebrew lessons, and school. It's no fun. I just want play outside with my friends."

"Now you listen up, young man, do you want to be like me?" cautioned Shmuel.

Shmuel was old, an octogenarian, but he never stopped working. Known as a soft-spoken guard at the market, he was also responsible for checking on locked doors and collecting money from shopkeepers. If anyone stopped by to say hello, he had a familiar rant: "I still walk straight and upright, but I sit in this little shelter wedged between two shops. You think this little roof protects me from the cold and rain? I go from door to door every Friday and pull on door handles and try to collect my weekly wages. Some of these merchants are not so good at paying and you know what they tell me? 'Next week, Shmuel, next week.' I've been hearing that mishegas[14] from some of them for over ten years."

Berl tried to conceal his laugh, but he couldn't. Shmuel also smirked, but he continued.

"You need to take your studies seriously so you don't end up like me. You're a young person and you've got your whole life in front of you. Me, I got bupkes,[15] except for my clocks."

But Shmuel had a little more than just a shack. He had his clocks. He had a weakness for clocks. In total, he had seventeen of them in his tiny home. His best clocks were locked in antique cabinets: he had round clocks with Yiddish letters and he had ingenious alarm clocks made by craftsmen that kept perfect time and played sounds of birds and pleasant music.

---

14 Mishegas means foolishness, nonsense, or craziness in Yiddish.

15 Bupkes means beans in Yiddish. Usage translates to nothing.

CHAPTER 4:

Time to Grow Up

The Jewish people believe in one God. Like many religions, there are many movements or denominations within their own faith that differ in their views on various issues. The division of these denominations can take on different paths over time and in different locations it can sometimes lead to these groups becoming isolated and non-cooperative with each other.

Most Biržai Jews were considered part of the Mitnagdim[16]. The Mitnagdim focused on detailed and intellectual study of the Talmud while the Hasidim practices involved mystical teachings. By the mid-nineteenth century, the Mitnagdim and Hasidic Jews ended their struggles. The term Mitnagdim took on a positive connotation among non-Hasidic Jews of northeastern Europe and became almost synonymous with Lithuanian Jewry.

✡

The Magids were very much typical Lithuanian Jews. They were both family and spiritually oriented and led a very religious and pious life. After they left their temporary housing at the brewery,

---

16   The Mitnagdim/Misnagdim is the common name for rabbinical opponents of the Hasidic movement who were based largely in Lithuania, specifically Vilnius.

they moved into their new home at 27 Vilniaus Street, in an orchard in the shadows of the Astrava Castle and settled into a daily routine.

Moishe said his prayers three times a day. He got up at daybreak, prayed, and left for the villages to do business. He'd pray the Minchah every afternoon, then the Maariv at night when he'd return home. If there was not enough work to go around on a particular day, he'd drop into the synagogue, recite a couple of psalms, listen to the ongoing discussion of the *Mishnah* or the hair-splitting arguments over a page of the *Gemara*, the concluding sections of the Talmud. At the end of the day, he would enjoy a cooked dairy noodle supper, read the bedtime prayers and go to sleep.

A few years after the family had become entrenched back into life in Biržai, Moishe realized Berl-David was ready to join him in his daily routine.

"Berl," he called to him. "Do you remember the time in Kazan when I was almost killed? Well, let me remind you," he said before Berl could answer. "Shortly after the Bolshevik Revolution in 1917, the Tatars tried to kill me because of my business dealings. But a Russian saved me from certain death. Do you know why that happened?"

"No," Berl replied. "Why would anyone want to kill you?"

Ignoring his son's question, Moishe went on speaking, "Until the day that I die, I maintain that it was by virtue of the good deeds of my grandfather Naftali, that righteous rabbi. Because of him, I survived. And you, Berl, you survived the time when that sleigh ran over you in Kazan. You survived for the very same reason. We are both still alive because of your righteous great-grandfather in heaven. He stood by you and me."

"Abba, what do you mean?"

"I'm telling you it is time for your religious studies to begin. It is important to our family, our town, and for you as a Jewish boy. And it is my responsibility to ensure that you are raised as a proper Jewish male." Pausing for a moment to draw his son's full attention, he said proudly, "in other words, it is time for you to become a bar mitzvah."

Berl may not have understood the way his father was connecting the dots of their lives, but he was perfectly aware of just how religious the people in his family and around him were. Rosh Hashanah had recently passed, and Berl, as well as just about every Jew in Biržai, had been awakened by the shammash[17], who made the rounds at night knocking on everyone's shutters so that no one would oversleep morning services. The shammash's efforts worked. By two o'clock in the morning during the high holidays, the synagogues of Biržai were packed.

"Berl, listen to your father," his mother said. "After all we have been through, you think we survived just on chance or luck? It is because of our beliefs. It's time for you to learn the teachings of the Torah so you will understand."

Sheina was not just supporting her husband. She, too, was a pious woman. This was their faith and tradition. Because she was a force to be reckoned with, Berl knew he had no choice but to follow along. He knew it was because of his mother that the mikveh[18] at the Biržai municipal bathhouse was renovated. Originally the mikveh was made of boards with wooden stairs leading down to it. It was difficult to keep clean and eventually frogs moved in and jumped about as people bathed. No one wanted to be there—especially the women. At one point, Sheina had had enough of it. During a Sabbath, she interrupted the service.

"Stop," she had called out boldly. "Do not continue with this Torah reading. On behalf of all congregants, the mikveh needs to be updated. It's bad enough that we have these annoying frogs all over the place, but now I am getting splinters walking on these boards. Enough already." Shortly after his mother's demands were announced, the elders installed a wall in the mikveh and put in a smooth-glazed floor and steps.

---

17   Shammash means servant in Hebrew. Usage translates to the sexton or rabbi's assistant who runs the synagogue.

18   Mikveh is a Jewish ritual bath used for immersion to achieve purity.

Sheina was a strong woman but she was not just tough, she also had a reputation for her generosity. Her kindness made an impression on all and greatly influenced her children. One day Berl came home to find there was a poor stranger sitting at the family table eating. It wasn't unusual. Sheina insisted that the Magid house always had an open door. No poor man who'd gone from house to house looking for scraps ever left her house with empty hands, though the Magids themselves lived in poverty.

Berl sensed something different about this man, though. "Ima, who is this man sitting at the table? Why is he eating my lunch?" he asked.

"Berl-David Magid, you mind your manners," she answered sternly.

Obviously glum, Berl kept quiet as he ate the pauper meal of cabbage and watched the poor man eat the meat Berl felt should have been his.

The poor man finished his meal, and then complained he had a large family and he couldn't put everyone in proper clothes. Casting a glance at Berl, he lamented that he had a son just like him who had nothing to wear. Sheina immediately sent Berl into the second room and instructed him to find his suit. Berl did as he was told and then he watched as his mother gave the suit to the man. The poor man expressed his appreciation for the kindness of the Magid family and left. A couple of days later, Berl ran into an older neighbor who had a small re-sale business.

"You know, Berl," the neighbor said to him. "I have your suit. A poor man came in and sold me a sack of things. Among them I recognized your suit."

Berl explained to his neighbor how the man happened to be in possession of it.

"Ah, that's the way they are now, these beggars," his neighbor said with a wave of his hand. "So, do you want to buy it back?"

Berl chose not to take it back. He wanted to keep this little secret to himself and not do anything to dissuade his mother from being kind to the poor.

CHAPTER 5:

Being Jewish in Biržai

D aily spiritual life was important to all the Biržai Jews, not just the Magid household. In fact, the weekly Shabbat[19] celebrations and rituals highlighted everyone's week. No respectable Jew would ever think of leaving Biržai on a Friday. If they did leave during the week for some reason, they would be home by Friday. No serious business was conducted on Fridays. In fact, the merchant's wives would even send their grown children to tend the stores while they prepared their homes for Shabbat.

A centerpiece to the Friday preparation was a trip to the mikveh. Multiple hours were spent there telling stories of family, politics, and daily life. The poor and the rich, the young and the old, and the rabbis and the merchants, were all on equal footing in the bath house. This staple of Jewish life in Biržai didn't just provide good times with friends and family, but it cleansed their bodies, souls, and spirits as they embraced the spirituality of the Sabbath.

"Close the stores, close the stores, the Shabbat is approaching," the authoritative voice of the shammash would ring out every week. While a directive, the voice was still joyous and resonated in everyone's hearts as they dutifully began the festivities. The banging of closed shutters and the loud clacks of locked doors would be heard across

---

19   Shabbat, or the Sabbath, means rest in Hebrew and Yiddish.

Biržai as the excited merchants left their shops and marketplaces to head home. And within thirty minutes of the shammash's call, the streets would be cleared and the frenzied preparation inside homes replaced with a peaceful quietness.

Once out of their dirty work clothes and into their clean dress clothes, it was time to welcome the Shabbat. Following prayers during the day, families ate well with a sour cholent, the Shabbat stew that was placed in the oven before Friday evening and was eaten at the midday meal. Rising the next day as if experiencing Techiyas HaMeisim—rebuilding the old body from nothing—they tasted the cholent which left a sour aftertaste in the mouth, and afterward all would thank the Lord with several chapters of Psalms. As night fell after the conclusion of Shabbat, it was again a weekday. This was repeated, week in, week out, year in, year out, and thus it seemed to stretch into eternity.

Life was very predictable and for the majority of Biržai's Jews, it was also hard. There were a few wealthier property owners and some merchants, but as a general rule, earning a daily living was tough. They didn't always eat their fill, and they were short on clothes and shoes. Consequently, many of the young set out for bigger towns and the wider world outside of Lithuania.

CHAPTER 6:

Memories

At the heart of Biržai is Širvėna, the oldest surviving artificial lake in Lithuania. The lake's fifteen square miles feed the Aglouna and Apaščia Rivers that create natural boundaries through the center of town. On its banks sits Biržai Castle, and with the thick forests of tall birch trees, the result is a spectacularly beautiful landscape that vacationers have been traveling to since the sixteenth century. Even Napoleon was so awed by its beauty that he stopped to rest there during his march through Lithuania.

By the time Berl-David Magid and his friends were teenagers, the moat and massive high stone walls surrounding the castle had long disappeared, and the area became a favorite haunt of the young people for recreation and downtime.

Berl and his boyhood friends, Yehudah and Aaron Bass, Daniel Segal, Itsik Shek, and others, would sprint from the marketplace and across the bridge of the former moat, ducking snowballs from each other in the winter, and eager to race and play games in the summer. Perhaps they spent time telling stories and entertaining each other with tales about the history of the castle. When they were very young, they reenacted adventures based on the history of the castle, imagining invaders sneaking up on the castle at night, scaling the walls while the prince and his family slept. Then just in time, the boys as Biržai defenders intercepted them, unsheathing their sabers and scaring the barbarians away.

Existing diaries and memoirs from Biržai record tales of complaints about teachers, including one such memoir, *Der Hengst*. The literal German translation of "der hengst" is a stallion but the boys used its slang meaning of a young horse that jumps and strikes with its hooves. While the teacher never actually gave lashes, according to the records, he did keep his class in line by taking a foot and shoving the "guilty" students against the wall, and would then kick them with the other foot. The boys had nicknames for many of the teachers. One was Shmuel Monteglisker, whom they called "Pantoufle" behind his back because he wore traditional country shoes, or klumpes.[20] Then there was Betzkelevitch, known as "The Swan," and Yisruel-Khayim, whom they called "The Goat," because of his goatee. Berl topped all those nicknames though when his bar mitzvah rolled around and he began calling his tutor "Hairy Nails." As he explained to his friends, when someone asked the tutor a question, a translation from scripture, or the meaning of a word, if the tutor couldn't answer, he'd mumble some words that sounded like "nails with hair."

As typical Jewish youth in Biržai, they had no cares in the world as they approached their thirteenth birthdays and prepared for their b'nai mitzvah, when they'd become men, when they could start dreaming about their future work, getting married, starting a family, and living adult lives.

---

20   Klumpes are slippers with thick wooden soles.

CHAPTER 7:

Family in America

L eib Khait and his wife, Tame Bencelovicius, were well-respected citizens of Biržai (figure 12). Sometime after 1910, they left Biržai and visited the United States with an eye toward moving there. However, they did not like living in America and returned to Biržai when the exiled Jews were returned. By 1926, they were re-settled into their comfortable Biržai life where Leib still managed to stand out a little in town and at temple. He wore a Bukharan-style kippah[21] like the Sephardic Jews, in a traditional pillbox shape that gave it height and prominence. With his mid-chest length gray beard coupled with his kippah, he appeared to be very pious and rabbinical.

Berl's mother's maiden name was also Khait, but it is unknown if she was related to Leib. He and Tame had two sons, Samuel and Isaac[22]. Their sons were both "coming of age" around the turn of the century and subject to being conscripted into the Russian army. To protect them from military service, their parents cobbled together enough money to purchase visas for their sons to leave Biržai for America. Samuel and Isaac left Biržai in 1910. Samuel was a

---

21 Kippah in brimless, cloth hat in Yiddish. The Bucharian or Bukharan style is unique flat top style with a matching band from the Soviet Union.

22 Samuel and Isaac changed their surname to Chait in America.

shoemaker and went directly from Biržai to Boston, where he married Dora (nee Waranofski) and they had three children. Isaac took a different route. He became very friendly with Rose Dishler in 1899 just before her father, Morris, left for America and settled in Philadelphia (figure 13). Rose, along with two siblings, joined her father 1904. Her mother, Anna and the remaining four kids joined them in 1905. At that time, Isaac, who was a very pious and gentle man decided to move to Amsterdam to learn how to be a jeweler. Once trained in his new trade, he left Amsterdam, made a quick stop in Biržai, and in 1910 sailed to Philadelphia. He married Rose that same year, and they had five children.

Figure 12. Biržai residents Leib Khait and his wife Tame Bencelovicius. Reproduced by permission of Louise Chait.

As parents, Leib and Tame were happy for their sons who had the opportunity to have better lives in America. But they were also saddened they might never see them again. Before Sam and Isaac left, Tame baked challah in her home oven. Just before she had baked it, she ceremoniously pinched off a piece of dough and threw it right into the fire as an offering to God.

Figure 13. Biržai resident Morris Dishler. Reproduced by permission of Ted Kirsch.

That following Shabbat, Sam and Isaac were called up to the Torah in the synagogue. It had become a customary practice for the Jews who were leaving Biržai, presumably forever, to receive one last blessing. Afterward, Leib and Tame accompanied their sons to the cemetery to see their sons' tears when they said good-bye to their deceased relatives. Their tears became joyous ones when, back in the street, they walked throughout the neighborhood saying, "zei gezunt[23]," to all. All past sins were forgiven as they looked over the familiar streets of the shtetl one last time. The next day, with a final kiss on the mezuzah[24] hanging in the doorway, with broken hearts for those staying behind, each man left their family home and heartland. One of Isaac's sisters,

---

23 Zei gezunt means be healthy, be well, of farewell in Yiddish.

24 Mezuzah means doorpost in Hebrew. It contains a piece of parchment in a decorative case that is located on the doorways of Jewish households.

Taube, married a man named Borukh Meyer Bass. Together they had four children: Yehudah, Rivka, and twins Aaron and Gita (figure 14).

Figure 14: L-R (standing), Gita and Aaron Bass. L-R (seated) Taube Bass, Rivka Bass, and Yehudah Bass. Permission of Yona Shochat (nee Kaplan).

Isaac prospered as a jeweler in America, but he never forgot his family and his connection to his homeland. He frequently sent money home to his parents. Tame passed away in 1926, then Leib in 1927. Isaac continued to send money, redirecting it to his sister Taube. The charitable tradition continued when Isaac's son, Harold Chait, continued to send money to Taube's daughter, Rivka Kaplan (nee Bass), even after she married.[25] Harold's family in America didn't understand why he sent money to his cousins. After all, he had never met Taube or Rivka. He did it because his father had told him to do so. "They are family, and it was the 'right thing to do'." Harold replied, embodying the values of the pious, generous, and grateful people of his heritage.

---

25 The Khait family in America changed their name to Chait.

CHAPTER 8:

Flying Mail

Outside of Biržai, the world turned dark. The US stock market crashed on Wall Street in 1929 and the German people elected Nazis in 1932 making them the second-largest political party in Germany. In Lithuania, tensions increased within factions of the government as an independent Lithuania struggled to form a democratic government and constitution. In America, there was hopeful optimism for the New Deal as Franklin D. Roosevelt became president of the United States.

By the early 1930s, those who were boys after the Great War were now grown men. Of course, for the many Jewish males in Biržai, they were considered to be men since their thirteenth birthday. While that idea is rather symbolic in our time, it had real meaning in the Biržai shtetl in the early 1930s. Berl-David, Yehudah and Aaron Bass, Daniel Segal, Itsik Shek, and the others had completed their primary education and were expected to work. But finding work was very difficult, even for someone with high energy and motivation, and often it meant moving out of the area. Berl's brother Naftali learned how to make quilts and eventually moved to Klaipėda[26] and worked in a textile mill. Khatseh-Maneh, Berl's other brother, apprenticed with a tinsmith before immigrating to South

---

26   Klaipėda was also known as Memel in German.

Africa in 1929. Berl experimented with making caps and working with a Latvian shoemaker, but neither of those trades were well suited for him. He was good at drawing, so he began painting posters with oil paint for the movie theater and visiting theater groups, but that didn't provide much income. It did afford him spare time to volunteer in the Jewish library where he repaired damaged books. He also organized a soccer team of young players but because there was no money for real gear, they played with balled-up rags. Berl's shoe-making experience came in handy for them and he was able to sew an outer casing for the ball with scrap pieces of leather. With the little money they raised among themselves they bought a rubber inflatable tube to put inside the outer casing and then they played real soccer!

There were few jobs available for the young people in small towns. There were also few avenues for entertainment or social life. Many young men moved to bigger cities not only for a better chance for income, but because the urban centers provided a higher level of Jewish culture with Yiddish theater, lectures, and gatherings with Jewish political leaders, writers, and activists.

Unfortunately, not all cities were able to follow through on the promise of a better income. Berl Magid moved to Kaunas[27] where first he found a night job in a bakery, and later he worked sawing iron pipes with a handsaw. The jobs were hard and boring, and with low pay, leading many young men to give up after a year or so to return to Biržai. Berl Magid did just that, but he continued to struggle to find a trade in Biržai that afforded him the possibility to make ends meet. Eventually, he decided to enlist in the Lithuanian army. Twenty years earlier, Leib and Tame Khait had sent their sons Sam and Isaac to America to avoid military service, a common practice at that time. But now Berl was joining because it was increasingly becoming the only option for young men with few job prospects.

---

27 Kaunas is referenced by the Lithuanian spelling. It also is Kovno (Russian) and Kovne (Yiddish).

Before Berl left for Panevėžys to begin his service, he went to the castle with his friends when two boys approached them.

"Hey, what are you guys doing?" One of the boys asked as they drew nearer to Berl and his friends. They all turned to face the boys when Daniel Segal recognized them as two Lithuanian gentiles he had studied with in public school in Biržai. Berl and Daniel approached the boys and Daniel mentioned to them that they were giving Berl a final send-off as he was joining the Lithuanian army.

"That is great." One of the boys said. "I always wanted to learn how to shoot a rifle. Good luck." The two boys waved goodbye and went for a swim in the lake.

As Berl returned to his group, he saw a couple walking hand in hand by the lake. He recognized his friend Samuel Evans and gave him a shout. Sam saw Berl, but he and his friend hurried away quickly without acknowledging him. Berl thought that was odd and made a mental note to follow-up this snub later with Sam.

While Berl planned to go in the army, most other young men struggled to find work. Despite the hardships, many were thinking about other pressing issues that came with being a man—particularly the issue of marrying. Many marriages in small towns were a result of matchmaking because most young boys and girls were not bold enough to initiate romances. There were no textbooks for learning how to speak comfortably with girls and what to say or do. Sexual attraction was natural but expressing it was taboo until you were married or at least formally engaged. It was more difficult for girls as they were formally restricted by a patriarchal society where females at any age were limited to what they could say and do. And it was not proper for girls to initiate the conversation or interest. Therefore, boys and girls had to use a more inventive and unusual way to make a love connection—little tricks and games that resulted in good matches.

One such game was called "Flirt." The favorite place to play it was on the banks of Lake Širvėna, near the castle. Aaron Bass liked to facilitate the game. He'd gather a group of young people out by the castle and he would pull out what looked like a deck of cards, but it was really thick paper with lines of numbered questions and answers printed on both sides. In today's lexicon, the questions and answers could be viewed as pick-up lines. For the shy young men and women in Biržai, they were a method to flirt when they were not quite brazen enough to do it outright.

A shy boy would give a girl a flirtation card and mention a certain line number on it. For example, a card might have a number three on the card that read, "I love you! Your eyes are coral, your lips are like cherries, and your teeth are alabaster mixed with pearls." He would anxiously watch her face while she read it. Would she blush and ashamedly lower her eyes? After she accepted the card, and if interested, she would look for a suitable response in the flirtation deck to give it to him. Her card might have a numbered verse saying, "Do you mean this in earnest? Are you sincere?" He would then send her a card with a certain number for a line that might read, "Yes!"

The groups would spend evenings exchanging flirtation cards in a slow, anticipatory literary conversation. But it often worked. Many would become closer to one another; some were reported to have been seen sneaking off for a private rendezvous. Yet still others would find "the one" and swear eternal love to their matches.

Another game the young adults played to help them find "the one" was by assigning someone to be the shadchan[28]. Someone took on the role and delivered "secret letters" or "flying mail" to potential love matches. First, he or she handed out notepapers and envelopes made of pink paper to the young players. The boys and girls would write a secret letter on notepaper, seal them in an envelope, write a name on the top, and return them all into a hat. Once all the envelopes were collected, they would be delivered to the players.

---

28 Shadchan translates to matchmaker in Hebrew.

Figure 15. Berl Magid in military uniform with either Aaron or Yehudah Bass. Reproduced by permission of Yona Shochat (nee Kaplan).

Naturally, young people everywhere can be a little mischievous, and the same could be said of the young Jewish lovers in Biržai. There are reports that the game of flying mail was sometimes used by jokesters. For example, one young man sent a secret letter under someone else's name to a girl named Beila. He asked her to come outside to the courtyard and go to the well where he would be waiting for her. His language was colorful and over-the-top romantic:

"Come out to me, Beila, you beauty, you daughter of Zeus, you young woman of Biržai, come to thy sincere beloved, your Girsh, who waits for you outside with open arms and fluttering heart."

Unfortunately, when young Beila went to the well, Girsh was not there but the actual prankster and his buddies were, hiding in a corner, where an angry Beila caught them and chased them away.

CHAPTER 9:

Life Could Be a Dream

When Berl-David left Biržai for Panevėžys to serve his time in military service, life in the town continued to go on as normal—as it always had, almost oblivious to what was going on in the outside world.

Figure 16. Berl Magid in the Lithuanian Army in 1936. Source: Berl-David Magid, What I Have To Tell: Pages From a Life (Peretz Publishing, 1992).

Traditional meals that had always been eaten remained unchanged: potato and noodle kugels, challah bread, savory cholents, and gefilte fish. And a favorite treat that fed the neshomes[29] was matzah ball soup, where each matzah ball was filled with a chicken mixture at the center.

People continued to flock to the marketplace for commerce and gossip, and to the banks of the lake or rivers for relaxation. The young adults would do today's equivalent of "hanging out" in their favorite haunts along the Apaščia River, which created a natural border to the east side of the shtetl and meandered nicely from the northern mouth of Lake Širvėna. Lined by trees, it provided an ideal amount of shade and lush green grass alongside the gently flowing river. It was the perfect location to rest on any day but especially so on a warm summer day. This spot was ideal for children playing and splashing in the water or for young men just rolling a blade of grass between their fingers while pondering an uncertain future.

Social highlights revolved around family events. In the early 1930s, the Vinn family had a little girl named Leba Rivka. Then Motel Levitan and his wife, Chaya (nee Pesakhovich) had a little boy named Leiba. One day, Berl was crossing Karaimų Street, a young boy crashed into him and almost took him down. Berl grabbed hold of the little one and saved him from falling down onto the gravel. The boy briefly stopped, looked at Berl, and shyly muttered "thanks," and kept on going.

Berl recognized the boy immediately. "Wow, Leiba has really grown, but if he isn't careful, he won't see his next birthday," he declared jokingly to himself. He remembered Leiba Levitan was a newborn when he returned from the army in 1931. Here he was running the streets of Biržai the same way Berl did as a youth.

"Thank you," Chaya called out to Berl. She witnessed the small collision and acknowledged to Berl, "My son has a lot of energy." Berl looked back to see Leiba's mother and Motel Levitan pushing a baby stroller. He was introduced to Levitan's new baby, Golda, and he made a fuss over their little daughter. Berl asked Motel, "Are you still doing the lumbering job? I think that was in Dvaroniškis, right?"

---

29 Neshomes meaning soul in Yiddish.

"Yes, and you have a great memory," said a surprised Motel. "I used to live in the spare room of the forester's house before I was married, and I got to know the people really well, but now as you see I have my hands full here. There is one co-worker named Eduard Valintėlis that I still work with, and he and his wife Akvilina have two daughters, Regina and Elvyra. They are close in age to my Leiba and Golda so we get the families together from time to time. Eduard and Akvilina aren't much older than you, so when are you going to settle down and start a family?"

At the mention of marriage, Berl quickly changed the subject. "I gotta run Motel, nice to see you again." Berl quickly scampered off. If he had wheels for legs, he couldn't have moved any faster.

Meanwhile, more weddings were being planned. Whether engaged or dreaming of that "special" girl, the young Jewish men were well aware they needed to find a job to provide security for their future family. The need for work was not the only factor encouraging the young to start thinking about what the world had to offer outside their shtetl. The children who were born just before the exile, or during it, were adults now and they were very well aware that the outside world could, once again, infiltrate their quiet village. Unlike the generations before them, this generation felt the global influence encroaching on them, and whether it was a good one or not—they could not know for sure—they felt compelled to let it in, to learn from it, and possibly figure out how to protect their Jewish life if the need should arise once again. Like an ill wind, the global influences began to infiltrate their conversations, which now included discussions on politics and Zionist activities. Concerns grew as more and more Jews became interested in watching to see how the newly elected US president, Franklin D. Roosevelt, would deal with Germany's increasing activity and the rise of the Nazi party. Political organizations from every shade of Zionism worked to spread their message, while Yiddishists, anti-Zionists, and Soviet sympathizers also had their followers. Biržai was frequently visited by activists and religious figures of all kinds who spoke in the synagogues. Also, Jewish daily newspapers from several political parties arrived from Kaunas, Lithuania's capital city at that time. The result of this influx of new ideas, new thoughts, and new concerns resulted in people fighting among themselves. The marketplace wasn't just a spot for daily commerce and gossip; big commotions happened there over the issues of the day. The young adults began organizing groups and forming divisions among themselves according to political persuasion. The Hashomer Hatzair,[30] a Socialist-Zionist, secular Jewish movement grew a foothold in the area. Betar, another Zionist-based movement leaning toward the right wing, and the Gordonians, followers of A. D. Gordon, who founded Hapoel Hatzair, a Zionist movement based on manual labor and agriculture in Palestine, also grew very popular.

The idea of moving to Palestine became a driving force for many, including Naftali Magid, who, while Berl was away in military service, became a fervent Revisionist, a member of a Zionist organization strongly advocating emigration to Palestine. The Pioneer movement also saw increased attention and interest. As part of this movement, the Communist Party trained children in agriculture, hopeful that when they received authorization, they'd all immigrate to Palestine and be able to thrive there.[31] Berl was attending one of these meetings with his friends when he saw a group of people he went to school with including Batya Friedman and Rachel Vainer. He greeted them briefly and as the meeting started to break up, Berl caught up to Sam Evans and asked him to wait back for a minute.

"Hey Sam, remember back at my army sendoff, I saw you at the lake holding hands with a nice-looking girl, but you guys ditched us when I called out to you. Is everything OK?"

---

30 The Hashomer Hatzair is a Zionist movement that means The Young Guard.

31 Palestine was the name of the British occupied lands before Israeli independence in 1948.

Sam gave Berl a quick "sure" and started to head home but Berl was relentless.

"Hey, we've been friends since we were little kids. What is going on? I'm not letting you leave until you tell me."

Sam nodded to Berl and they sat down on a nearby bench.

"You know we are not supposed to date and marry non-Jews," Sam said in a low voice.

Berl nodded, signaling that Sam's statement was true.

Sam continued. "You know how much I love my faith and nature, but I met this beautiful girl that I love even more. Her name is Jadviga Šušytė-Pančkauskienė. She is beautiful on the outside with her amazing eyes and even more beautiful on the inside with her amazing soul. Berl, I am in love with a shiksa."[32] With the pain in his heart showing on his face, he looked intently at Berl. "My father, Aaron, refuses to let her in the house, so we can only meet after dark when nobody is around. We can't be seen together, or people will tell my parents. You need to promise me that you won't say anything. Promise me."

"Of course, Sam, you can count on me. We are friends." Berl shifted lightly on the bench and asked in a near-whisper. "What will you do? How long can you two go on like this?" Berl understood how serious a matter this was within the Jewish families and community.

"We have talked about this a lot. The reason that I go to many of the Zionist group meetings with you is because we have discussed making aliyah[33] to Palestine. We want to go and get married there and start our lives together there."

Berl was impressed by his friend's commitment to Jadviga but he was very concerned about how the future would unfold for them. Nevertheless, he would support his friend. With a firm handshake,

---

32 Shiksa means gentile or non-Jew in Yiddish.

33 Aliyah means ascent in Hebrew. The immigration of Jews to the Land of Israel.

Berl swore to keep Sam's secret, and promised to help him in any way that he could.

Other young couples didn't have such hurdles to cross. Abram Alzutski and Jenta Shtein married in 1932. The wedding ceremony was officiated by Rabbi Yehuda Leib Bernshtein under a chuppah[34] in the synagogue courtyard. Candles glowed in the windows, music played in the klezmorim[35] style, and there were even fireworks. It was quite the festive event, especially for a Tuesday night! After Abram stomped on a wrapped glass and everyone shouted, "mazel tov!" the whole wedding party left the synagogue and danced in the streets until they arrived at the bride's house. Sore Leja, her mother, was already standing on the porch with a large braided, twisted loaf of challah in her hand, singing for all to hear:

"Thank you, Gottenyu.
Thank you that what I wanted, you made happen,
You made it happen,
That I should live to see it."

The crowd pushed its way into the house and soon packed all the rooms. The dancing to the klezmorim continued, cognac flowed freely, as did wine and vodka. Young girls stood on tiptoes to see over everyone's shoulders, trying to catch a glimpse of the groom. He was considered to be a true "beauty," or "monarch," as they giggled to each other.

Abram's father, a very tipsy Izrael Alzutski, grew tired of dancing and sat in the corner with a bunch of the young men.

"Wasn't that a great sermon that Rabbi Bernshtein delivered?" Izrael asked. "I'd have him marry all of my kids, any day of the week."

---

34 Chuppah means canopy in Hebrew. Jewish couples stand under the chuppah during their wedding ceremony.

35 Klezmorim is an instrumental music tradition of the Ashkenazi Jews. Includes dance tunes, ritual melodies, and improvisations played at weddings and other social events.

The boys looked at each other, with that "OK, I should be leaving now" kind of look, but they were too slow to leave.

Izrael continued at a quick pace. "Hey, did you guys know about the previous rabbi in Biržai before Rabbi Bernshtein?" The boys all shifted their eyes toward each other and then slowly nodded "no." Izrael didn't really wait for their answer and pressed on. "Let me tell you about the great Rabbi Pinchas Lintup. He was in Biržai when I had my bar miss…vah…" Izrael's slurred speech made the words sound something like bar mitzvah. Attempting to focus himself and get serious for a second, Izrael continued. "He was one of the great rabbis of Biržai. No, no, no, of all Lithuania. He was sharp and well versed in the entire treasury of Jewish law, he knew almost the entire Talmud by heart, and more importantly he was pious and zealous."

Rivka Bass caught a glimpse of what was going on between the intoxicated father of the groom and her trapped friends, so she came over in an attempt to rescue them, but Izrael wouldn't hear of it. "I have a couple funny stories for you guys, but not for mixed company." Rivka wandered off and left her friends with no way out. Izrael continued, "Rabbi Lintup had a student named Menachem Mendel Frieden who was sent to Biržai to study with the rabbi. The house was just like our houses, very small, and the rabbi and his wife Slova had three daughters and three sons at the time. So, the daughters start to, how should I put this…mature," as he gestures in air quotes. "In the cramped hallways of the house, Menachem would be stopped by the older daughter and then they would kiss and grab a squeeze." The group howled at this story, especially Izrael, which now caught the attention of others from the wedding. Izrael waved for others to come over for he was just getting started.

"Menachem and the Rabbi's son became really good friends. They went together to the synagogue to study because the house was crowded and uncomfortable," pausing to wait for the snicker. "The synagogue was a tall and wide building and sometimes empty during the day. The two of them would both study and sing out loud and the echo of their voices would carry very far. One day I was walking by the synagogue and I hear this beautiful song of the Talmud and I see two people huddled by the door. I walked over and just listened for a few minutes taking pleasure in the sweet sounds coming from Menachem and Rabbi Lintup's son." Izrael ended this last story with a devilish smile and a wink, then he hugged all the boys for coming to the wedding and for listening patiently to his stories.

Seeing the coast was clear, the bride's mother and father, Sore Leja Shtein (nee Khait) and Paltiel Shtein, came over to also thank the young men for coming.

"You know, you boys are not that much younger than Abram and Jenta, who are now both twenty-four years old. You should really be thinking about settling down. It's easier for the boys to marry. It is so much more difficult for the girls because they are the ones who have to wait to be asked and at twenty-five, they are considered old. Jewish girls would work respectably around the house, milking the cow, the goat, driving them to the field, and even leading a cow to a rendez-vous when nature required it or when the cow had the urge to mate."

This prompted laughter from all the boys, probably imagining how their friends who were girls would manage cow mating.

Continuing her remarks to these future grooms, the bride's mother added a final cautionary advisory. "There is no great future for the girls in the shtetl. Our only goal is for them to make a match, we are not worrying about careers and jobs. If we can't find a young man from Biržai, there is always a nearby shtetl we can visit for making an arrangement."

"Thank you, Mrs. Shtein." Almost all of them said in unison. The boys were attracted to the girls, but they were focused more on find-ing work to support themselves before they could consider a marriage. Sore Leja is ready to move on to mingle with other guests, but then a thought came to her so she again addressed the young men.

"You know, we have a lovely daughter named Reiza who is just about your ages and I'd be happy to make introductions..." She couldn't finish her thought, though, because Paltiel smiled and politely guided her toward the other guests. A non-verbal thank you from the boys was politely signaled to Paltiel.

Paltiel, the bride's father, isn't quite done yet. "This has been a great day for the Shtein and Alzutski families. I am glad all of you could be here to celebrate with us. I know everyone is in a pinch trying to find work amid all the things that are going on around us and out of our control. But here is a little story I think will have some meaning for you as you try to find your way. There is a man named Leib who is primarily a tailor, but he is also the shammash, or caretaker, at the synagogue where our children got married. He knew the wedding was coming and his two workers, Leizer Portnoy and Motel Winer, and their wives Dine Portnoy and Hena Winer, needed money to buy clothes for the wedding. Leib is a man of few words, more like a man of action. He is very generous, and he spends more time at the synagogue in support of the congregation than he does at home. The supervisor of the synagogue is very slipshod at paying Leib and his workers, but Leib never asks for the money. This day, his workers come to him very concerned about getting paid because they want to buy proper clothes worthy of the bride and groom. Mrs. Shtein and I do not require fancy clothes to attend the wedding, we just want people to come and share in our joy. When the workers came to Leib and asked him for the money, he told them, 'God will help us,' and thought that would end the discussion. Not that the Leib's workers didn't believe in God or the power of him, but they were skeptical." Here Paltiel paused and checked to see if the boys are still following him. Heads were nodding all around.

Paltiel continued, "A few days before the wedding, Leib sent his wife to the market and when the workers saw Leib they started in on him about the clothes they needed and told him their wives were getting angry with them because they did not receive their back pay from the supervisor. Making sure the coast was still clear and his wife was still at the market, the man of very few words dug into his pocket and pulled out some money. He motioned the workers to come to him and presented each of them with a ten ruble bill. As Leib sat down at his workbench to start his work, he saw their shocked and joyous faces as they had their money in time just as Leib told them. Truly, God must have intervened and influenced the supervisor to pay since they all knew Leib would never ask for the money. What they didn't know is that against every bone in his body, Leib had gone to his supervisor and insisted on receiving their six months of back pay."

"Did Leib tell the men that he asked for the money?" asked Berl.

"No," said Paltiel, laughing slightly. "He just sat down at his desk and started singing 'How good it is to live in your house, Oh Lord.' He never told his workers, and he hoped this little experience would help them also find God.

At this moment, Paltiel changed his smile into his serious face and said to all the young men, "This is the message I want you to remember as you approach your struggles. Put your faith in the hands of the Lord and good things will happen. Bless you and thanks for coming to the wedding, even though half of you weren't invited." At that, they all laughed a good laugh.

CHAPTER 10:

Changing Places

Shortly after President Roosevelt took office in America in January 1933, he was immediately faced with difficult and disturbing events in Europe. Hitler's rise to power included systematically rounding up political prisoners and anyone deemed anti-Nazi. There were so many arrests made, the conventional prisons were overwhelmed, and concentration camps were constructed. In March of 1933, SS[36] leader Heinrich Himmler became police president of Munich and he led the construction of an SS-run concentration camp in Dachau.

In the summer of 1934, when German President Paul von Hindenburg died, the Nazi party illegally declared the authority of the president to be transferred to Adolph Hitler who soon became Chancellor of Germany. In the next few years, Hitler's Nazi Party established the Nuremberg Laws (1935), stripping Jewish people of German citizenship and civil rights, violated the Treaty of Versailles by rearming Germany, reinstituted conscription of more than 500,00 soldiers, and allowed German troops to occupy the Rhineland. These actions threw the European allies, especially France and Britain, into a state of confusion. At the same time, tensions were also rising in the Soviet Union as Joseph Stalin led

---

36 SS is an abbreviation of Schutzstaffel, German translation of Protection Echelon, Nazi's elite guards.

the "Great Purge" involving the imprisonment and executions of minorities, government officials, and anyone deemed as a threat to him and his authority.

In Biržai, changes slowly started creeping in. They were very positive, at first.

The Magid family took in a boarder that summer, Pinkhus Girshovich from Kaunas. He was an engineer who was hired to help design water lines, plumbing, and central heating for the Biržai public high school that was under construction. He was very religious and when he came to Biržai, the first thing he did was go to the synagogue and ask the rabbi if he could find him a room in a home that kept kosher. The rabbi referred him to the Magids and said, "If they will take you in, you can be sure of the kashruth[37] of the house." Pinkhus and Berl-David became fast friends, and because Berl knew how to draw, Pinkhus hired him to draw the plans for the radiators, toilets, washbasins, and other hardware connected to building the gymnasium.[38] Berl was happy for the work but once the construction of the building was completed, he was unemployed again.

Berl's brother Naftali had moved to Klaipėda, a town on the Western coast of Lithuania on the Baltic Sea. Naftali had been undergoing preparatory training for a life of farming in Palestine and was hoping to receive permission to emigrate soon. Since Naftali knew that Berl liked to paint and was good at it, he found a job for Berl in the color-dye section of a large textile mill where he would learn to be a master dyer. Berl soon discovered that assembling the necessary colors to weave cloth according to the complicated formulas was nasty, dusty work, and when the red color emerged from the dust it burned his eyes and nose. Because of the working conditions, Berl left the textile mill and his brother and returned home.

---

37 Kashruth means kosher state in Hebrew.

38 A gymnasium in Lithuania is equivalent to a secondary or high school.

Knowing he had an affinity for artistic work, Berl embarked on a career in photography and retouching pictures. He paid a small fee to learn, and worked unpaid for a year, but he came away with useful preparation and experience about the photography craft which he soon came to love. He eventually acquired his own equipment and started a new career. He photographed streets, interesting corners of the town, and natural landscapes from the outlying areas during all seasons. In the spring and summer there were meadows in bloom, fields of rye, and forest paths. In the fall and winter there were cloudy skies, muddy paths, and nooks in the forest covered with snow. Unfortunately, there was little work for photographers in a small town so once he had mastered the craft, he took his photo portfolio and headed back to Kaunas again. This time he got a lucky break and received small jobs from several studios on the town's main street, which landed him on his feet. Life was momentarily good, especially in the bigger city, which was culturally rich with bookstores, a theater, and movies. Berl was enjoying making new friends, reading newspapers, and keeping in touch with what was happening in the rapidly changing world.

✡

Time rolled on. However, life in Germany continued to worsen for Jews. The Civil Service Law passed by the Nazis in 1933 forbade non-Aryans from working in many various sectors. That was soon followed by many more anti-Semitic and racist laws under the Nazi regime, and Germany's state-sponsored persecution of Jews began. In September 1935, shortly after Berl arrived in Kaunas a second time, the Nuremberg Laws stripped German Jews of citizenship and gave them the status of subjects. Jews were also prohibited from marrying Aryans or having sexual relations with persons of "German or related blood."

In 1937, Berl was in Darshunishok, Lithuania, in the home of a local Christian friend. Without any warning, an old gypsy woman appeared and opened the door. Berl was slightly perplexed asked his friend what she wanted.

"She wants to foretell our future with cards," he answered.

Berl, not one to normally engage in superstitious nonsense, agreed to let the old woman stay. She sat next to Berl at the table and said, "Take out a lita[39] and I'll tell you your future."

After Berl put down the lita, she gazed deeply into his face and eyes. Berl felt an odd shudder go through his entire body as he held her gaze. This was the most unusual sensation he had ever experienced.

"Make it two and do I have stories for you," she said.

Berl's friend, not knowing the torment that was going on in Berl's head, abruptly stood up and was about to throw the woman out when Berl put down the second lita. She took out a pack of cards, and slowly and deliberately placed them on the table.

She methodically took the cards out and shuffled them, mixing the cards throughout the deck. She then pulled off cards from the top of the deck and turned the cards face up on the table. She said nothing for what seemed like a long time. Berl could hear his own heart beating and felt like his heart was going to explode.

She finally spoke. "You have a heart of gold and worked hard for every centu[40] you have earned, but your fingers have a light touch as though you haven't worked hard."

"That's it, that's all you got?" Berl roared, incredulous. "Give me back my money before I throw you out." He stood up and the gypsy woman abruptly raised her hand toward him.

"Wait!" the gypsy woman responded. "Sit." Berl very slowly eased himself back into the chair. Berl's friend watched the scene play out in total disbelief.

---

39   Lita was the official currency of Lithuania until 2015 when it was replaced by the euro.

40   Centu was 1/100th of a lita.

The gypsy woman continued. "You will lose your parents and two young women. Sisters." Pausing, she took a long shallow breath, then said lowly, "I see you hanging between life and death, closer to death than to life, but still staying alive wandering over the world."

Berl looked at the gypsy woman with a wry smile. To relieve the tension, he derisively laughed out loud at her prophecies. Once he left his friend's house, he immediately dismissed the matter.

In 1938, the Magid family living in Biržai consisted only of the parents, Moishe and Sheina, and the two young daughters, Perl and Zelda. Berl was a photographer in Kaunas, Naftali was at the coast, learning agriculture, and Khatseh-Maneh had successfully immigrated to South Africa.

Khatseh-Maneh was not alone in his wish to emigrate from Biržai to South Africa. Between 1923 and 1939, 7,200 Jews left Lithuania for South Africa. Among the many Biržai Jews attempting to migrate to South Africa was 11-year-old Samuel Ferber, whose letter (figure 17) to his relatives was read by Khatseh-Maneh. Some of Sam's family had migrated to South Africa and he wanted them to come back to Biržai for his bar mitzvah in a of couple years. He was also looking for help with obtaining permit papers because the Ferber family was looking to move to South Africa. Berl watched the cycle continue as the youth of Biržai became "men" at an early age and then struggled to find work. He hoped 11-year-old Sam would be successful and not have the same challenges he and his friends experienced.

Khatseh-Maneh Magid frequently sent British pounds back home along with letters expressing his concern for the well-being of his family. Aware of what was happening in Europe, he once, along with money, sent papers about the process for immigration to South Africa. Berl thought they lived on a quiet island surrounded by storms brewing on either side, but he was certain the Jews of Biržai could weather the storm. The immigration papers wound up in the family's trash.

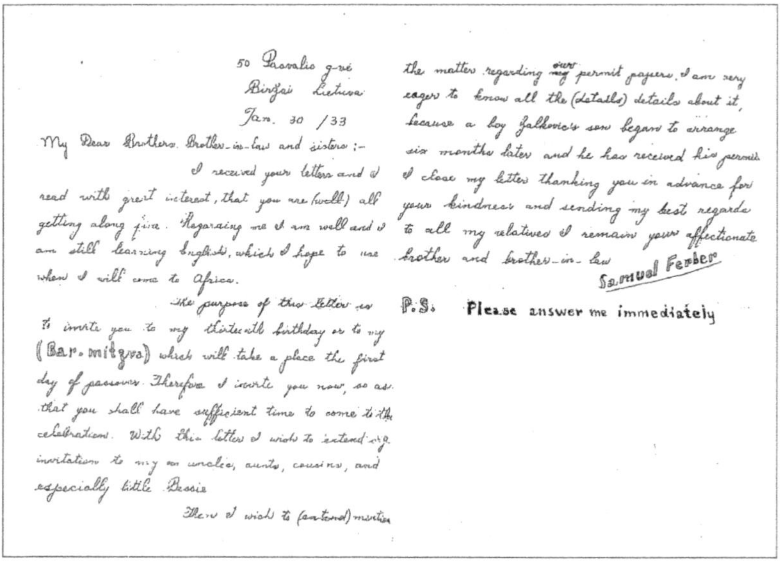

50 Pasvalio g-vė
Biržai Lietuva
Jan. 30 /33

My Dear Brothers. Brother-in-law and sisters :-

I received your letters and I read with great interest, that you are (well) all getting along fine. Regaraing me I am well and I am still learning English, which I hope to use when I will come to Africa.

The purpose of this letter is to invite you to my thirteenth birthday or to my (Bar-mitzva) which will take a place the first day of passover. Therefore I invite you now, so as that you shall have sufficient time to come to the celebration. With this letter I wish to extend my invitation to my uncles, aunts, cousins, and especially little Bessie.

Then I wish to (extend) mention the matter regarding our permit papers. I am very eager to know all the (details) details about it, because a boy Zalkovic's son began to arrange six months later and he has received his permit. I close my letter thanking you in advance for your kindness and sending my best regards to all my relatives I remain your affectionate brother and brother-in-law

Samuel Ferber

P.S. Please answer me immediately

Figure 17. A letter than Samuel Ferber wrote to his family in South Africa in 1933. Reproduced by permission of Cyril Ferber.

Later one night, after he had returned to Biržai, Berl left his parents' house with a full belly and his soul re-charged from another traditional home-cooked meal. He headed over to see Sam Evans. On the way, he bumped into his three good friends, Aaron and Yehudah Bass, Daniel Segal, and Itsik Shek who joined him on the way to Sam's. An outdoor theater was set up at the castle, and soon all of them headed there together. Like young men everywhere, they enjoyed their time together, catching up with their experiences with work, girlfriends, and current events. As the conversations wound down, Sam subtly motioned to Berl with a slight flick of his head to indicate he wanted to have a private conversation. The two friends stood up, said their goodbyes to the others, and headed off together. As soon as they were out of earshot of their friends, Sam abruptly grabbed Berl by both shoulders, turned toward him, and looked him straight in the eyes.

"Have I got some unbelievable news for you," Sam insisted.

Shocked by his friend's abrupt enthusiasm, Berl couldn't muster a response.

"I am going to America," Sam continued, and he let the words hang in the air for a few seconds.

"What? When? How?" Berl's eyes were now wide as saucers.

"I went down to the administration building to apply for a visa to visit the United States. I was only planning to take a trip to visit America, not to immigrate. But, as I was waiting in line, someone announced that all the visas were gone. We were told to leave. I walked out of the building and a woman saw me and called me over."

"What did she want?"

"She told me that I looked so dejected as I left that it broke her heart, so she wanted to give me some special information. She said the Americans allowed only fifty immigration visas for Lithuanians per year and she knew that someone who had one but decided not to use it. She told me if I went back in there right then, I'd get it. So, I went right back into the building."

"And, what happened?" Berl asked, shaking with eagerness to learn what happened next.

Sam reached into his pants' pocket and pulled the visa out of his pocket.

"What?" Beryl almost shouted this time. He gripped his friend in a strong embrace. When he released Sam, Berl looked perplexed. Sam knew exactly what he was thinking.

"I plan to send for Jadviga when I am settled," Sam said. "We are as fully committed as ever in our love for each other. You know how difficult it has been for us because of my parents. Berl, I need you to promise me something. And I am very serious."

"Anything, Sam. Whatever you need," said Berl.

"I need you to look in on Jadviga when I am away and help her in any way that you can. Can you do that for me?"

"I'd be happy to, Sam. You know I will do everything I can. I come home to Biržai from Kaunas regularly to see my family, so I can look in on Jadviga for you." Berl tapped the visa in Sam's hand, thrilled just to touch what seemed like a ticket to a new world. "I am so excited for you! Promise me, you will keep in touch and that I can visit you in America."

"Yes. I promise you both those things." Sam replied enthusiastically. "I really hope you will come to America to visit Jadviga and me. That would make me so happy."

So it was, armed with a visa and a camera, Sam Evans left for America in 1938. First, he settled in New York, then he moved to Hollywood, California.

CHAPTER 11:

World War Again

The day Sam left in 1938 was a very melancholy day for the friends and family he left behind. However, the parallel events happening in Eastern Europe made it seem that maybe Sam had the right idea about leaving for America. Hitler wanted to acquire the Sudetenland territory, a northern section of Czechoslovakia, where the majority of people who were considered to be ethnically German lived. British, French, Italian, and German leaders met in Munich in an attempt to avoid war. An agreement was made to annex the Sudetenland to Germany in exchange for a pledge of peace from Hitler. The president of Czechoslovakia resigned in protest to show how strongly he opposed his country being on the wrong end of an awful deal when they weren't even invited to the negotiation table.

A month after the Sudetenland annexation and the Munich Pact was signed, a massive, coordinated attack was conducted on Jews throughout the German Reich on the night of November 9, 1938, a night infamously known as Kristallnacht, or The Night of Broken Glass. Hitler and Minister of Propaganda Joseph Goebbels used an incident in Paris to incite Germans while he exalted them to "rise in bloody vengeance against the Jews." Mob violence broke out as the regular German police stood by and crowds of spectators watched. Nazi Storm Troopers, along with members of the SS and Hitler Youth, took liberties against the Jews. The Jews were beaten, murdered, and robbed. The homes of Austrian and German Jews were ruined. Women and children were brutalized all over Germany, Austria, and other Nazi-controlled areas: Jewish shops and department stores had their windows smashed and contents destroyed. Vandals targeted synagogues. Sacred Torahs were desecrated. Hundreds of synagogues were systematically burned, while local fire departments stood by or simply prevented the fire from spreading to surrounding non-Jewish buildings. The reaction outside Germany to Kristallnacht was such shock and outrage that a storm of negative publicity in newspapers and among radio commentators successfully isolated Hitler's Germany from the civilized nations and weakened any pro-Nazi sentiments in those countries. Shortly after Kristallnacht, the United States permanently recalled its ambassador.

In March of 1939, Hitler demanded that the Lithuanian port city of Klaipėda, called Memel in German, a large seaport town on the Baltic Sea, be returned to Germany. It had been a part of the Prussian and German empires before the Versailles Treaty was signed to end World War I in 1919. German Foreign Minister Joachim von Ribbentrop demanded the annexation of Klaipėda on March 20, 1939, citing the ethnic German population in the city as the reason for its unification with Germany. The German Navy with Adolf Hitler aboard the battleship Deutschland *steamed toward Klaipėda to back up Ribbentrop's demands with force. After failing to secure support from other European powers, Lithuanian President Antanas Smetona submitted to German demands, announcing the bloodless surrender of Memel to Germany.*

When Berl-David heard about the events in Klaipėda, he immediately went to visit his brother Naftali, who was living and working there.

"I am worried about you," Berl told Naftali. "What will you do?"

"I need to get out of here, that is for sure," Naftali replied. "But I am still preparing for my immigration to Palestine. Granted, this action by Germany strengthens my fortitude, but I don't yet have a plan. I'll continue with my preparations until I can find work."

Berl, alarmed by Naftali's situation and cavalier approach, gave his brother a directive. "No! You must leave at once. You can go home to Biržai and live temporarily with Ima and Abba, or you can join me in Kaunas. But you cannot stay here. I insist you leave this place and protect yourself. I'm not leaving until you do."

"Little brother, I appreciate your concern. I'll accelerate my plans, thank you for your love. We Magids are strong. We stick together. Now, give me a hug." Berl and Naftali embraced before Berl headed back to Kaunas alone.

As Berl and Naftali strategized on their future, Russia and Germany, unbeknownst to the world, worked together on theirs. In August of 1939, Germany and Russia signed a non-aggression pact called the Molotov-Ribbentrop Pact. In this agreement, both parties agreed not to take any aggressive action toward each other for ten years. This agreement took the world by surprise and heightened tensions throughout Europe. With the new deal signed and Germany no longer worried about fighting a war on two fronts, Germany invaded Poland from the East a week later, while Russia invaded Poland from the West. Soon afterward, Britain, France, Australia, and New Zealand declared war on Germany. World War II had officially begun. In just a few short weeks, Poland surrendered, and new borders were established as the country was now split between Germany and Russia.

The escalating situation in Eastern Europe made the cold, snowy winter of 1939-1940 more harsh and bitter. The weather severely affected Berl's photography business. He was without work again and without a way to make living. Naftali, meanwhile, had taken Berl's advice to leave Klaipėda. He found work at a tuberculosis sanatorium in Ramėnai, a town near Kaunas. The news of this filled Berl with joy and peace, especially since Naftali was now closer to Biržai and the family. Naftali, then, switched roles with Berl, and pleaded for him to join him in Ramėnai.

"Come to Ramėnai! The people who are receiving treatment here where I work at the sanatorium want to be photographed. You will find work here. You can come celebrate the Shabbat with me and then on Sundays you can take the pictures. You can't say no, little brother."

Berl indeed couldn't come up with a reason why he couldn't take up his brother's offer. "I see we are cut from the same cloth. We seem to find a way to say the right things to get each other to act. I will take you up on your offer, Naftali, and thank you." Berl agreed to join his brother, in part, because it was still close to Biržai and he was able to meet his commitment he made to Sam Evans to keep a protective eye on Jadviga.

On Shabbat, when Berl arrived at Naftali's home, he noticed things seemed a bit tidier. He also spotted a women's shawl on a chair. Soon, Naftali introduced him to a beautiful young woman named Miriam Oppenheimer. She was a nurse from Vilkovishk who was working at the tuberculosis sanatorium where Naftali directed one of the departments. Naftali told Berl that he really liked Miriam and he could one day see the two of them getting married and moving to Palestine. The work at the sanatorium was steady. Berl was pleased to discover he had underestimated the demand. There were many residents interested in being photographed. He would bring his equipment to take the pictures in one week and then he would bring them the finished photos the following weekend. It all made for a very modest living. Berl was able to sleep in a corner of a public room and eat a daily meal of a bowl of soup with a meat dumpling in a cheap public kitchen. It was a pleasant existence in the bigger city where he met men and women of his own age group and had a good social life. They would all go together to the social hall to see the Jewish Theater Organization. There, an amateur theater group gave fine performances and a chorus offered concerts. Berl also dated; often they went out to the movies and danced in the evenings as they all hoped for better times.

Taking into account the fact that Nazi Germany had occupied Poland, and that the Second World War had started, the economic situation in Lithuania wasn't very bad. The people still felt they were on a quiet island with a storm brewing around them. Every day the newspapers brought news of the frightening fate of the Jews in Poland. Jewish refugees fled into Lithuania with news of the Nazi savagery directed toward the Jewish population. In Lithuania, however, life flowed on without change. People did not engage in any additional speculation. It looked like the Non-Aggression Pact between the Soviets and the Germans would spare Lithuania the threat of war. At least it was what people tried to convince themselves to be true. Many came to believe this foolish fantasy, while they were really living on the edge of a precipice from minute to minute.

Following the invasion and the surrender of Poland, Russia and Germany continued with additional conquests in Europe. On the eastern front, the Russian army invaded Finland in late 1939 and set their sights on the Baltic States. Lithuania signed a treaty with Russia in October 1939 that allowed the Soviet army to send 20,000 troops to be stationed in Lithuania, which was part of Poland at the time, in return for Vilnius. The Lithuanian army also marched into Vilnius, setting up a showdown between the two countries. To end tensions, Prime Minister Antanas Merkys made a speech in December 1939 stating a treaty was signed in October with a "friendly Soviet Union." On the western front, in the spring of 1940, Germany bombed a naval base near Scotland, and then in succession invaded Denmark, Norway, France, Belgium, Luxembourg, and the Netherlands. The Germans entered Paris in June of 1940, and France surrendered.

The young working people of Biržai were politically on the left. They believed that their salvation would come from the Soviets who, as it turned out, didn't keep them waiting very long.

PART II:

Changing Landlords

"When you choose the lesser of two evils,
always remember that it is still an evil."

Max Lerner

81

CHAPTER 12

An Old Friend Comes to Town

As soon as the hard winter of 1939–40 ended and while the world was focusing on the German occupation of Paris on June 14, 1940, the Russians issued an ultimatum to Lithuania demanding free entry for an unlimited number of troops. With 300,000 Russian troops amassed on the eastern border and the previous 20,000 troops already in Vilnius, it was impossible for Lithuania to mount a defense. To avoid bloodshed in a potential unwinnable war, they unconditionally accepted Russia's ultimatum. The next day, the Lithuanian government capitulated and the president left the country. Russian troops entered Biržai in June, beginning a very difficult and challenging period for the Jews of Biržai.

What is someone to think when their country is invaded by a foreign power? Is it ever a good thing? No, it isn't. With the havoc that Germany was waging on the eastern border of Lithuania, a western invasion from Russia looked better, maybe even positive. The townspeople of Biržai viewed the Soviet occupation as the lesser of two evils and they tried to remain optimistic. The Soviets began a constitutional metamorphosis by first forming a transitional "People's Government." A month after their arrival, following illegal amendments to the electoral laws, they rigged local parliamentary elections for the "People's Parliaments," conducted by local Communists loyal to the Soviet Union. The laws were worded specifically that the Communists and their allies were the only ones allowed to run. The election results were therefore fabricated with the results having already appeared in print in a London newspaper a full twenty-four hours before the polls closed. The newly-occupied Baltic States' new "People's Parliaments" met on July 21—each with only one order of business—a request to join the Soviet Union. When the motion was passed unanimously, the Supreme Soviet of the USSR "accepted" all three requests, receiving Lithuania into the Soviet Union. The official Soviet propaganda was that all three Baltic States carried out socialist revolutions and voluntarily requested to join the Soviet Union.

Other acts adopted in these early sessions concerned nationalization of virtually all larger enterprises, real estate, and land, and other Sovietization policies. The laws were adopted with virtually no discussion. While these legislative changes were happening across all of the Baltic States, the people of Biržai were trying to figure out what the impact would be on their lives and livelihoods. Naftali Magid and Miriam, along with the Bass, Magid, and Khait families, got together one Shabbat following the Russian occupation of Biržai. While this was normally a festive and celebratory occasion, this particular gathering was more somber as there was still much unknown about how life would change under Soviet rule.

"Miriam and I couldn't help but notice all the Soviet posters and red flags on the streets and buildings announcing solidarity and peace," Naftali said to the others as they sat around the large dinner table.

"That's just a minor change," Moishe said. "Since the Soviets rolled into town, they've brought nothing but trouble. Our friends up the road have a large house that the Soviets deemed had too much living space for them, so they moved officers and their families into it and just took the rest of it. At the beginning, there was one family, but then another was added. Eventually they put in a Soviet Air Force officer and his wife and their small daughter. If that wasn't enough, they took over another part of the house and put a Lithuanian Communist leader in there who had a child that was difficult. They brought in a teenage girl from the Ukraine to be her nanny. The Ukrainian girl told my friend that the Russian families can't live this way with all of these people in 'their' house and he and his family should prepare to go to Siberia."

"What does that mean?" asks Berl-David. "Can they just waltz into our town and take our properties and treat us this way?"

"Welcome to Communism, comrades." Naftali said. "I hope all of Biržai is against this type of behavior, but if they are for Communism, they should keep quiet about it."

Naftali continued. "Nah! Those sympathetic with the Soviet system are vocal about it. Jews and gentiles alike! And they're loud about it. Maybe they think that will advance their career or move them forward in this new society. They are out and about tearing Lithuanian symbols from buildings. Those against the Soviets are more subdued because the terror is here and there is no sense in starting trouble and openly resisting. I think we should just keep our voices and our heads low, and hopefully we can survive this occupation."

"Agreed brother," Berl continued. "There definitely are people, independent of religion, who are collaborating with the Soviet occupiers. I can't tell if there are more Jewish sympathizers than Lithuanians."

Following the meal, Moishe Magid, as patriarch of his family, felt he should say a few words to help calm and reassure the families. Trying to ascertain the best way to communicate with everyone, he figured he would start out with a story to lighten the mood.

"As many of you know, we have many out-of-town students from different yeshivot[41] who come to Biržai to study with our great rabbis. These students have very limited means, and it is our tradition to invite a few students once a week for a home-cooked meal. Otherwise, how

---

41   Yeshiva (Yeshivot is the plural) means sitting in Hebrew. It is an orthodox college or seminary.

could they study with their bellies rumbling and distracting them? We have maintained that tradition and we are happy to do so going forward. Our faith tells us that we should do tzedakah[42] for the poor and less fortunate."

"Abba, that is great, but why are you telling us this now?" asked his youngest daughter, Perl.

"Good question, Perl, let me tell you. You see, there once was the biggest and most intimidating man in the synagogue named Nacham. He was an imposing fellow, who also liked to talk all the time, especially during prayer time, and many of the religious Jews had issues with him. So, they decided to make him the one in charge of order and decorum."

"Wow, isn't that ironic," said Naftali. "The loud and boisterous one is the man they pick for the job. Why did they select him?"

"Ah, remember I also said he is a large man and he looks very intimidating. He was also a man of high character and known for honoring his commitments, so as soon as he was given the job, he took to it like a fish to water. If anyone received a quick gaze from Nacham it would immediately stop anyone's conversation and return tranquility back to the service. No one would dare to speak just based on his appearance. The point I am trying to make is that the biggest joker and talker at the synagogue is now the strictest keeper of order during services. Another thing people didn't know about him was that the students loved the meals Nacham prepared for them, and they looked forward to them. He had three boys every Friday who told all their friends the best meals of the week were with Nacham. So, for our current situation, using Nacham as an analogy, let's not judge the Soviets the same way. We didn't judge Nacham by his appearance and demeanor. Let's see what happens and make our judgments later. Nacham looked large and intimidating before you got to know him, but we found out that he was a gentle giant."

---

42 Tzedakah means righteous behavior in Hebrew. Tradition is providing support for those in need.

"Abba, you have much wisdom and you have presented a great lesson to all of us to think about," says Naftali. "As everyone knows, I was in Memel when the Germans arrived there, and now we are together as the Russians arrive here. We can hope that Abba's story translates to our situation."

Everyone nodded in agreement and the mood was happier. Naftali took notice of the pleasant faces and continued with a different subject. "Now, for some happier news, I want to let everyone know that Miriam and I are to be married." The room erupted in choruses of mazel-tov as Naftali and Miriam were hugged and kissed by the families. The last and strongest hug was from Berl, and the embrace between the two brothers seemed to last for minutes. After slowly releasing Naftali, Berl embraced Miriam. He whispered in her ear and she let out a huge laugh. Naftali looked at Berl and asked what he said to her. "Oh, nothing really, I just wished her congratulations and told her that she picked the wrong brother." Berl rose from his chair as Naftali chased him playfully out of the house.

The parents were joyous about the engagement announcement of Naftali and Miriam and glad everyone was able to celebrate together under these trying times. While everyone was still together, Rivka Bass, the youngest of the four Bass children, also had something to announce to the families. "I want to let everyone know that today is Uncle Isaac Khait's birthday and he is celebrating it in Philadelphia. Also, he and Aunt Rose will be celebrating their thirtieth wedding anniversary later this year (figure 18), and we should raise a glass to them while we are all here together." A second round of mazel tov and l'chaim chants resonated throughout the small house as the families of Biržai often looked to any occasion for some joy and peace.

Following the dinner and celebrations, the mood was temporarily high but things around them were just beginning to change. Berl left the family gathering and met with Yehudah and Aaron at their favorite spot on the lake as they tried to figure out how things were going to work out.

Figure 18. Isaac and Rose Khait's wedding picture from 1910 in Philadelphia. Reproduced by permission of Reba Kirsch.

"Has everyone lost their minds?" asked Yehudah. "The people here think Soviets occupying our town is a good thing. They greeted the Soviet tanks with flowers. People are rejoicing the new regime. Haven't they paid attention to what is in the newspapers? What do you think?"

Berl answered first. "With the storm the Nazis have unleashed upon Europe, there seems to be only two choices for the smaller "neutral" lands: the Germans or the Soviets. I believe Jews are settling with the lesser evil of the Russians. The poor Jews, workers, and leftist intellectuals are in heaven. Let's see if their joy will last."

Aaron joined in on the conversation, adding his concern. "But I don't think it will. We are already seeing a shortage of goods, the exploitation of work, and the meager wages the Soviet 'Order' has brought us. At first people loved the assuring words and were very influenced and intoxicated by the Soviet propaganda: open theaters and movie houses, rallies, and catchy slogans. The concerts had a strong effect on audiences at the beginning. The talk about the liberation of the working class and the friendship between nations went on and on, and all of it spoke to the heart of us, to all of us, to the Jewish youth who saw no future for themselves in the villages."

Yehudah interrupted his brother, "That is what I'm talking about. I also heard some Jewish businesses elsewhere are being nationalized and people are being fired from their jobs. All of the Zionist parties and youth organizations and several community institutions were disbanded. The Hebrew school became a government school with Yiddish as the teaching language. Is this the way it is going to be for us?"

"I hope not." Aaron responded. "I hear some Jewish families have changed their family language from Yiddish to Russian and the other Lithuanians resent that. Why would they give up Yiddish, and if they are doing that, then why don't they switch to Lithuanian? Yiddish and Hebrew speaking doesn't bother anybody, but speaking Russian is an insult to our neighbors."

Wanting to be heard, Yehudah spoke up firmly. "I have heard a Jewish father and son speaking in Lithuanian. There are some families that went to the Lithuanian language. I also saw a Jewish girl writing in Lithuanian because she just didn't know Yiddish that well. However, I do agree with you Aaron, there is a sense of betrayal with the Lithuanians because they thought the relations between Jews and other Lithuanians were good, and they didn't see the reason why parts of the Jewish community are acting this way, in particular the younger generation."

Berl summed up the feelings for all just before they disbanded. "We need to be careful here. We have a lot of tension with both the Russians and the Lithuanians, and we must be watchful how this plays out across the Jewish community."

One thing was clear and ominous to nearly all. The Jews of Biržai were still consoling themselves with this one thought: 'At least they're not the Germans.'

CHAPTER 13:

A New Boss

In an ironic stroke of fate, Berl-David later found work painting banners praising the new order and the happiness that simple folk had found. When this work in Kaunas dried up, Berl faced that familiar question of what to do next. As Berl considered what to do, he ran into a non-Jew from Biržai named Paungsnis who was now an influential man with the new regime, having previously served ten years in a Lithuanian prison for Communist activities. After renewing their friendship, Paungsnis advised Berl to immediately return to Biržai where he would find him work. This was not only a fortuitous meeting for Berl, but Paungsnis was also able to help out Berl's sisters as well. The Communist Youth Organization would not allow Sore-Libe to work because she had been an active Zionist in the Maccabee movement. Paungsnis was able to find jobs in the cooperative workshops for not only Sore-Libe, but also for Perl and Zelda.

When Berl returned to Biržai, the municipal administration gave him the propaganda job of selling cards with pictures of leaders of the Soviet government. He was also given the task of painting more banners in praise of the new authority. The appeals of spurring the population to work more diligently to speed the establishment of the Communist order were written in Lithuanian, Russian, and Yiddish. The posters were hung at meetings, theatrical presentations, and concerts. The new Communist rulers sought to confuse the population with fancy language promising a bright future so people would not notice products and goods were getting scarce in the stores while at the same time everything was getting more and more expensive. The people of Biržai quickly realized it was a smart thing to remain quiet about such trends under the new Communist administration.

Following a Shabbat service in the fall of 1940, Moishe asked Berl to wait behind while they waved on the rest of the family to continue home. Sitting down in the almost empty synagogue, Moishe leaned into his son and talked in hushed tone. This took Berl by surprise. "Son, your supervisor in the Soviet administration is making life difficult for all of us. And believe it or not, that Motke Kerbel is Jewish. I don't understand how a Jew could be so harsh to his own people. I ran into him in the street and he tells me 'he who doesn't work, doesn't eat.' He tells me I have been given a job, but it means I must work on the Shabbat."

"Abba," Berl replied in a quiet voice, "I'm not sure if you know, or remember, but Motke was imprisoned eight years for Communist activities. It is no surprise he is now an important figure since the Communists took over. People in town are afraid of him. He is using his influence with the Communists to become a powerful man." Then he paused a moment, looked into his father's eyes, and spoke earnestly. "You cannot work on Shabbat. You are the most holy and righteous man."

Motioning with his hand for his son to stop speaking, Moishe placed his other hand on his son's shoulder and said in a flat voice. "I need to work and make money for the family. I will sell our horse and wagon and then I won't be able to work, especially on Shabbat."

"No!" Berl exclaimed a bit too loudly as his voice echoed off the now empty synagogue ceiling. "You've toiled for us enough. You shouldn't have to work. It's enough that I work on Shabbat. Go to the synagogue on the Shabbat, say your prayers, and recite the psalms. I will give you money to live on. Ima knows how to run the household very efficiently and make ends meet on a very modest budget.

Keep the horse and wagon, do what you like, and spend your time in synagogue, but you are not working on Shabbat."

Moishe's voice began to rise as he spoke again. "Son, I won't have it. You barely have enough money to feed yourself. You need to have pocket money for yourself. You are young and still struggling. You do not need to be taking care of your parents."

"Abba, it is not up for discussion. You and Ima have raised me to be a mensch[43]. You have brought strangers into our house and fed them when we didn't have enough food for all of us. You have given them a bed to stay, clothes to cover their bodies, and help in any way they needed. So, now this mensch is doing the right thing and I am taking care of you and Ima, so you will not be working for Motke Kerbel. There is no need to mention this discussion ever again." Moishe knew there could be nothing else he could say to his son to change his mind. At this moment, he knew his son was now the man he wished him to be. He stood and embraced his son as he tried to hide the tears rolling down his cheeks. "It's fine, Abba," Berl said to his father. "My shirt is wet also." Those were the final words spoken between them on the subject.

As father and son composed themselves and walked home to the Magid house for the Shabbat meal, Moishe shared news with Berl. "Remember back in the synagogue when you mentioned how we take in strangers? Well, we have new guests that I want to tell you about. Since you and your brothers and sister Sore-Libe are no longer at home, we now have more space and we have taken in a group of yeshiva students from Białystok. They were previously lodged as Polish refugees in Vilnius but when the Soviets arrived, they were told to move from the city to a smaller town. They found asylum in Biržai and now some of them are staying with us; others are staying in apartments in the town."

---

43 Mensch means someone to admire and emulate, someone of noble character in Yiddish.

"Wow. Abba, how many are staying with you?"

"We have the head of the yeshiva, Rabbi Shapiro, with his two unmarried daughters, two sons, and another daughter with her husband and small son. His son-in-law is Rabbi Levin. Your mother was seriously concerned about their tenuous situation and she assumed responsibility to get them settled in and help them in any way she can. I am sure none of this comes as a surprise to you."

"No, Abba, not at all. I am just not sure how long you can last with all of those additional mouths to feed while you are now 'retired.' You and Ima have the biggest hearts. I am amazed by your continual generosity."

Just as they turned the corner to Vilniaus Street they saw a young girl who had fallen and scraped her knee. Berl and Moishe came over to check on her to see what they could do to help. The girl was crying slightly and trying to be brave in front of these two men, who might have looked intimidating to her as she was sitting on the gravel road.

"Can I give you a hand, young lady?" offered Berl as he stretched out his hand to the girl.

The young girl looked up and gently placed her hand in Berl's. Together, Berl and Moishe gently lifted her up, helping to brush off the rocks and dirt from her dress. The two Magid men didn't recognize her and they introduced themselves. She replied, "Thank you for helping me. I was playing with my friends and I slipped on the dirt and they left me here on my own. I am new to Biržai, my name is Regina Batvinytė. My family moved here a year ago from Braškiai village and we live just over there by the bridge and the synagogue on Apaščios Street."

"Well, it's very nice to meet you Regina," Moishe said as he comforted the girl. "Let me guess. You must be about twelve years old, and it's just about time for you to start studying for your bat mitzvah. Is that right?"

"Close," she says now smiling, "I am thirteen, but I don't know what a 'bat miss vah' is."

After Moishe explained to her what a bat mitzvah is, she told them her parents have many Jewish friends and they seem nice. Berl and Moishe laugh and so does Regina. "Can we walk you home, Regina?"

"No thank you, I have to run home. We listen to the radio on Saturdays and I am late. It was nice meeting you." The skinned knee didn't seem to have any lasting affects as young Regina bolted home and left the father and son in a trail of dust. Moishe and Berl just smiled at each other and then continued home for the Shabbat celebration.

When Berl and Moishe arrived home, there were lots of introductions to be made. It turned out Rabbi Shapiro and his sons and daughters were soon able to secure travel to America by way of China. His son-in-law, Rabbi Levin, would remain in Biržai at the Magid house with his small family.

✡

Following his father's retirement, Berl went to meet with his supervisor Motke Kerbel who had chosen an additional job for him.

"Berl, I want you be the representative on all matters to Biržai's MOPR."[44] Berl never heard of this term and asked Motke for clarification.

After giving Berl the basic definition, Motke further explained it was an organization to help political prisoners detained for Communist activities in capitalist countries. The organization received funds for that purpose. Until the arrival of the Soviets, the MOPR group was illegal, but now it could carry out its activities openly. Berl took to this assignment without enthusiasm, and further had the unfortunate "pleasure" of reporting back to Motke that among the new members of MOPR were former fascists, Lithuanian members of the

---

44   The Russian literally translates to "International Organization for Assistance to the Fighters of the Revolution" but the acronym using the Russian letters spells MOPR. It is also referred to as International Red Aid.

semi-military, and persons who belonged to other organizations run by criminals. Motke told him it didn't matter because they would soon become good Soviet citizens, even though Berl knew they were really fifth columnists: people involved in acts of sabotage, disinformation, or espionage carried out by secret sympathizers.

Sometime later, Motke assigned additional responsibilities to Berl. In the past, records of births, marriages, divorces, and deaths of the townsfolk were all documented by the rabbis and the priests of their respective faiths. But now the Communists wanted to introduce civil recordkeeping. For a wedding, as an example, it was now required the bride and groom and their two confirmatory witnesses appear before the Soviet authorities to affirm that neither the bride nor the groom were already married before the couple was declared married. Berl's new job was to furnish these young married couples with apartments, by forcing people who had large dwellings to surrender a room or two to a young couple. This unpleasant task implemented by the Communist Party also applied to foreign religious elements who were forced to give up their apartments to those designated by the party. This edict also applied to the yeshiva students from Białystok. While the Magid family was already helping the rabbi and his family, Berl would be helping more students to find accommodations. When the Germans repatriated themselves back to Germany, their apartments were made available to the Russians streaming into Biržai. This is how the process transpired toward the end of 1940. The nationalization of the larger houses and all businesses was a very difficult episode in the history of Lithuania and Biržai. The former owners of shops and homes wandered around town in a bleak depression wondering how they would make a living since they were banned from their own workplaces.

✡

Elsewhere, German troops continued their westward advances with the bombing of England and the invasion of Romania.

Italian and British troops faced off against each other in Africa, and the Tripartite Pact, also known as the Berlin Pact, was signed creating an alliance between Germany, Italy and Japan. Following Winston Churchill's June 1940 speech in which he proclaimed England "Shall never surrender," it appeared England was now the main combatant against the German war machine.

As New Year's Eve approached, the Germans were in the midst of one of their most devastating bombing raids on London and it appeared Europe would fall to the Germans. As the calendar prepared to roll over to 1941, the people and Jews of Biržai were in a precarious position. They were still hopeful for better times to come, but they found it more difficult to envision that an end to the turmoil and upheaval all around them would come anytime soon.

CHAPTER 14:

Signed, Sealed, and Delivered

The beginning of 1941 saw more international drama in Europe and in Africa. In Europe, British forces arrived in Greece while a coup occurred in Yugoslavia which overthrew the pro-Axis government (those countries aligned with Germany, Italy, and Japan). In North Africa, Tobruk fell to British and Australian soldiers, forcing Germany to send its "Africa Korps" to support its Italian ally. The German army led by General Erwin Rommel prepared to re-take Tobruk.

In March 1941, the Russian government decommissioned the lita as the official currency in Lithuania and replaced it with the Soviet ruble. The conversion of 1 lita equaled 3–5 rubles, so such an exchange rate provided greater profits for the Russian military and party officials. Trying to protect the value of the currency, people started to massively buy any available products. This run on goods, together with a downfall in production following nationalization, caused additional material shortages and did not improve an already difficult situation.

In April 1941, as Passover was drawing near, observant Jews in Biržai worried how they were going to purchase or bake matzah now that bakeries were nationalized. Access to the bakeries was in hands of the city administration. During a visit to his parent's house to see the family and check on the yeshiva guests, Berl-David had a conversation with his parents about matzah. Every Jew in Biržai understood this unleavened flatbread is a remembrance of Jewish faith and was an integral element of the Passover tradition since God commanded the Israelites to eat only unleavened bread during the first Passover.

"Some of our neighbors and prominent citizens came to us with concerns about Passover and matzah. They want to know how we are going to have matzah for the holidays if the Russians operate the bakeries," remarked his mother. "You need to do something so we can have matzah for Passover."

"Would you like me to talk to my friends in the administration?" asked Berl.

"Yes, your father and I would like your help on behalf of all the religious Jews in Biržai."

"And for the yeshiva students of Białystok," said Rabbi Levin, launching his voice from the other room.

After leaving his parent's house, Berl began envisioning a plan. First, he must find a way to get the keys to the bakery. He knew it was one thing to get the keys, but yet another to acquire the ingredients to make the matzah. He would carefully approach getting the materials for the matzah one step at a time: he would begin with his Jewish supervisor, Motke Kerbel. Walking to work, he was contemplating his plans in his head and totally engaged in his own thoughts when he ran into Sonja Beder (figure 19). Berl and Sonja, who hadn't met for a while, warmly greeted each other. Berl told her what was going on with the matzah situation.

Sonja shook her head in disbelief and asked Berl if he remembered when their families got together after his return from Kazan, and he nodded his head and smiled.

"Let me tell you a story that always sticks with me from growing up." Sonja began. "My family had been in Biržai for some time. You may remember my grandfather, Leizer Gordon, was a doctor who used to help out the poor. My grandfather wanted us to be able to have our butter. With eighteen cows you'd think we should be able to have plenty of butter. The idea was we would have our own fresh milk, fresh sour cream, and be able to make cheese and butter. But the family used to laugh at ourselves when we needed milk and butter, because we would have to send the children to the market-place to buy it."

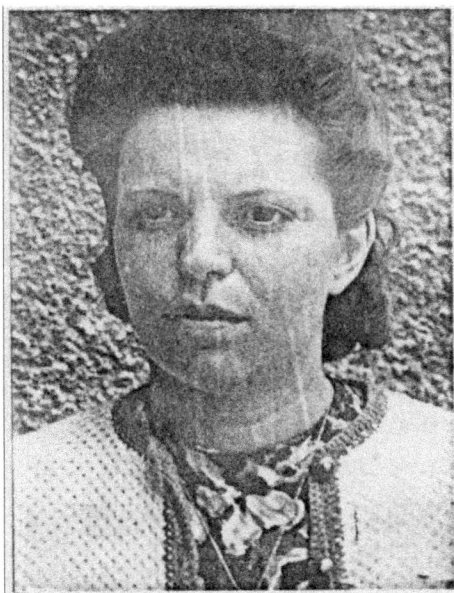

Figure 19. Sonja Beder. Reproduced by permission of Yad Vashem.

Berl, interrupted her story. "So, because he was a doctor, he was bad farmer. Is that why, Sonja?"

"Oh no, they were great farmers. They were just so generous to the local poor people and gave it all away and they had to go buy butter for themselves. That is what is so ironic to me about this matzah sit-uation, my family gave all our food away to the peasants until we had to go out and buy our food. And now the Russians won't even allow us to make our own basic necessities." Showing passion in her eyes, she added. "Berl, don't let these people stop you from doing what is needed. That Kerbel is such an amoretz."[45]

"Thank you for the story Sonja. Now I am even more motivated to work this out with my boss. I am heading there right now. Wish me luck." Just before he walked away, he asked her, "What are you up to?"

"I am heading to Kaunas for a couple months. I got a job as a typist for a Lithuanian engineer in the building commission. I am going to miss my family and Biržai but jobs for women are so hard to come by that I couldn't pass up this opportunity. The time will hopefully go quickly and then I will be home before long."

"That is great," Berl answered sincerely. "I will look forward to seeing you again and hearing about your time in Kaunas. I spent some time there and I'd be happy to share my experiences with you." They said goodbye to each other and Berl headed to work.

As Berl walked into the office to address Motke about baking the matzah, he was hopeful his boss would have some sympathies for the situation as he was also a Jew and because of the good work Berl has done for the administration. Berl greeted Motke and he quickly got down to the matter at hand. Berl explained the situation and then awaited his response. Motke didn't need much time to think or render his decision. His response was quick and disappointing. Motke replied instantly.

"There is no need for matzah. That is religious obscurantism and nationalistic superstition," he added sharply. Berl argued to the contrary that his parents and the Jewish people did indeed need matzah and they would not eat bread during Passover. He also told Motke they would work at night when nobody was around. Unfortunately, all of his arguments to Motke fell on deaf ears. Berl would need to revise his plan.

After some quick thinking, Berl turned to a couple of non-Jewish Lithuanians on the city council for support. The council's conclusion

---

45 Amoretz means numbskull or ignoramus in Yiddish.

was letting Jews into the bakery at night to bake matzah would require a letter of permission from a higher authority. After hearing their ruling, Berl went to visit his good friend Paungsnis, who had previously helped him and his sisters. Paungsnis wrote a note for Berl and told him to give it to the Russian official from Moscow who alone could grant the permission needed.

"Comrade," said Berl, as he met the official with a facade of loyalty. "Paungsnis wrote this note to you and it explains we are looking for keys to the bakery." The official read the letter very closely, rubbed his chin, and signed the letter of authorization without a single word. Berl took the letter and was about to leave, but he looked down at it and saw only the official's signature, not the official stamp. Thinking this could jeopardize the plan, he stopped, turned back and asked, "Is it possible to also have the official stamp?" Again, without uttering a sound, the Russian applied the stamp and with a thud it was all completely legal. Berl did not say a word to him about the real reason for the bakery keys, baking matzah, as there was no point in giving him a reason to say no. He was filled with excitement. Just as he was leaving the office to go home to show his parents the approved permit, he approached the room where Motke Kerbel was sitting alone. Berl walked into the office and laid the permit on his desk.

"Look," he said, "Signed and sealed!"

✡

Now that the keys were secured, it was time for part two of the plan: how to get the flour and the wood for the fire. Berl bartered with the department that distributed wood and exchanged a couple of bottles of brandy for thirty cubic meters of wood which he turned over to the Jews who would be doing the baking. In addition, they would buy their own additional flour from the mill. The left-wing Yiddish youth movement was opposed to the matzah baking movement, so

Berl went before them to advocate on behalf of the righteous Jews of Biržai.

"We're all Jews," he told them. "It's enough that we suffer anti-Semitism from the Russians, should we also cause trouble for our own older generation? We must take their customs into account." The final agreement allowed those who wanted matzah for Passover to have it and the Yiddish movement withdrew their opposition.

On April 6, 1941, while Berl was navigating through the matzah dispute and just one day before the start of Passover, the Nazis invaded Greece and Yugoslavia. Before the conclusion of Passover, Yugoslavia surrendered to the Nazis.

✡

Even in their late twenties, Berl and his friends still returned to walk by the lake and the castle when they needed to re-center themselves. As they got out of earshot from others, Itsik Shek blurted out, "Did you hear the news? The Nazis are getting closer to us and they are in our backyard now. How much longer until they invade Lithuania and Biržai?"

"Whoa, whoa, whoa! Hold on there, Itsik," Aaron answered, motioning with his arms. "The Soviets and the Nazis have an agreement in place. The Nazis aren't coming here." Speaking more from hope than with any real certainty, Aaron continued. "I know those flowers laid down at the tracks of the Soviet tanks have long since wilted and died along with our optimism, but I think we are still OK. Don't you agree?"

Yehudah chimed in, "I don't know what to believe, but I do know Europe is a mess. The Germans seem to occupy almost all of it now. Maybe the smartest of all of us was Sam, who got out of here and moved to the United States. That doesn't seem like such a bad idea after all."

"Well, I don't see that as much of an option for us, at least now anyway," says Berl. "At least the Yeshiva director, Rabbi Shapiro, and his sons and daughters are on their way to America."

"Mazel-tov," they all said in unison.

"Finally, something to cheer about," said Yehudah.

"I do have some news, though," offered Berl. "My 'friends' at the Soviet administration office have asked me to..." Berl paused and tried to muster his best Russian accent, "join za party." With that statement, the group let out a much needed laugh they feared was heard clear across the lake.

"Details, details. Tell us what great things you are doing for the party, Comrade Magid," joked Yehudah.

Berl waited for the second outburst of laughter to subside before continuing. He explained all the jobs he had been doing for the Soviets, including his creativity in solving the matzah crisis. "The Communist party members in the city council proposed I join the party. They gave me a questionnaire to fill out with a lot of questions. I told them I'd think about it, even though I had no intention of joining. I was fortunate the party had other pressing issues to deal with, like contraband leather, especially with Jews."

Berl continued telling his friends about two more situations where he had to intervene. "A Jewish doctor was arrested for possessing contraband leather. As a result, the doctor's daughter, Bunia, was expelled from the Communist youth group. She came to me asking what she should do. I went to my good friend Paungsnis and told him about this doctor's situation and that he happened to be an old member of the MOPR cell. The daughter has a sister in Russia whom she hadn't seen in twenty years and she was taking her a little piece of leather as a gift to repair shoes because leather was in short supply in Russia. To make it short, my conversation helped."

"I know what you mean." Itsik said. "They arrested a prominent doctor in Biržai for possession of leather, are you kidding me? Would they do that to a Lithuanian gentile?"

"Exactly the point," Berl replied. "Lithuanian gentiles who hide goods, even guns, are hardly bothered. Jews, on the other hand, are pursued for the most trivial matters, like leather. It is quite clear that anti-Semitism plays a big role in who is arrested. There was another incident with leather. This time with a Jewish quilt maker. He was found with some cured leather and they threatened to exile him to Siberia."

Yehudah interrupted Berl. "Why do they hate us? What have we ever done to anyone?"

Berl continued, "Before the Russians arrived, Lithuanians would say all Jews were Communists. Now, with the Soviets in power, all we hear now is that Jews are capitalists and rule the country. The hatred for Jews is constant and everywhere, and the anti-Jewish rhetoric spewing out of the Lithuanian Activist Front isn't helping."

Aaron listened to Berl's stories and with concern in his voice, said, "So to be clear, Berl, you do this great work, you intervene to help Jews in trouble, and you think they will just let you not join the party?"

"Right. Motke knows that I am not going to join the party and he lets it drop. I suspect that when I was recommended for a position as a photographer in the Soviet militia he intervened. The job was dependent on the approval of a Russian and I didn't get it, probably because Motke wanted to keep me in my current job. Also, I sensed the Russian in the militia was against hiring me because I was a Jew. Look, I don't want to work for any of the Soviets, but we need to survive, and I need to support my parents. All options are unpleasant at this point."

As the group headed back toward the castle, now gloomy and pessimistic, their recent laughter seemed like ages ago. Yehudah sensed the group needed a little levity to break the tension, so he recounted a story he overheard in the pharmacy. "Hey guys, I have a funny story I want to tell you." This got their attention and they urged him to proceed.

"I head into town one day to talk about my 'condition' with Gidal Dibobes, the pharmacist. While I am waiting in line, these two tough looking boys come in and head to see the pharmacist where there are a couple girls waiting at the counter. I see these tough guys talking to this man who I don't recognize. I can see on the man's face that he is confused, then the two boys lean in some and whisper to him. He finally nods like he understands, and he calls out very loudly to the pharmacist, 'Gidal, do we have, conservat... conservatives... conserva...' and he can't figure out the right word. So he says in Lithuanian 'prezervatyvai.'[46] The two girls start laughing and the two tough guys are so embarrassed they turn a great pink color when everyone turns to look at them."

Aaron and Berl look at each other, a little perplexed. Yehudah snickered as he explained to them this guy just shouted condoms across the pharmacy while these two "tough" guys were trying to quietly make a delicate purchase. Aaron and Berl joined the laughter.

Now heading home with smiles on their faces, they see many people assembled at the outdoor theater erected on the castle grounds. They stopped to listen to the speakers, knowing the speakers would be arousing public opinion for the Soviet power. The speakers praised the Soviet state and the new "socialist order" as the most "just" society in the world. They pledged the Soviets would continue to establish Communism where the workers would live in prosperity and happiness; that everybody must work diligently, fulfilling and exceeding work norms. All the speeches ended with the same refrain: "praise for the father of all peoples, the greatest and wisest sage in all humanity, our friend Joseph Stalin." Everybody in the crowd listening rose upon hearing Stalin's name, joining together with long applause and accolades. Berl and his friends looked at each other and shook their heads in disgust and resumed their walk home.

Heading home, Berl was lost in his thoughts wondering what was going on here in Biržai. The economic situation in Lithuania was getting worse day by day. The newly arriving Russians who were coming to Biržai said things were even worse in Russia. When comparing Russia to Biržai, they said Biržai was like America. The Jews of

---

46   Prezervatyvai means condoms in Lithuanian.

Biržai felt the political situation around them was getting so oppressive it would soon knock them off their feet. Those in power, the party officials making these speeches, pretended not to know what was happening beyond Biržai.

Shortly after the end of Passover, on April 27, 1941, the noose tightened. Greece surrendered to the Nazis.

CHAPTER 15:

Rising Tensions

Sonja was looking forward to starting her job in Kaunas. She was, however, apprehensive about the events that were taking place in the region while she was away from home and her family. In mid-May, as she was getting settled in Kaunas, the German Luftwaffe launched one of their most devastating air attacks on London with over 1,400 killed and a vast amount of acreage burned, including damage to their Houses of Parliament. The war was expanding everywhere.

When Sonja first arrived in Kaunas, she met with her new boss, Antanas Ratziukaitis, who was an engineer for the building commission. Upon arriving in the office, he greeted her warmly and made her feel immediately at ease. One day, toward the end of her shift, Antanas peeked his head out of his office and inquired, "It is a very nice evening. Do you want to go for a walk?" The question took Sonja by surprise so she hesitated, and then replied in a stammer, "No. I... I have plans." Not wanting to potentially jeopardize her job, she added, "But maybe some other time, Mr. Ratziukaitis. Thank you for asking me." Unaccustomed to being flustered, she was distracted and hadn't noticed that he had come around to her desk and gently put his hand on top of hers as he said, "No problem, Sonja, enjoy your time with your friends and please call me Antanas."

Soon, Sonja was enjoying the cinema, the theater, and all the places Berl-David had told her about. While things were going well socially with her new friends, she was concerned because the invitations from Antanas continued throughout her employment. She had some trepidations about the continuing proposals she was receiving from him. He was forty-four years old and she was eighteen, and he was her boss. She was also not comfortable with being too friendly with a non-Jewish man. She was a proud Jewish girl, comfortable with her faith and Jewish culture. She was hoping she could maintain a professional relationship with him, but he continued to ask her out on dates. One day, after she politely declined his offer once again, he grew irate with her. "Sonja, why do you keep rejecting my offers? I have been nothing but nice and gracious to you! Can't you be more friendly toward me and accept one of my offers?" Sonja didn't like his demeanor, yet she needed to hold her ground. "Mister Ratz, er, Antanas, yes, you have been very nice to me, however it is not proper for a Jewish girl to go out with a gentile. I hope you can understand that. In addition, you are my boss. What will people think?"

"What about when you no longer work for me, when my work dries up here because of this crazy war and your assignment ends? What about then, Sonja? Will you go to the theater with me then, when I am no longer your boss?"

Not wanting to take too many risks with being alone with him in his office, and not wanting to incite any more anger from him, she spoke in a non-committal and disarming way. "Let's discuss this when my work is done." Taking a page out of his book, she gently tapped him on his back between his shoulder blades.

"You're fired then." He announced abruptly. Sensing her shock and surprise by the look on her face, he quickly added. "I was just kidding, Sonja. You see, if you no longer work for me, then we can go out together. You know that I am very fond of you and your work here is excellent." Lowering his head, he spoke softly. "I won't bother you anymore, I'm sorry to have scared you. Have a good evening." With those final words, he left the office. Once he was outside, she let out a huge sigh of relief for having avoided another of his advances and for keeping the situation under control.

As May rolled into June and spring was turning into summer of 1941, things remained unsettled for Sonja in Kaunas, Berl in Biržai, and for all of the Jews in Europe. The tightrope of tension everyone was walking on was getting very wobbly and something would need to change very soon for the better, if people had any chance of improving their situations and getting onto firmer footings.

CHAPTER 16:

Things That Go Bump in the Night

T he townsfolk of Biržai—gentiles and Jews, though all religious, were still burdened with their old superstitions of broken mirrors, black cats, spilled salt, and such things, so they certainly kept a cautious watch every calendar year for the occasional bad-luck Fridays. In the middle of this Shabbat evening on Friday the thirteenth, June 1941, their superstitions were aroused with the rumble of trucks traveling along the uneven streets of Biržai. Berl-David was awakened by the sounds of the trucks through the night, some closer to home, but he fell back to sleep. His mother, Sheina, was typically the first one to rise and she enjoyed the quiet morning as she prepared to get her family and her guests awake, fed, and off to synagogue to celebrate the Shabbat. She was deep in her own personal meditations and lost in her thoughts when her peacefulness was suddenly interrupted. The rumbling she heard during the night in the distance was now thunderous and very close to their house on Vilniaus Street. Arriving at the window ahead of her, Berl was suddenly wide awake and aware as to what the raucousness was all about.

Berl and Sheina tried to comprehend what they were seeing. They slowly turned to face each other, both with their mouths wide open, but they couldn't utter a sound. They were unable to move. Seconds seemed like an eternity to those now awake including Moishe and Rabbi Levin who were standing behind them looking for answers.

"What is going on here?" Sheina inquired, nervously. "What are they doing out there? We need to go out and help them. Come on Berl, let's go."

"Ima, wait!" Berl pleaded with her, "First, we need to find out what is happening."

"What? What are you seeing?" asked a very concerned Moishe. "Please tell us now as we are going crazy. What is happening out there?"

Berl explained what he and his mother had seen on their street. "There was a Russian army truck with uniformed soldiers carrying rifles with bayonets. The Russian soldiers on the truck had the Gendler and Beker family members surrounded. It looked like there were about eight of them and the families looked very frightened, especially the youngster Itsik Beker."

"What is going on?" said an increasingly agitated Sheina. "Have they done something wrong? Is it just them that are being captured or are there others? We can't go through this again like when we were sent to Kazan, I won't."

As if on cue and just as the words finished rolling out of her mouth, there was a pounding at their front door. In a loud, aggressive voice, a soldier at their front door demanded the door to be opened. Everyone was in a state of shock, and there was no immediate movement toward the door by anyone in the house.

"Berl, you talk to them and tell them to go away. We have not done anything wrong. This is some kind of mistake," his mother's voice was shaking as the pounding continued and the voice outside grew louder and more forceful. Berl went to the front door of the house and opened it.

"We are here for Rabbi Levin. Hand him over to us and you will not be harmed," a Russian soldier commanded.

"What has he done?" Berl calmly asked the first soldier while noticing more soldiers standing in the background ready with rifles to storm the house. Trying not to show his fear at the presence of angry men with guns, Berl stood his ground. "Why do you come here on the Shabbat to take him and other families? What is the meaning of this and where are you taking them? He is not going anywhere until you provide us with some answers."

"I don't need to explain myself to you. I have my orders. Rabbi Levin can pack a bag, bring food, clothes, shoes, or whatever he wants, but he is getting on this truck in five minutes."

"It is the Shabbat," Berl explained to the soldier. "The rabbi will not do any sort of work, including the packing of a bag."

"So be it, then," the soldier said impatiently. "He can just get in the truck with nothing, and we will be off to the train station."

The rabbi heard the commotion and resisted, saying. "What about my family? My wife and my daughter are here with me. I am not leaving them."

"Fine, the more of you we take, the better." The soldier responded, his anger growing as he wagged his finger at them. "The more anti-Soviet dissidents we can remove from here, the better. Let's go. Now!" Pointing at the rear of the open bed of the truck already crowded with several families, the soldier gave his last order. "You and your family will get in the truck."

The Magid and Levin families shared a quick and tearful set of hugs, ending the sudden calamity that ravaged the calm and peaceful Shabbat morning. The loud, noisy truck filled with the Levin family and others, and accompanied by soldiers with their bayonets mounted, turned the corner and headed to the train station.

"Why just the rabbi?" was Berl's first question to no one in particular. "Do they have a specific list of people and what are the criteria? Are we safe or will they come back here for us? Will they take anyone directly off the streets?" He then sadly realized the other yeshiva students may also be in danger. "We need to go help our friends."

Moishe had seen that look in Berl's eyes before and he knew what it meant. Moishe was not going to be able to stop him, yet he was not letting him go alone. "It is not safe for you to go but I will not let you go alone." Berl and Moishe headed to the train station to ascertain what exactly was going on in their town and how they could help.

CHAPTER 17:

Russia Revisited

When Berl-David and Moishe arrived at the train station, the scene was chaotic. In a normal situation, the station and its surroundings are scenic, with the building nicely set back in a wooded setting. People regularly used the train system to connect with other parts of the world for business or pleasure. But not today. There was no pleasure to be seen, but unseemly business was transpiring.

The first thing that struck them as odd was that the cars attached to the train engine were boxcars used for freight, not passenger cars. Many of the doors on the freight cars were already closed and shouts could be heard from inside. The only opening for air were three small slits on the side wall toward the back of each freight car, carved out next to the Soviet initials CCCP and the hammer and sickle symbol painted on the cars.

They realized later how fortunate they were that most of the doors were already shut because it saved them from witnessing how tightly packed their fellow townspeople were in these cars, and how they were being treated like cattle. People were standing nose to nose in the cars and there was no place to sit. Soldiers were pointing their bayonet-tipped rifles toward the people, forcing them into the full cars. People were reaching out for air and help as more and more people were being added and pushed into the cars. The cars were so fully packed that some of the bags people had brought with them were removed and taken away by the soldiers.

The situation on the platform was not much better. Trucks with families continued to arrive as other empty trucks left and headed out to bring more and more families to the station. Families not on trucks were being herded on foot by soldiers with rifles. Some people carried cloth travel bags, others were in their Shabbat clothes, and many were still in pajamas after being dragged out of bed in the middle of the night. Children clung to their mothers who got down on their knees and pleaded with the soldiers. All in vain. The constant screaming and crying reached new crescendos whenever guards would force people back at gun point and slide the door closed, sealing their fate.

Figure 20. A chaotic scene depicting Jews forcibly deported to Russia on June 14-15, 1941. Reproduced by permission of Biržai Region Museum Sėla.

Father and son could barely fathom what they were witnessing. "Abba," Berl said fighting back tears, "I can't believe what is happening here, this isn't right."

Berl looked at his father, waiting for a response, but Moishe just stood there, motionless with his hands over his nose and mouth. "Abba, are you all right?"

Snapping out of his momentary daze, Moishe replied, "No, I am not all right, this is not all right. This is fercockt."[47]

"Where are they taking everyone?" Berl mumbled as he looked at the chaos in front of him. "What can we do to stop this?"

Among those being deported, Berl and his father recognized many leading Lithuanian and Jewish political leaders as well as wealthier Jews and Lithuanians whose homes, businesses, and enterprises had been nationalized. They saw one soldier who appeared to be in charge reading through a list and making notes. Berl was about to approach the soldier when he saw Motke Kerbel from the municipal council standing on the station platform. He walked quickly to Motke.

"Motke, what in God's name is going on here? The Russians have no right to do this, these are innocent people. You are in the administration—I demand you stop this immediately." Berl's anger was obvious as his voice grew louder and stronger.

"How dare you talk to me in that way! It's a good thing you didn't speak like that to the soldier," Motke said. "He would have found a space for you on the train."

"Let him," replied a defiant Berl. "You didn't answer my question, what is this all about?"

Motke smirked and handed Berl a document and walked away from him. Berl unfolded the document with his father standing next to him. He read it and then told his father what was happening.

"Let me tell you some of the 'highlights' of this Russian rubbish," Berl began. "A month ago, the USSR adopted a resolution[48] to purge the Baltic states of anti-Soviet, criminal, and socially dangerous elements. They are being arrested, having their property confiscated, and being sent to camps for a term of five to eight years. After serving their sentence in the camps, they will be exiled to

---

47 Forcockt means all screwed up in Yiddish.

48 In October of 1939 Soviet Minister of Internal Affairs signed a secret NKVD order for deportation of anti-Soviet elements from Lithuania, Latvia, and Estonia.

settlements in remote areas of the Soviet Union for twenty years. This includes former policemen, gendarmes, landowners, factory owners, former high-level government officials, as well as their family members. The arrest and deportation operation will be concluded in three days."

Moishe shuddered at what he just heard. "Do they mean Siberia? Are they sending them to Siberia?"

As the anger was heating up inside Berl, his father noticed the group of yeshiva students on the platform being escorted by soldiers. Berl and Moishe hurried over to them as they were being loaded into a boxcar. Just like Rabbi Levin, the yeshiva students carried nothing with them as they were not prepared for this deportation. Moishe tried to convince the students everything would work out and he told them he would go home to put together a package for them and Rabbi Levin. That was all he could do.

The turmoil in Biržai was intense as the lives of Jews and Lithuanians were brutally interrupted. In less than a day, on a truly black Friday the thirteenth, many were packed into boxcars and exiled to Siberia. Their journeys would last weeks, sometimes months, always in unsanitary conditions with little or no food. Everyone was in jeopardy of perishing on the trip, let alone not being prepared for the conditions waiting for them on the other side of the journey.

When Berl and Moishe started to head back home, there was a commotion coming from the other side of the platform. Above all the wailing and misery, there was a distraught man that could be heard pleading over and over again, "Take me! Take me! Take me, I'll go," he cried, "I just don't want to be without my family." A soldier went over to the man and asked him what was going on. The man explained that when he saw the soldiers coming, he ran away for his own safety, thinking they only wanted him and wouldn't take his family. But the soldiers took his family anyway and he wants to be with them. The soldier was more than happy to oblige the man and escorted him to the last open car.

As the last group of people were herded into the final boxcar and the door was shut, the train whistle screeched ominously through the Biržai sky. The white puffy smoke grew denser as the train lurched forward, slowed, and lurched again, probably knocking all the people into each other and even some off their feet onto the floor. The stop and go, stop and go, rocking motions continued like a cruel dance, entertaining only the devilish souls who design such horrors. As he watched the train pull away from the station, Berl was left with his thoughts of his journey back to Biržai from Kazan. He didn't recall his earlier journey in 1915 from Biržai to western Russia. He was too young to recall the misery of that exile. He didn't know what was in store for these people, but he knew it would not be pleasant. Berl and Moishe embraced on the platform, pausing to say prayers for the more than three hundred poor souls on the train.

Berl and Moishe surveyed the station platform and the surrounding grounds before heading back home. Strewn about were suitcases, bags, and packages that didn't make it onto the train. Soldiers were picking up the items left behind and loading them onto the now empty army trucks. Berl looked around and saw a small stuffed teddy bear laying on the ground, and he could not hold back a tear. Moishe noticed how emotional his son had become and he put his arm around him and gave him a strong squeeze. "Thanks, Abba," Berl spoke quietly. "You always know the right thing to do. What do we do now?"

Ever positive, Moishe instantly thought of the needs of the Rabbi and his students. "When you were talking to Motke, I saw on his papers that a troop train is leaving tomorrow. We need to get home, pack some things, and get them on the train for Rabbi Levin and the yeshiva students. Let's go home and get to work."

When they got home and told Sheina what had happened, she immediately sprang into action, baking and getting food together, even on the Shabbat. Moishe felt he had a special mission to help Rabbi Levin and the yeshiva students, so at dawn on Sunday morning he snuck out of the house and delivered luggage and supplies to the train station. He waited for the troop train that would take the soldiers and arranged for the items to be taken. His joy was great as he thought that he had been able to perform a true mitzvah.

✡

People were unsure if the deportations would continue and how the selections were being made. This was not just happening in Biržai but throughout all of the Baltic States on these three days in June 1941. The railway system soon became overwhelmed and in need of some relief, so the deportations were paused. On June 17, 1941, following the paused deportations, the People's Commissar of State Security, Vsevolod Merkulov, submitted a memorandum to Stalin, in which he reported a total of 15,851 people were deported from Lithuania.

Back in Kaunas, Sonja Beder came into work and was met by Antanas Ratziukaitis, who had created yet another approach for trying to move his relationship forward with her. He was aware of the ongoing deportation to Siberia, so he offered his help to her and her family as the continuation of the deportations remained uncertain. She declined this new advance, disguised as help, and looked forward to the end of June and the end of working for him.

CHAPTER 18:

Strudel

Following the events of the surprise deportations, the town of Biržai, along with many towns in the Baltic region, were in a state of shock. Middle of the night arrests and thousands suddenly deported in a weekend terrorized hundreds of communities. While the people who remained in Biržai were concerned about the fate of those deported, they also had to focus on their own prospects for survival.

Just as Berl-David was preparing to head to his job at the administration building, he bumped into his father in the hallway and pulled him aside. In a very hushed tone just above a whisper, he asked his father, "Do you think it is safe for me to leave the house and go to work with the Soviets?" He paused for a moment. "Do we know if these deportations are finished? And are we safe?"

His father faced his son and said softly, "These are questions I don't have answers to, but I do know one promising fact, son." Berl didn't respond. He just raised one eyebrow and tilted his head to the side to indicate he is ready to hear what his father had to say. Moishe continued, "On Saturday, when we were at the train station during the madness of it all, we both had a chat with your boss, Motke. He and his colleagues had the opportunity to arrest us and provide us with a one-way ticket to Siberia and they didn't. Thank God."

"He didn't then," Berl said quickly, "but maybe there is a second wave, and we could be on the list for today, or tomorrow! Who knows what their plans are for the rest of us? You saw the document he showed us. Maybe they view all of us as 'socially dangerous' elements and we could be next."

Moishe did not have any reassuring answers for his son but he wanted to comfort him. "Berl, you are resilient, strong, and confident. I am not so young anymore, but my strength and belief come from God," he pointed to the sky, "and I know we are fine. They had their chance to take us and we are here and safe. That I am sure of. What I am not sure of is whether the others in town may be next. I also know some of the people from our shtetl have had their families ripped apart and we need to do something for the people who remain."

"Yes. We need to be strong for the ones who need help. What are you suggesting?"

Sheina heard the hushed tones out in the hallway and came out of the bedroom. "What are you two up to?"

"We were trying not to wake you, my dear," Moishe answered. "Come downstairs and I will tell you all what I am thinking."

Moishe explained his plan to his wife and children. He suggested the young people coordinate a grassroots effort to pull together a pool of money of small donations from the townspeople, to buy or make things for the relatives of the families involved with the deportations. Berl and his sisters were excited and agreed to the idea. They left the house with a new sense of urgency and importance as they headed to their groups of friends. Berl headed directly to the Bass house and along the way stopped at the Shek and Segal households. He continued knocking on doors and spreading the word of their plan to the Shoket, Levitan, Khait, Melamed, Tabakin, and other families in the shtetl. He also included gentiles as the Lithuanian families were also affected and he stopped at many of the houses of his acquaintances. By the end of the day, a solid plan had been implemented and the people were engaged in this idea initiated by the Magids of Biržai.[49]

---

49 Magid means a preacher in Hebrew. The play on words is Berl Magid's memoir enabled the story about the Jews of Biržai to be told.

Following the fundraising, the making and baking, and the purchasing of goods, the recipient families of Beker, Fridman, Gendler, and Lipshitz, to name a few, were ecstatic with the generosity of the townspeople and their spirits were lifted for this act of love and kindness. Between the generosity of the shtetl and the completion of a much needed Shabbat celebration, the people were, at least for a moment, filled with gratitude and peacefulness. Berl went to bed on Saturday night with a hint of a smile on his face, satisfied they were able to bring some joy to families that, just a week earlier, had loved ones deported to Siberia.

What Berl thought to be a nightmare awoke him from a sound sleep, but it turned out to be shocking reality. Rubbing his eyes, he could not wrap his brain around the contradiction of the apparent thunder he was hearing with the clear blue sky of the bright new day. He realized that the thunder was emanating from the ground, and not from the sky. Their small house swayed from side to side with each clap of thunder. The entire family, now up and awake, rushed outside to see what was happening.

There was no storm, no thunder, and no clouds. However, the bright blue sky was filled with black planes circling very high up. Off in the distance, there was black smoke rising from the ground at multiple locations. The Magid family, completely shocked, was standing in the street. They were not alone; every family on the entire block was outside, all of them staring up into the sky in disbelief.

Suddenly, five planes flew at low altitude over the town of Biržai. The buzz of the propellers replaced the temporary silence from the bombings with a hum and a rumble they had never heard before. As the planes turned and banked toward the east, the yellow tipped wings was not the most distinctive feature of the planes. There was no mistaking the black crosses outlined in white and the swastika on the tail. These were German war planes.

Although these five planes were closer to the ground than the others, they were still relatively high, but it didn't stop some Russian officers from firing their pistols at the planes. The Russian pistols were ineffective against the planes, but the shooting made everyone around them terrified, seeing both gunfire and German planes in Biržai.

There were some Lithuanians who were not terrified. They viewed the invading Germans as liberators of their Russian- occupied country. In their minds, if the Germans were here to liberate Lithuania, it could mean the deportations had ended which would be a positive outcome for some.

The thoughts of peacefulness and goodwill for those few hours quickly and abruptly ended. The surprise attack of Operation Barbarossa started at 3:15 a.m. on June 22, 1941, as Germany invaded Russia through Lithuania. The partnership and non-aggression pact between Germany and Russia was shredded, just like the formerly peaceful skies over Biržai were shredded by the propellers on Hitler's Luftwaffe.

CHAPTER 19:

Caught in the Crossfire

Sunday June 22, 1941

Berl-David was joined on the street by Aaron and Yehudah after they finally stopped staring at the sky full of metal birds. They'd had discussions in the past about life, jobs, and girls, but what had just transpired introduced an abrupt new topic. Trying not to sound trite or overstate the obvious, Aaron instead asked, "What do we do now?"

"I have an idea," Berl addressed Aaron. "Abba and I met a girl last year around the time when he stopped working because of the new Soviet rules. I think her name was Regina."

"OK. How is that going to help us?"

"Well, she mentioned she needed to get home because her family listened to the radio on Saturdays. We can head over to her house and ask them if they have any news, or maybe we can listen to the radio together with them. What do you think about that?"

Aaron looked at his brother, then turned back to Berl, "That's a good idea. Do you know where they live?"

"Regina didn't want us to walk her home, but you know Abba, he insisted we at least follow her to make sure that she got home all right. I know where she lives. Let's go."

Berl, Aaron, and Yehudah briskly walked to Regina Batvinytė's house. They walked up to the front door and just as they were about to knock, the door opened and there stood Regina. "Hi, Berl," she said with a smile, startling him because she remembered his name. "Come on in, we are all inside listening to the radio." Berl and the Bass brothers walked in and were introduced. Inside was a large group of adults and children belonging to the Racemor, Orka, and Batvinytė families. The three new visitors moved as close as they could to the radio, but it was still hard to hear. Berl leaned over to Kazys, Regina's father, and asked him what happened. He said Joseph Goebbels, the Nazi propaganda minister, gave a speech announcing the invasion. "You are not going to believe this." Regina's father said to Berl. "Hitler said he is a 'man of peace' and Germany will destroy Russia in three months."

"Wow! God help us all if that is the case." Was Berl's solemn reply.

Kazys continued, "Russian's Minister of Foreign Affairs, Vyacheslav Molotov, is about to give a live radio address from Russia." Berl and his friends moved closer to the radio in the small room now crammed with people in the summer heat. The speech started and no one made a sound.

"Citizens of the Soviet Union. The Soviet government and its head, comrade Stalin, have ordered me to make the following announcement:

Today, at 4 o'clock in the morning, German troops have entered our country, without making any demands on the Soviet Union and without a declaration of war. They have attacked our borders in many places and have subjected our towns—Zhitomir, Kiev, Sevastopol, Kaunas and some others—to aerial bombardments during which more than 200 people have been killed or wounded. Hostile aerial attacks and artillery barrages have also taken place on Romanian and Finnish territory.

This attack is unheard of and is a treacherous act that has no equal in the history of civilized peoples. The attack on our country was launched despite the fact that a non-aggression treaty between the

USSR and Germany has been signed and that the Soviet Union has observed all conditions of this treaty in full honesty. The attack on our country was launched despite the fact that during the whole period this treaty has been in force, the German government has never once been able to dispute our observance of this treaty. The whole responsibility for this raid on the Soviet Union lies in its entirety in the hands of the Fascist German government."

Some in the room covered their mouths, others raised eyebrows as the speech was delivered and Kaunas, which is just 100 miles to the south of Biržai, was mentioned. The loud boasts of these two military powers, pounding their proverbial chests and proclaiming they will annihilate each other, left the people of Lithuania and Biržai feeling deeply concerned and fearful they would become collateral damage as the two powers fought across their borders. As the speech wrapped up, Berl turned his ear back toward the radio to hear the closing remarks:

"The government calls on you, citizens of the Soviet Union, to close the ranks around our triumphant Bolshevist party, around our Soviet government, and around our great leader, comrade Stalin even further.

Our cause is just. The enemy shall be defeated. Victory shall be ours[50]."

The young men left the Batvinytė's house and thanked Kazys for allowing them to join his family for the breaking news. Kazys told them they could come by any time to hear war updates on their radio. Berl, Aaron, and Yehudah were speechless as they walked in silence back to their families. They were deep in their thoughts, not knowing what to say. All of the times in the past when they pondered the future, their only solace was that "at least it wasn't the Germans."

50 Radio speech by Molotov, TracesOfWar.com.

Now that mantra was no longer the case. What was once a glimmer of optimism was now dramatically downgraded to a heavy dose of pessimism following a week of hellacious events. The news, stories, and rumors they were told by people, saw in the newspapers, and now heard on the radio were about to descend upon their hometown. What would life become for the people of Biržai? Sadder days for the Jews of Lithuania had begun.

CHAPTER 20:

Out in the Fields

Monday June 23, 1941

The surprise and utter swiftness of the initial German attacks completely destroyed the Soviet's ability to communicate and to manage a defense against the German invasion. The German Luftwaffe had free rein in the skies over Lithuania, from where they targeted and destroyed Soviet troop locations, supply depos, and airfields with no resistance. They destroyed almost 1,500 planes on the first day of the invasion and over 3,000 total at the end of the third day. The German Army Group North ground forces had the responsibility to invade the Baltic States and they attacked the Soviet northwestern front. The Soviets launched a powerful counterattack on June 23 at Raseiniai, about 100 miles from Biržai, a hallmark tank battle known in Soviet lore as one of the key border defensive battles. While this battle was ongoing, multiple German armies were streaking east toward the Russian border, with a northwest trajectory that put Biržai directly in their path.

The Jews in Biržai were panicked at the prospect of the Germans arriving in their hometown. Many Jews from the surrounding towns of Pasvalys, Radviliškis, Tauragė, and Kupiškis entered Biržai, bringing the total to 6,000 Jews. While many people were arriving, many Jews of Biržai had already fled the town in an attempt to make it across the Russian border to get as deep into Russia as possible, hopefully before the German troops arrived there. The idea of fleeing became a heated discussion among the townspeople. The Bass and Magid families met to discuss the prospects for fleeing to the Russian border.

"I am not leaving again," Moishe said emphatically. "The Russians deported us almost thirty years ago and Biržai is my home. Sheina and I are in agreement and we are staying. We will deal with the new regime as we have before. We will pray and ask God for help."

Taube Bass, the mother of Gita, Aaron, Yehudah, and Rivka sided with Moishe. "I agree with Moishe and Sheina. I don't want to be schlepping through the forests and trying to get to Russia. My dear husband Baruch has been gone for almost fifteen years and this is my home. I am staying. We need to decide what the kids should do. What does everyone think?"

Aaron spoke first. "Ima, your 'kids' are in their twenties. We are strong and can survive the journey, but should we leave and abandon you and everything that you and Abba built for us? I don't think we should." Looking at his siblings, then directly at his Ima, Aaron said. "Since you have decided to stay, Yehudah and I are staying with you. The question is what should the girls do?"

"I am getting out of here," Berl's sister Sore-Libe stated firmly. "I don't know how much of what I have heard is true or not, but I don't think this is a safe place for young women during war time. I would rather take my chances on the run than wait here as a sitting duck."

Her sisters Perl and Zelda jumped up and hugged their parents. "We are not leaving you. We will stay also."

"OK, then it is settled. What about you, Gita? Rivka?" Aaron asked his sisters. Rivka didn't hesitate and said she is going with Sore-Libe. "I am with Sore-Libe. I don't want any Nazi getting his hands on me. I am ready to go. Gita, are you coming with us?

"No, I am staying. I agree with what Ima said. This is our home, and we shouldn't be chased away. You go and we will stay with Ima."

✡

Tuesday June 24, 1941

It was agreed that Rivka Bass and Sore-Libe Magid would attempt to flee Biržai and head east to the Russian border. Berl, Aaron, and Yehudah would canvass the shtetl and talk with other families in an attempt to get groups to travel together to support and protect each other during their journey. As they were going from house to house and approaching the Beder's house on Vytauto Street, Berl-David suddenly remembered Sonja Beder was in Kaunas, a city bombed by the Russians, and he was worried about her. Berl, Aaron, and Yehudah walked up to the Beder house to talk to the family. Aaron knocked on the door. They exchanged greetings with the family and just as they were about to mention their plans to them and why they were here, Sonja walked toward them from the kitchen and greeted them with a huge ear-to-ear smile.

"Wow!" Berl was excited when he saw her. "I can't believe you are home. It must have been so frightening for you. We were all so worried about you. How did you ever survive and get here?"

Sonja was just as happy to see them. "Come in and take a seat. I have stories to tell you." Sonja began to tell them of her experiences of traveling from Kaunas to Biržai.

"As soon as the war started, I decided I had to leave Kaunas and return home to Biržai. I walked some, ran a bit, and got rides on wagons. While I was coming north to Biržai, there were plenty of people I came across heading east to Russia." She paused, looked down with sadness on her face, and then continued.

"They looked frantic. In the villages, on the roads, and in the forests, there were armed bandits with guns trying to prevent Jews from escaping. But I knew that I would make it home. I had to."

Berl interrupted her. "Germans, right? The 'bandits' that you saw were German soldiers with guns, right?"

Sonja stood up for dramatic effect and said loudly. "No! They were Lithuanians and they were shooting at us. They killed Asne and Leib Fridman near Rokiškis."

"Lithuanians killed the Fridmans? Lithuanians? I find that hard to believe," Berl was in shock. "What is going on here? I thought the Germans were the enemy. Why would Lithuanians be shooting and killing us?"

"I was told there were some travelers who made it." Sonja added happily. "But there are still many remaining out in the towns and villages closer to the northern border of Latvia. The partisans are getting more and more intense and they are killing Soviet soldiers. The German army is all over Lithuania and by now they must be at the Russian borders. They are taking Soviet soldiers as prisoners and they are forcing Jews to return to Biržai."

Berl, Aaron, and Yehudah sat silent, overcome with shock and disbelief.

Aaron finally spoke. He asked the same questions Berl asked earlier. "Lithuanians, really? Our neighbors could really be out there and shooting at us? Why would they do that?"

"It is true," Sonja said emphatically. "This is what I think. We Jews always saw the Soviets as the lesser of two evils, right? But the Lithuanians see the Germans as their saviors. They see them as their liberators from Stalin and the Russians. For the last year the Russians were here, many Lithuanians continued to spread their anti-Semitic rhetoric that Lithuania was ruled by the Jews. Armed with confidence, soon the Lithuanian Activist Front (LAF) also spread the same propaganda."

Berl let Sonja's words settle in his mind, then he questioned her again. "So, you think a large number of Lithuanians warmly embraced the German invaders as their saviors and believed the Germans saved them from further deportations to Siberia? And since the propaganda was that everything was 'our fault,' the new German occupiers found many sympathizers in the ethnic Lithuanians."

"Exactly. If they believed the lies and propaganda being spread that we were all Communists, the opportunity now presents itself to target and get rid of us Communists."

Berl's next words were prophetic. "We know of Hitler's hatred toward the Jews, it is well documented. So, what will happen when he brings his anti-Semitic beliefs to a country that is already blaming Jews for their problems? If Hitler convinces sympathizers to help him to carry out his plans, this really does not bode well for the Jews of Lithuania. We need to do something and quickly."

Still standing, Sonja shared one final thought. "Let me tell you a story. Like many of us, our family didn't have any bathrooms in our house, we had outhouses. So, one cold winter's night I wake up and I have to go to the outhouse. Earlier in the day my mother had put laundry on the line, including the boys' long underwear. As I rolled out of bed and headed to the outhouse, I looked up and thought I saw men standing near the clothesline. I screamed and almost had an accident, doing my business right where I stood. What I saw was the boy's long underwear completely stiff and frozen on the line and their white outlines against the black sky made them look like bodies."

At first, everyone was breathless envisioning the story Sonja had painted for them, but just as quickly they became hysterical when she explained what caused her nightmare. Laughter replaced fear when they pictured poor Sonja freaked out in the middle of the night thinking she had seen ghosts fluttering in the night sky.

"My point here is that the phantoms of my childhood are nothing compared to what I witnessed as I traveled back home. With tears in her eyes, Sonja pleaded with them all. "We need to get ourselves and our families out of Biržai now, before it's too late."

Soon after, the German army arrived in Kaunas and Vilnius without any resistance.

✡

Wednesday June 25, 1941

There was a lot of activity on Vilniaus Street and a number of people assembled at the Magid house. A wagon was sitting in front of their house. This was a bittersweet farewell for the Magid and Bass families. On the one hand, they were leaving Biržai with a chance to be safe but on the other hand they were leaving their families and their hometown. Sheina had put together a care package for Sore-Libe and her traveling partners.

"I packed you some bread, milk, cheese, and a little bit of wine." Sheina said nervously. She was not her normal self, always firmly in control. "I also have some bagels. I know how much you love those bagels. Oh, and a little bit of sweets. You need to have some sweets. What else should I pack for you, dear? Let me run back in and see what else we have." So much nervous chatter hiding a breaking heart.

"Ima, you have done enough." Sore-Libre said. "I love you. We will be fine. I am more worried about you and Abba staying here than of me leaving. Are you sure you don't want to come with us? There is room in the wagon."

Last night Berl shared with his family the stories that Sonja had told him the day before and it added to the tension and nervousness. Everyone took their turns exchanging well wishes, hugs, and kisses as the time approached for their departure. Sore-Libe Magid and Rivka Bass were joined by an entire Jewish family and others on their horse drawn wagon.

Sore-Libe was about to board to the wagon when Naftali took her aside for one final goodbye. "You have been a great big sister to all of us and a brilliant shining star in the eyes of Ima and Abba. You mean so much us, and your safe passage is so important to the community. This is definitely not a goodbye, just a 'see you later.' Let's all plan to meet in Palestine following all of this madness. Be safe sister, we love you."

With tears in their eyes, Sore-Libe and Rivka climbed on the wagon, holding hands, and carrying the precious goods prepared for them by Sheina. As the clip-clop sounds and the sight of the horse and wagon slowly faded from view, the families knew exactly what was needed at this moment. They all followed Moishe to synagogue to pray for the safe passage of Sore-Libe, Rivka, and all the other Jews trying to escape Nazi cruelty and to make it out of Biržai to a safe place in Russia. After prayers, Rabbi Bernshtein stopped Berl and asked him to wait and do him a favor in the synagogue. Berl told the family to go on without him.

Later as Berl walked home alone, he saw a big truck and a large group of young people gathered around it. He walked up to the truck and saw a school friend, Mina Fridlender.

"What is going on?" he asked her.

"The ten of us are leaving and going to Russia. It is not going to be good when those Fascist occupiers come to town. Come with us, my friend. Look inside, there are several of our classmates here. We have room for you on the truck. It is now or never. Are you coming with us?"

Berl was momentarily stunned and unprepared for the simple question. He had contemplated leaving a couple days ago when Operation Barbarossa first started, but he decided to stay for reasons he rationalized to himself and shared with his family. Before, it was a theoretical scenario he played out in his mind. This was different. There was a truck sitting before him with an actual opportunity to leave. Many thoughts began racing around in his head. He felt he was in the swirling bands of a hurricane. Could he leave? Could he abandon his family after telling them he would stay? What about Zelda and his youngest sister Perl? Could he just get on a truck, leave town, and not let his family know of his intentions or his whereabouts?

Mina leaned out from the truck and reached out with her hand, "It's time, take my hand, we are leaving." Berl steadied himself, placed his foot on the tire, reached up, and placed a hand in Mina's hand, but it was not his hand. A distraught young woman had arrived and was agonizing that her bicycle had been stolen and it was her way out. Berl placed the young woman's hand into Mina's and helped her onto the truck. He waved to them as the truck pulled away. He knew he was in the eye of storm, calm now, and he was comforted knowing he kept his word and followed his own advice.

✡

Later that evening, Aaron and Yehudah went to the Batvinytė house to get radio updates on the German invasion. As they approached the house, they noticed how very dark it was and wondered if the family was home. After gently knocking on the front door, they were greeted anxiously by the family. Kazys looked all around and he hurriedly whisked the boys into the house.

"Were you seen?" He asked the brothers. "There are all kinds of bandits and partisans out on the streets with guns looking for Communists, Jews, or anyone they think is against them. If they find you it could be very bad."

"Thank you, Kazys," Yehudah responded. "Can I ask, why is it so dark in here?"

"We have sealed off the windows, we are keeping the radio very low, and we are being very quiet so the bandits don't see or hear us."

"But you are not Jewish. Are you still concerned for your safety?"

"We don't know what they are thinking and we are not taking any chances, plus who knows what will happen when the Germans get here and fuel these bandits with their hatred."

Aaron and Yehudah moved in closer to hear the radio. The news from Moscow provided updates on the raging tank battle in Raseiniai. The Germans occupied Dubno and Lutsk, towns in Ukraine and Baranovichi in northern Belarus. Many of the Soviet troops in Lithuania retreated and their positions moved east toward the Russian border as the German offensive was streaming toward Daugavpils, a town in southern Latvia, close to the Lithuanian northeastern border and ninety miles from Biržai. An update was also being provided on the provisional Lithuanian government. It had secretly formed in April by members of the LAF and just announced on Monday, June 23, 1941. The provisional government asked the people to guard public and private property; the workers to organize protection of factories, public institutions, and other important objects; and policemen to patrol their territories preserving the general public order. The message was repeated several times in Lithuanian, German, and French.

Seeking some opinion on unfolding events, Aaron asked Kazys, "When do you think the German troops will arrive in Biržai? It seems some have already reached towns farther northeast and southeast of here. Will they skip smaller towns like ours in their quest to take Russia?"

"We can hope Aaron, we can hope," he said with a wistful sigh. "For now, please be very careful when you go home." As they approached the door, Yehudah stopped and knelt in front of a frightened Regina. "Don't worry, sweetie, it will all work out."

As they walked the couple of blocks home, they had a heightened sense of awareness following the warning from Kazys. They began looking out for armed bandits, slinking behind walls, crossing streets slowly and carefully, stopping multiple times to survey their surroundings. As they turned onto Dagilio Street, close to their house and the synagogues, they heard the rumble of engines and then saw a sight that caused them to freeze in their tracks. What they saw took their breath away. It was not the soldier sitting on the black motorcycle with the muddy boots, or the long black overcoat, or the rifle that was slung over the soldier's back that sent shivers down their spines. No, it was the Stahlhelm—steel helmet, with goggles sitting at the brim of that distinctive shaped helmet that told Aaron and Yehudah they were looking at German soldiers. In Biržai.

"Uh-oh," was the single utterance that came out of their mouths at the same time.

CHAPTER 21:

Protection Squadrons and Yellow Stars

Thursday June 26, 1941

The motorcycles Aaron and Yehudah saw were the leading edge of the German troops arriving in Biržai. The scope of the German military and paramilitary included Einsatzgruppen A, supported by the SS, Order Police battalions, Wehrmacht units, and Lithuanian auxiliaries. These German forces quickly combined with the Lithuanian nationalist activists and formed a new Biržai administration. The local auxiliary police forces, supported by the partisan units, were often recruited from former Lithuanian riflemen's organizations that had formed when the Soviets' retreated.

The local auxiliary police forces were known by many names such as Lithuanian auxiliaries, policemen, white armbands, nationalists, rebels, partisans, or resistance fighters, but they were all part of the Lithuanian TDA Battalions (Tautinio darbo apsaugos batalionas). These battalions were paramilitary units organized by the Provisional Government of Lithuania at the onset of Operation Barbarossa. The TDA battalions were intended to be used for the future independent Lithuanian Army but they were taken over by Nazi SS officials and reorganized into the Lithuanian Auxiliary Police Battalions called Schutzmannschaft. The auxiliary police wore white armbands with the letters TDA in black on their sleeves. The term Hiwi, the German abbreviation for the word Hilfswilliger or auxiliary volunteer in English, became synonymous with collaborationism. Just as the rapidity of the German invasion surprised the Russians, so too were the Biržai Jews about to be stunned by the changes that would be implemented in their town. However, unlike the commencement of the invasion which was clearly signaled by low flying airplanes and explosions rocking the country, there was a different and more menacing means of communication that would soon become clear to the residents of Biržai.

At the same time, Elvyra Valintėlytė and her father Eduardas were on their ten-mile-long market trip from Dvaroniškis to Biržai to shop at the Liberman's store at the intersection of J. Basanavičiaus and Kilučių streets. Shmuel Liberman was married to Zelma (nee Ilman) and they had three sons, Zundel and twins Haim and Berel, who were frequently in the shop helping their father.

On the journey, Elvyra kidded her father. "Dad, we don't go very often to Biržai but when we do, we always seem to go to the Liberman's store. You must really like shopping there."

"Yes, they are very nice people and they always take good care of us." Eduardas said as he tied his horse to a post and helped his daughter down from the wagon.

"I am so excited to be here, and I do hope the twins are here, they are so cute."

The Liberman family warmly greeted Eduardas and Elvyra as they walked in, but Eduardas, knowing Shmuel for many years, sensed something was not right. Eduardas took Shmuel aside to talk as ten-year-old Elvyra played with the twins.

"Shmuel, what is going on?" Eduardas inquired. "Is the family OK? Is business good?"

Shmuel answered him in a low voice. "I have a bad feeling about what is going on with the German attack of Russia and what it might eventually mean for us, and by us, I mean Jews. My friend, you are out of town in your nice place in Dvaroniškis and you are Lithuanian, so you don't have anything to worry about. But we Jews are very worried."

"What can I do? We have space up at the farm, why don't you come and join us. You know that Motel Levitan worked for me as a forester and he used to live in our spare room. You could bring the family there and get away from here until things cool down in Biržai."

"Thank you, thank you, Eduardas. You are a good friend indeed. But I wouldn't dream of imposing on you. Why don't you help yourself to as many store items as you would like to have?"

"Shmuel, you too are a good friend. I am not taking anything for free, I can pay. I insist. Plus, I haven't even paid off the radio you sold me." The topic of conversation changed and the visit neared an end. Eduardas and Elvyra settled up for their purchases, said their goodbyes, and headed home. Just as they were preparing to leave, a platoon of cyclists, who were German soldiers, arrived in town with the inscription, 'Vaterland,'[51] on their bikes. The soldiers dismounted their bikes and approached a store owned by a Jew named Elijah Nankin. Booming sounds echoed through the streets and reverberated through Shmuel's store as the German soldiers proceeded to break through the metal door and rob Elijah's store. There were children who had gathered outside, and the soldiers gave them everyday items such as socks and coins they had robbed from Elijah's store.

A visibly scared Elvyra was comforted by her father. "Daddy, that was so loud and scary. Why did they do that?"

"I am not sure, sweetheart," he told her. "But I know it is not safe here in Biržai. We need to quickly say goodbye to the Liberman family and get back home to our farm." Maybe, he thought to himself, there was something to be said for Shmuel's intuition about the future.

---

51 Vaterland means Fatherland in German.

✡

Berl-David was up early and upon leaving his house he didn't notice anything different on his short walk to visit Dr. Avram Zalman Levin. Aaron and Yehudah had told Berl about the German soldiers they saw the previous night and so he was on high alert. He was greeted by Dr. Levin and welcomed into their house at 4 Vytauto Street. The doctor's wife Sore (nee Dorfan) and their son Eliyahu, who also is a physician, were also at home. Berl immediately noticed that Avram and Sore looked worried.

Figure 21. The Levin family (L-R): Dr. Avram Levin, his wife Sore (nee Dorfan), and son Eliyahu. Reproduced by permission of Yad Vashem.

Berl and the Levin family exchanged pleasantries and then Berl asked, "What's going on?"

"Nothing, Berl. I'm just anxious about what's happening here, I heard about the arrival of the Germans and we are concerned what will become of us and other families in Biržai."

"I know some people have already left, and more are considering leaving, if that is still an option. Do you think it is safe to stay?" asks Berl.

Before Dr. Levin could answer, his wife Sore interjected, "Do you know the people in Biržai refer to my husband as Dr. God? Dr. God. He is a well-respected doctor in this town, and he has built a great reputation for almost twenty years since we left Vilnius. Nobody will touch him." Her husband attempted to say something, but Sore wasn't finished.

"Berl, let me tell you a story about my husband. One day I was walking down the street when an older woman stopped me. She knew Avram was my husband and she told me Avram saved her mother and relatives from death. I know he is a great doctor, so it was not a huge surprise to me. I asked her how did he do it? She told me he wrote her a prescription with a note, and he told her to hand both papers to the pharmacist. Do you know what was on that note? It said if the family ran out of money, Avram would pay for it himself. That is the type of mensch my husband is, a true mensch."

Dr. Levin leaned in and sweetly kissed his wife on the cheek. Berl was pleased to hear the story about Dr. Levin, but he didn't get his question answered directly so he assumed they weren't leaving. Trying a different approach, Berl asked them what they thought the Germans would do next.

"Berl, this is what they do," answered Dr. Levin. "They come to a town, they steal people's gold and valuables just like they did at Elijah Nankin's store, they make threats to intimidate the people, and they feel like big shots. Why do you think they say they will kill 200 people if one German is killed? To frighten us. To keep us from fighting back or from forming an uprising," insisted Dr. Levin.

Berl thought that Dr. Levin might be right, but he was still not sure about everyone's safety, including his. Changing the subject, he asked about their daughter Ester.

"She is doing great," said the now beaming Sore. "She is in her last year of medical school studies at Vytautas University in Kaunas. She recently called us while in transit to say that she was traveling with a troop train to Russia." Berl was saddened to hear the news from

Dr. Levin and thought it more likely Ester was possibly fleeing from Kaunas. He left their house in terrible spirits. What options were there for anyone in this predicament? He continued to agonize over his decision about staying in Biržai and he wasn't sure about the best course of action for himself, his siblings, and his mother and father.

As he left the Levin house to make the short journey back home, he ran into two brothers, Lithuanian gentiles, who he knew from high school. Even before they were within a handshake distance apart, one of the two brothers called out to him. "Berl, don't let yourself be seen in the street. It will be bad for you."

Berl, already feeling despondent about recent events, asked the brothers for more information. "What do you know? Has anything happened since the Germans arrived? Please tell me." The brothers looked at each other and then slowly turned toward Berl. "The German Wehrmacht is the army, navy, and air force that fights the armed forces of other countries. Are you familiar with the Einsatzgruppen?"

"No," Berl replied. "I haven't heard of them before."

One of the brothers explained who this group of Germans were. "They are a paramilitary group of the SS and they don't fight other armies. Their mission is shooting and killing civilians; to eliminate those people who they view as threats, or whomever they please to kill. In Poland, they killed thousands of government officials, clergy, teachers, nobility, prostitutes, mentally ill, and…" A long pause followed, and the brothers slowly turned to look at each other. Then they turned back toward Berl, their faces betraying their indecision whether to say more.

"What is it that you need to tell me?" insisted Berl. Though he was now fearful to hear what was going to be said, he knew he must know what this awful thing was that was too awful to be said aloud.

"Jews. They targeted the killing of Jews in Poland." These were the awful words Berl heard explode in his head. "Look Berl, we don't know all the details of why the Einsatzgruppen are here, but we did hear they are targeting people affiliated with the Russian Communist Party and Communist supporters. You worked for the Russian administration; you had some business with them. It's possible they're looking for you and others who did similar things. Like we said when we first saw you, it could be bad for you. You need to get out of Biržai."

Berl, sensing that the brothers had more information to share, could only nod his head to encourage the brothers to continue. Once again, they looked at each other but this time they said nothing. Reaching into his pocket, one of the brothers handed Berl a crumpled flyer they received earlier that morning from an auxiliary police officer. They witnessed all of the color drain from Berl's face, replaced by a terror-stricken shade of white. Berl stumbled, awkwardly reached out his hand to shake their hands. "Thank you. Thanks for the information. I… I need to get home." He turned and walked hurriedly, then began to run toward his house, barely hearing the "good luck" uttered in unison by the brothers.

As he hastily entered his house, destroying the peaceful morning, he stumbled into the living room facing his very startled parents and sisters. First out of her seat was his mother who immediately rushed over to him. "What message does this ghost trembling before me bring us?" Sheina asked. Berl, winded from his sprint home and still digesting the information, handed the crumpled flyer to his mother. Witnessing the exchange, the rest of the family all rose up and gathered around Berl, Sheina, and the crumpled flyer. Not a single word was uttered as they all silently read the flyer held in the shaking hand of Sheina Magid.

Finally, Moishe spoke. "Yellow stars? Are we really being ordered to wear yellow stars on our clothes? And a black letter J signifying Juden, a Jew, to be placed on our homes. This is outrageous."

"And the pavement!" said Perl. "We are not permitted to walk on the pavement any longer? We must walk only in the streets like dogs." Almost in tears, she asked in disbelief. "Abba, can they do this to us?"

The list continued with restrictions: Jews were forbidden to leave their homes without an official permit; to engage in any form of business; or to attend the market. Jewish stores would be closed down. There was also a warning that if one German soldier were killed, then in turn the Germans would kill 200 Lithuanians.

Moishe responded to Perl and the family with much pain in his heart. "Sadly, my dear Perl, they can do as they wish as they are in power and the Germans and Lithuanians are working together. It is a very sad time for the Jews of Biržai."

Berl, trying to compose himself, related to the family what the brothers had told him about the Einsatzgruppen and their theory about them targeting Communists and potentially him, since he worked for the Soviet administration officials. Sheina then threw herself on Berl in despair. "Berl, leave the house. Run away. They're going to look for you. I don't want to be the one to see you shot."

As word spread through the town about the new Jewish laws, people stayed in their homes and the streets of Biržai were barren of Jews. However, the streets were filled with many armed Hiwi who were out enforcing the rules and who were also looking for "rich Jews" to rob. Many of the Jews who fled from Biržai for the Russian border started to return because the borders were closed. When they returned, they found themselves detained by the armed Lithuanians and their houses looted of all of their possessions. The window of opportunity to leave Biržai seemed closed. The questions of what to do and where to go under these circumstances didn't have any quick and easy answers. Without agonizing on the decision he recently made to stay, Berl knew he needed a new plan, since he was a marked man. Even though the Bass house was not far away, he thought it was too risky to head over there in the daytime. Instead, he went across the street to the Shek house and he was happy to see Daniel Segal was also there. It was time to make a new plan.

CHAPTER 22:

Peaceful Sabbath

Friday June 27, 1941

Israel Shek was from Belarus and his wife, Sara Bliuma (nee Mikhalovich), was from Vilnius. They arrived in Biržai in 1922. Of their seven children, the six oldest were boys and not born in Biržai, while the youngest named Shulamith was a daughter born in Biržai. Israel owned a sweets shop and the two oldest sons were barbers, including Itsik. The Magid and Shek families became close when the Sheks arrived in Biržai and lived a few houses away.

Zundel Shek, the youngest son who was about eighteen, Daniel, and Berl-David huddled in the corner of the Shek house to discuss the recent events since the Germans arrived in Biržai. When their new plan was finalized, Berl went home to his family to let them know the plan. Berl lost track of time while they were deeply engaged in planning and when he walked into his parents' home, he was shocked that it was after midnight. Nobody was sleeping, so he sat down at the table and unfolded his plans.

"The Sheks know three boys from Rokiškis, which is about forty miles southeast of here. They are coming to the Shek house at 3:00 a.m. and Daniel, Zundel, and I will travel with them toward Rokiškis, but we will only go as far as Papilys, which is halfway, about twelve miles. From there, we will try to reach the Russian border."

Sheina was the first to speak. "That is very dangerous, especially with all of the new laws that have been passed. Have you thought this through, and do you think it is a good idea? Moishe, what do you think?"

But before Moishe could answer, Berl said firmly. "We will do anything we can to get away from Biržai, where the Lithuanians are rejoicing at the arrival of the Germans and where they seem very eager to unleash their hatred of Jews upon us. Ima, I understand your concern, and I have my own, but we must try something." With these words, Berl spent his last few hours with the family and they all said their goodbyes. He went to the Shek house and waited for everyone to join him. While waiting, Berl asked Itsik if he would look in on his parents and sisters while he is gone and Itsik agreed.

At 3:00 a.m., seven of them—the three boys from Rokiškis, Daniel Segal, Zundel Shek, another boy from Biržai, and Berl Magid—began their journey on foot toward the Russian border. At noon, they reached Papilys. Just as Aaron and Yehudah had told Berl a few days earlier, they saw German military riding around on motorcycles with their sleeves rolled up tightly as if they were in a military parade. There was nobody shooting at the Germans. On the contrary, the Lithuanians stood by with flowers in their hands and they showered the Germans with flowers. It truly was a parade, identical to how the Lithuanians welcomed the Russian liberators. This heartwarming scene did not fill the seven boys with much confidence. Instead it left them feeling sad and dejected.

✡

Back in Biržai, the new joint German-Lithuanian administration was just getting organized. However, the Jews were witnessing robberies, people being detained, and armed guards patrolling the shtetl. The Beder family was financially well-off and they were concerned the Hiwi would come to their home or business and steal all of their possessions. Sonja had an idea: she would take her gold, jewelry, and other precious and valuable family items and hide them at a friend's house. She knew her parents would never agree with the plan because it would be too dangerous for her to leave the house; so, she decided she would not announce her plan to the family. She went methodically from room to room without being spotted and placed all of the family valuables into a bag which she hid in her room. She planned to wait until darkness and deliver the valuables to her friend for safe keeping.

✡

In Papilys, Berl and his six traveling partners were watching a German parade from a veiled location. Once the parade passed and the street was cleared, they moved on toward Russia. Berl caught sight of a woman he recognized from Biržai named Pesa. She was wringing her hands and screaming, "My children, what's going to happen?" She stood there, a lost soul who was distraught about her daughter and her two grandchildren who were all taken away in a truck. They had disappeared. Would this woman ever see them again? Now it appeared the hysterical woman could no longer go on living: it was too much for her to bear. In that moment, Berl felt as desperate and despondent as he ever had in his entire life. He couldn't tell if his desperation was due to his compassion for poor suffering Pesa or if it was for his own dire situation. He reached into his pocket and felt the cover of the razor blade that he had brought with him for protection. Spurred on by Pesa's anguish, he thought about ending his life. It would be better to be dead by his own hand than to be murdered by the Germans or the Lithuanians. He knew from his father's teachings that suicide was incompatible with Jewish law. He thought long and hard about ending his life by cutting his veins with that razor. He stood there awhile, a lost soul, agonizing about his situation, and then he made a decision. No, he wasn't going to do any favors for the anti-Semites trying to rid the world of Jews. He did not know what fate had in store for him but just maybe he would have the good fortune to survive the hardships that were in his future. It was at this point that he harkened back to what the gypsy lady had told him four years earlier. "I see you hanging between life and death, closer to death than to life, but still staying alive wandering over the world." All right then, Berl thought to himself, here's to staying alive. He breathed in a large gulp of fresh air, an elixir, and put the suicidal thought out of his mind.

✡

Later, after hours of walking, the boys were tired and were in need of some water. Berl saw a well in a courtyard of a Jew named Cantor. He knew him as an agent for the Singer Sewing Machine Company; his mother had once bought a machine from him. Thinking this would be a safe place to rest and grab a drink of water, the boys headed toward the well.

"Hey," Mr. Cantor bellowed, "All of you. Get out of here right now. I'm serious. Get out of my courtyard or I'll alert the Hiwi!"

Normally, sharing water with travelers was a normal courtesy, but this was a growing problem. Everyone, including Jews themselves, were so terribly frightened of what would happen if a group of Jews gathered around their house. "What are we going to do?" asked Zundel.

Ignoring the owner's demands to leave, Berl told his friends. "We are going to drink some water and then we will leave. Now drink." They all took turns drawing some water from the well in the courtyard as Mr. Cantor yelled and pleaded with them to leave quickly, as soon as possible. After they drank their full and satisfied their thirst, Berl turned toward Mr. Cantor and said, "They will indeed shoot us, but you won't avoid death either."

Leaving the Cantor house, the boys continued on their journey toward Rokiškis. They saw a peasant with a horse and wagon, and they considered it safe to approach him about a ride. Much to their surprise, they were able to hire him and his wagon and he took them a little way further toward Rokiškis. When the peasant needed to turn off and go home, he handed them some bread and milk, dropped them off, and refused to take any money from them. The boys were amazed at this act of kindness and thought maybe their luck was improving. Since he wouldn't take any money for his efforts, they rewarded him with the only other item they had of value, a wristwatch. The boys then continued on foot once again toward Russia.

As the boys were walking not far from the village, the shock of their lives occurred when they were suddenly stopped by a German on a motorcycle. Without exchanging a word, they all believed that this was the end of their lives.

"Stop," ordered the German. The boys froze. "I know that you are all Jewish and you are heading in the direction of Rokiškis. Don't. Don't go there. It is not going to be good for the Jews."

The German army had just arrived in Rokiškis and they were exerting their presence as they did in Biržai. The boys figured perhaps hell had broken loose on the Jews and they marveled at the kindness of the German. He could have easily ended all of their lives right then and there. Not knowing much German, Daniel mustered a quick "Danka," and the boys headed further away off the path and continued to go deeper into the woods. When their heartbeats returned to normal, they stopped to catch their breath.

"Can you believe what just happened?" Zundel said to everyone. "We were dead men, yet we are still breathing. We need to figure out what to do with this gift we just received." The boys from Rokiškis decided that since they were so close to home, they would disregard the warning from the German soldier and keep on going toward home. Zundel, Daniel, and Berl decided to return to Biržai. Feeling a little bit stronger thanks to the bread and milk provided by the peasant driver, they started walking. Who knew what fate awaited them back home, this is not the plan they had when they left in the middle of the night. Their spirits were gloomy and bitter thoughts penetrated their minds as they started their journey back home.

It was around the same time, approaching 11:00 p.m., that the boys fell fast asleep in the woods outside Rokiškis, when Sonja Beder quietly sneaked out of her house to hide the family treasures. She went to Hela Savitzky's house near the Jewish cemetery. In normal times, the walk wouldn't take very long, but there was nothing normal about what was going on in Biržai. Typically, she would just head straight on Vytauto Street toward J. Basanavičiaus Street as that was the only way to cross the Apaščia River. She decided to take a long loop behind the Biržai Castle, walk along the banks of the lake where she had so many great times and memories, and paused at J. Basanavičiaus Street at the base of the bridge. Checking to see if it was all clear, she crossed the river and immediately dropped herself down into the brush. She sat still for a few minutes while she tried to catch her breath, continuing all the while to shift her eyes from side to side to see if she had been spotted. When she determined she was safe to proceed, she continued on her mission toward Hela's house.

✡

Saturday June 28, 1941

When Sonja arrived at Hela's house, she was relieved the house was all dark and quiet. She moved to the agreed upon location at the back of the house and much to her delight, everything seemed to be in order. She placed the family's valuables gently into the hole where they fit nicely. She picked up the shovel and very quietly filled the hole with the dirt pile provided by Hela. She was nearly finished when she saw a light come on at the neighbors' house—the door swung open, and then a male voice rang out in the still night.

"Hey, what are you doing over there?" She dropped down quickly to the ground and stopped breathing.

"Go! Go get her, boy. Get her off my property." The man shouted. Sonja heard the scraping of claws and nails on the walkway and then the panting of the dog as it came running directly toward her. As she lay motionless in the grass, the dog launched itself off a large rock in the backyard and leaped directly over her prone body in its single-minded pursuit of a forest animal of some kind or another.

"That's right, boy, chase that critter out of my garden before I grab my gun and kill it myself." Other lights turned on as the commotion stirred up a few neighbors.

"Will you lay off that vodka and go to bed. We are trying to sleep over here," yelled a disgruntled neighbor.

"Fine." The first man answered, then addressing his dog, he called out in the dark. "Come here, boy. Come. Daddy has a bone for you."

Sonja couldn't believe her undoing was almost caused by a drunk and his dog, and not from a Hiwi pointing a rifle at her, threatening to kill her. Finally, the dog returned home for his midnight snack and all the lights went out. Sonja remained in the grass for some time to make sure it was safe to return home. As she was about to get up, the quiet night was interrupted by automatic gunfire nearby in the direction of her house. While her reaction should have been to stay down, she immediately sat up and looked toward the gunfire, expecting to see something. The gunfire stopped as fast as it started and there was nothing for her to see. She hurriedly finished her task and started home, now spooked by the close gunfire. The trip home was less eventful and she snuck back into her house, satisfied she was not spotted by any family members. She quietly slid into bed, and the last thing she heard before her eyes shut was, "Where were you, young lady? Shabbat Shalom." Sonja's father gently shut her door and went back to bed.

CHAPTER 23:

All Bets Are Off

Saturday June 28, 1941

A full day had passed since Berl-David visited the Levin house and also since he departed from Biržai. The Levins enjoyed a restful evening and slept peacefully in their bed, dreaming of better times. But their quiet evening, dream, and even their existence was twisted into a living nightmare by a pounding on the front door.

The loud banging on the door immediately woke up the household. A startled Eliyahu came bounding into his parents' bedroom. Dr. Levin told Sore and his son to stay in their bedrooms and to keep the door shut, telling them he would see what the noise was all about. He went downstairs to see who was beating on his front door and waking up his neighbors.

"All right, all right, I'm coming," he said. "Keep the racket down."

He rushed into the front room and opened the door to see two Lithuanians standing at his door. They barged roughly past him into his house. The two men were very agitated and didn't ask any questions, they just walked into his house and started making demands.

"You need to come with us right now. Someone is sick at headquarters. Let's go!" one of the men shouted. They approached Dr. Levin very aggressively. He backed away, tripped over the foot stool, and fell to the floor. When he looked up, he saw Sore and Eliyahu standing in the room at the bottom of the stairs.

"Someone is sick, and they have come to me for help," Dr. Levin said, as he managed to stand up. Dr. Levin was skeptical about this request to help someone sick and he was hesitant to go with these men.

"Abba, let me go with you." His son said. "We can both help whoever is in distress and then we can return home and get back to bed," said Eliyahu.

Dr. Levin thought this was a good idea, so he started speaking to the men. "I need more information about the patient before we leave here…" But he could not finish the thought before he was struck in the face by the first goon while the second came from behind and hit him across the back with a chair. Dr. Levin was stunned and fell down. The room began to spin and he couldn't lift himself up off the floor. Unfortunately, he received unwanted help. The man who threw the punch grabbed him by his shirt and violently lifted him up. The doctor felt like his feet weren't touching the ground; the goon was now nose to nose with him.

"I'm not going to tell you again, let's go. Now!"

Sore was stunned to see her husband treated this way. Eliyahu took a step toward his father but he was intercepted by the other Hiwi. "Not one more step, either of you, or you get the same treatment."

"OK, OK," Dr. Levin said, in a hushed tone, which took all the strength that he had just to get those two words out. "I will go with you, alone, and we can help the sick patient. Just leave my family alone, do you understand?"

"Let's go then. And if you try anything fancy, there is more of this for you," he said, while holding his large, closed fist up in front of the doctor's face.

The door to his house was still open as the two goons shuffled out into the street with Dr. Levin sandwiched between them. Sore looked out and last saw them walking on Vytauto Street toward the marketplace, when she shut the door. Still speechless and in shock, and not knowing what else to do, she and her son cleaned up the room. She walked upstairs to return to bed when she heard gunshots. Since this was happening frequently these days since the German occupied Biržai, she dismissed it, never possibly thinking she had heard the sounds of her husband being murdered.

PART III:

The Null Hypothesis

A null hypothesis in research would state there is no difference when examining two groups. In Biržai, would the fate of the Jewish people be better if they stayed in town or left? Location has no effect on fate.

CHAPTER 24:

Dr. God

Saturday June 28, 1941

The large tank battle that had been raging at Raseiniai since the start of Operation Barbarossa had finally concluded. The Red Army tried to contain and destroy the German troops, but they were unable to prevent them from advancing. The result of the battle was the destruction of most of the Soviet armored forces of the Northwestern Front which cleared the way for the Germans to attack and gain the Russian border. This would make it more difficult for the Jews to escape Lithuania and enter Russia.

B erl, Zundel, and Daniel woke up after a very exhausting twenty-four hours on the run, and they were hungry. While they had the food their parents gave them for the journey and also had received more from the peasant driver, they were trying to conserve their supply. After nibbling on some bread and cheese, they started out again on the way back to Biržai. Later in the morning a horse and wagon approached them and as they stepped aside, they heard a timid voice ask, "Hey, are you Zundel Shek?" The wagon stopped and the boys recognized the Rotsamer brothers from Biržai with their wives and children. Berl-David and his companions had many questions for those in the wagon who were returning home to Biržai. "Are you all right? Where were you trying to go and what happened? Where are you going now and what was it like out there?"

The Rotsamer families explained they were one of the first families who attempted to leave Biržai when the Germans arrived, and they headed for the Russian border. They were making good progress with not many issues along the way until the German troops quickly took control of the borders and turned everyone back. Berl's heart sank as he thought of his sister, Sore-Libe, and Rivka Bass and worried about them, not knowing yet of their fate.

"We can't take all of you with us, you see the wagon is very packed. But I think we can squeeze in Zundel. Do you want to join us, if you are heading home to Biržai?"

Daniel and Berl embraced Zundel, said their goodbyes, hugged each other, and helped Zundel onto the wagon. From the original seven who started out, only Daniel and Berl remained as they started out walking again in the summer heat. Sometime later, tired from the walk, they were approached by a peasant asking them if they wanted something to eat and drink. He treated them to bread, milk, and cheese and the boys were once again amazed by the kindness of a stranger. But while they were enjoying the food and rest, he suddenly pulled out a revolver and pointed it at Daniel and Berl.

"I could shoot you and no chicken would crow. Jews don't have any rights now. But I'm not going to do that. I'll give you a warning instead. Go through the field. Otherwise, you'll have to pass the monastery. Lithuanians who are helping the Germans are staying there."

The sight before the peasant's eyes inspired him to add, "Close your mouths, finish up your food, and move along." The boys didn't need to be told twice. They hurriedly thanked the peasant for the kindness of the food he gave them, and for not killing them.

Berl and Daniel found a secluded spot in the forest and collapsed in the grass. One minute they are rejoicing in the kindness shown to them by a stranger in these crazy times and then seconds later they are staring down the barrel of a gun. The tightrope of tension which had previously been swaying now seemed to be fraying, above a safety net that had been removed, leaving the people to teeter between life and death.

✡

Sunday June 29, 1941

Through the night, Sore Levin tried to stay awake and wait for her husband's return, but she was too exhausted, both mentally and physically, so she fell asleep. In the morning, when she was downstairs in the kitchen, she heard a knock on her door in very rapid succession, followed by the sound of someone calling her name. "Sore! Sore, open the door! Sore, please."

She shuffled slowly over to the door. "OK, OK already, I'm coming."

Sore opened the door and saw her neighbor, Muse Drumlevich, standing there.

"Sore, I need you to listen to me, and listen to me very carefully. I need you to sit down." Sore was dumbfounded, not understanding why she was being asked to sit down. Muse gently directed Sore to the couch. "Sore, I have to tell you something. It's very serious."

Sore looked into Muse's eyes and felt Muse supporting her by the shoulders but she couldn't hear her saying anything. Nothing. Then a single tear began a slow, quiet journey from the woman's eye. Sore remained silent but her chin fell down and her mouth opened as she realized the woman was communicating to her about Avram. Sore suddenly shrieked a painful and elongated, "No..." and fell into Muse's arms and immediately began sobbing. Sore's son, Eliyahu, heard his mother cry out and rushed downstairs. He didn't yet know what had happened, but he saw his neighbor holding his distraught mother and he knew it was not a good sign.

"What happened to my husband?" Sore weakly asked her neighbor.

"He is dead." Muse answered quietly. "His body was discovered this morning, laying on the street in a pool of his own blood."

Sore's mind went numb at first. Who would kill her husband? Why? Then she remembered the incident that occurred last night, and the two men who took him from the house to heal someone.

"Those brutes!" she bellowed, her emotions quickly turning to anger. Muse was confused and asked Sore what she was talking about. Sore explained the events of the previous days, providing the details of the previous night. While Muse was trying to digest all of the facts, Sore suddenly tilted her head sideways and looked at her without saying anything. Just staring at her but not seeing her.

"What is it, Sore?"

"Did you say my husband's dead body is lying in a street in his own blood?"

The neighbor slowly nodded her head and looked away from Sore, unable to make eye contact with Sore after confirming her words were correct.

"Take me to him." Sore requested in a spiritless voice.

Sore and Eliyahu quickly dressed and followed Muse outside. On the way to the marketplace where Avram Levin was murdered, Muse explained to her why no one had moved his body. It was known the Germans and their local collaborators wanted to frighten and intimidate the Jews of Biržai and a part of that intimidation was to leave Avram's body in the street for all to see. They believed if the leaders of the Jewish population were neutralized—imprisoned or killed—all others would become submissive and not fight back.

When they arrived in the marketplace, there was a small gathering of people standing around Avram's body. As soon as the people recognized Sore, they moved aside to allow her to pass through to her husband. She knelt on the ground and pulled him to her, hugging him tightly. She laid him back on the ground and extended her arms to Eliyahu who had brought their best white bed sheets to cover Avram Levin's body. The sheets quickly soaked up all of Avram's blood as the lifeless outline of his body remained motionless on the streets of Biržai.

The news of Dr. Levin's murder spread quickly throughout Biržai. Jews and Lithuanians were both shocked and saddened.

✡

While Biržai was dealing with the loss of Dr. Levin, Berl and Daniel were trying to survive on the road and not become casualties of war. After their episode with the peasant, the boys went through the field and back out onto the road. They had a heightened sense of awareness and caution, but motorcycles moved much faster than a horse and wagon.

"Jews, stop!" they heard shouted at them just above the roar of a motorcycle. They were stopped by two Lithuanians with white armbands on the sleeves of their left arms. They were not interested in small talk. "Empty your pockets," they demanded.

They boys didn't have much to offer so there was nothing of interest to the Lithuanians. "You don't look familiar. Are you from around here?" they asked. Berl and Daniel explained they were headed home, back to Biržai. The Lithuanians waved them off, sending them on their way. Berl and Daniel didn't fully understand the intention of the white armbanders who stopped them; they believed they were going to be shot. Nevertheless, they took off and started running as fast as they could, feeling as if their feet were not touching the ground, feeling as if they were flying. When they were totally exhausted and couldn't run any longer, they arrived at a bend in the road and stopped. Breathing heavily, they looked back and were extremely pleased to see the Lithuanians and their motorcycles had disappeared.

After several minutes of trying to catch their breath, Daniel asked Berl, "What was that all about? We have run into Germans, Lithuanians, and peasants who could kill us, but somehow, we are still alive. Are they toying with us?"

"I don't know, Daniel," said Berl. "Did you see that white armband on those two Lithuanians? Are they working for the Germans? How could they be so organized? The Germans have only been in town for a few days. I am really worried about what might be going on at home. We really need to keep moving."

The boys continued toward Biržai. Their pace was very slow because of the many dangers to be avoided along the road but they pressed on. As nightfall approached, they looked for a place to sleep. They came upon the house of a Lithuanian and as they approached the doorway, he refused to let them inside, but he allowed them to sleep in the hay in the barn. This was much better than sleeping under the open sky in the field. As they laid down in the barn, their heads were filled with bitter thoughts of their situation, but they were exhausted and they soon fell quickly into a deep, much needed sleep.

CHAPTER 25:

A Spider's Web

Monday June 30, 1941

The rest for the boys was much needed for their bodies, and for their minds, and especially their souls. The sun was up and shining brightly outside but their souls were dark and dreary. As they rested on the hay, they contemplated their next steps. "What do we do? What will become of us?" asked Daniel.

"Do you see how a spider in the spider web waits for a fly? We're also surrounded by a spider web. As long as we lie here, we are safe. Outside we have to protect ourselves from falling into the spider web."

"OK, that's very helpful," Daniel remarked sarcastically. "But how long can we stay here lying on hay? Plus, I am hungry."

"We can't stay here." Berl's voice was stronger now after some rest. "We must remain men and we must leave here and face our destiny," Berl-David stood and Daniel followed him out of the barn, and they continued their journey back to Biržai.

✡

At the same time Rabbi Yehuda Leib Bernshtein and his wife Liba Sheina (nee Dverovich) were enjoying a nice, quiet breakfast following their morning prayers in their Biržai home.

"Yehuda," his wife asked, with unusual concern in her voice, "do you think it is safe for you to continue to conduct services at the synagogue? It is now against the rules and if they catch you, what will those murderers do to you? You saw what they did to poor Dr. Levin. Let us pray to God it never happens to us, keinehora."[52]

"Liba, all our fates are in God's hands. I will continue to follow our teachings, read from the Torah, and celebrate the Shabbat until my last breath passes through my mouth," her husband answered, then they shared a hug as she moved to the kitchen to refresh their cups of tea.

Liba had just entered the kitchen when the peacefulness in the house was abruptly ended. The house shook violently as the front door was obliterated without any warning. Shocked by the unexpected explosion of sound, the rabbi fell off his chair onto the floor. "Him, that's the one," yelled one of the armed bandits who burst swiftly into the Bernshtein house. "He is the one who reported me to the police for breaking the windows in their Jew church." The same bandit now pointed directly at the rabbi who still hadn't gotten off the floor. "Now you will pay," he added loudly.

The bandits rushed over to Rabbi Bernshtein and they yanked him roughly to his feet. "You are coming with us," they said heading him toward the door.

"Stop. Where are you taking him?" shouted a distraught Liba. "He hasn't done anything or harmed anyone. He is a rabbi."

"Don't worry, we will bring him back right after he meets with the new administration. It will be all right," one of the bandits assured her. Unable to stop the men, Liba could only watch in tears as the two bandits, one on each side, lifted him under each arm and carried him outside where they were joined by a mob of other Hiwis. But they were not going to the administration building to meet with officials, they were headed to the Jewish Cemetery by Lake Širvėna. When

---

52 Keinehora means knock on wood in Hebrew. Usage translates to wishing no evil eye on someone.

they arrived by the lake, they forced him to kneel on the bank of the lake. "What is the meaning of this? I am a rabbi, and you have no right to treat me this way. I demand you take me back to my home." But he was immediately cut off by a swift smack across the face. "Shut your mouth, you have no rights here, Jew."

The leader of the group then read a proclamation. "Rabbi Bernshtein, you are guilty of all of the sins Jews have committed against the world." He then gave a nod to the two accomplices who were holding onto the rabbi. They dunked his head into the lake, and held his head underwater, only bringing him up after the leader gave the signal. Dripping wet and gasping for air, Rabbi Bernshtein coughed and tried to catch his breath. He couldn't even speak to tell them to stop. The leader continued with his rhetoric. "Rabbi Bernshtein, you are responsible for the sins of all the Jews of Biržai." Again, the signal was given, and the rabbi was dunked into the lake. This time he was held under a little longer and when they brought him back up, he was in worse condition. After the water torment, the murderers continued their torture of the renowned rabbi by lighting his beard on fire and burning his body with hot irons before finally shooting and killing him. The killing of Dr. Levin and Rabbi Bernshtein marked the beginning of pogroms and other atrocities against the Jews of Biržai.

✡

Later in the evening, Berl and Daniel were winding down another day of slow, careful, and now methodical walking. They were getting closer to Biržai when they recognized a Jewish student who was studying at the public high school in Biržai. After exchanging greetings, the student asked, "Are you heading back to Biržai?" Berl and Daniel nodded yes. "Don't go there." The student warned. "I heard they have started killing prominent Jews in town. A couple days ago it was Dr. Levin and today I heard it was Rabbi Bernshtein." Berl's mind was racing as he played back in his mind the last conversation he had with Dr. Levin a few days ago. It appeared that things were spiraling out of control. And now Rabbi Bernshtein…Berl was having trouble understanding why anyone would kill a respected doctor and a rabbi? The boys thanked the student for the information, wished him good luck, and continued on their way. After hearing the news, Berl and Daniel wanted to go home immediately, contrary to the advice they received. They developed a more purposeful and quicker pace to get home faster.

According to their calculations, it would take five hours to get home if they kept a brisk pace. As dusk was nearing, they liked their chances of travelling in the dark, so they decided to rest for a while and wait for the darkness. Once it was fully dark, Berl and Daniel started out toward Kupreliškis, using the moon as their flashlight. As they approached the edge of the village, they saw two Lithuanians with rifles and white armbands on their left arms. At first, Berl and Daniel became frantic, thinking they would be captured by these guards. But as they approached, Daniel and the two Hiwis recognized each other. Daniel and the two Lithuanians attended high school together and were in the same class in Biržai.

"Daniel, is that you?" called out one of the Lithuanian nationalists.

"Yes. Yes, it is. We are so glad it is you guys," Daniel replied with great relief. "Do you remember meeting my friend Berl back in Biržai when he was leaving for the army?"

"No, not really." One of the men replied.

"That's OK, it was a while ago. Anyway, we are heading back to Biržai. Do you have any advice for us on getting home safely?" asked Daniel. The two Hiwis, who initially had their rifles strapped on the shoulders pointing upwards, now lowered their guns and pointed them at Berl and Daniel.

"What are you doing?" asked a bewildered Daniel. "It's me, Daniel Segal. We are friends. We went to school together. What is this, some kind of joke?" The two men did not lower their rifles.

"The only difference between you two Jews and all the other filth is we know your names." They motioned toward Berl and Daniel with their rifles. "Now, move!" The two high school "buddies" arrested Berl and Daniel and led them into a formerly Jewish-owned supply shop that had once stored flax and seeds. It appeared the outstretched spider web had succeeded in capturing Berl and Daniel. Now what would the spiders do with their prey? That became the question; it was the last thing that went through their minds as they fell asleep on the hard floor of the flax and seed store, now hastily transformed into a prison.

CHAPTER 26:

Home, Not So Sweet Home

Tuesday July 1, 1941

The situation in Lithuania had worsened. As June ended and the calendar flipped to July, Operation Barbarossa continued to make steady progress: the German Luftwaffe began bombing Leningrad and the German ground forces captured Minsk. Happening at the same time, and much closer to them and therefore a bigger worry to the people in Biržai, was the Lietūkis Garage Massacre in Kaunas where fifty Jewish men were killed with iron bars. Everyday, Jews were disappearing, either being imprisoned or shot. Anybody capable of working was forced to do horrible menial tasks while being berated and beaten. Residents were also returning from their failed attempts to flee into Russia.

Aaron and Yehudah were very worried about the state of affairs in their town after the brutal murders of their doctor and rabbi. There was still no word on the fates of Berl-David and his sister Sore-Libe or their cousin Rivka who had all recently fled Biržai. Aaron and Yehudah had not returned to the Batvinytė house since the Germans arrived in Biržai the previous week, and they decided to go over for a visit. As they arrived at the house after carefully walking the short distance, they noticed a woman standing outside talking through the window with Marijona Vinclavaitė-Batvinienė. When they approached, Marijona said hello to the boys.

"Why don't you come in?" Marijona said to the boys and the rabbi's wife. "It is dangerous to be standing outside here in the courtyard."

Once they were in the house, she asked the boys if they knew the wife of the rabbi and their faces quickly turned pale. Yehudah reached out to her and said, "We are so sorry to hear about your husband."

The rabbi's wife spoke, "I see why your color has drained, but I am married to a different rabbi in the town. It was truly horrible what happened to Rabbi Bernshtein. I have been to their house since the horrible incident, and poor Liba Sheina is devastated."

After an uncomfortable pause, she continued, "As you know, our customs do not permit Jews to enter buildings of Christians. My husband and I follow the strict rules of the faith."

"Yes, I understand the custom, but surely these times allow an interpretation for safety?" said Marijona.

"The barbarians can choose how they wish to act, and I will also choose how I wish to behave," said the rabbi's wife.

Marijona nodded in agreement and wisely changed the subject. "Can you tell the boys about the guests that arrived at your house?"

The rabbi's wife told the Bass boys that a group of about ten to twelve young men from the yeshiva in Romania had arrived in Biržai and they were all staying at her house. Marijona started to laugh and explains, "My husband and I call them 'half-rabbis' because we know they are students, but we didn't know the word 'yeshiva.' They are very attractive men, all so tall, handsome, with black hats, wearing black coats, and black suits. They definitely look like they were selected for the teaching they were receiving. Among them there was one small man, not very tall at all. We always admired all of them and watched as they walked to the synagogue."

They all shared a much-needed laugh. "'Half-rabbis.' Now that is funny; but it does describe it very well," observed Yehudah.

"They all go to the synagogue, every day. Your house," Aaron remarked as he pointed to the rabbi's wife, "is behind the bridge, so they also pass by our house every day on their way to and from the synagogue."

Even though the strictest of regulations were enforced in the German-occupied Biržai shtetl, the yeshiva students risked their lives every day to visit the synagogue to pray and to continue learning the teachings of the Torah. Fortunately, because they were refugees and not registered as residents in Biržai, they were spared the beatings and humiliations of working on public projects for the new administration.

✡

A group of Jews, including Sonja's brother Motel-Yosel and a friend, Tevye Tabakin, worked at one of these public construction projects at the gymnasium. Whenever the Lithuanians assembled the workers, they would beat them with their whips and sticks. Even as they waited for instructions to start the job, they were sadistically tormented and harassed, both physically and mentally.

"Pay attention, Jews," was the call to order from the Hiwi leader. "You see this pile of bricks. All of these bricks must be carried to the fourth floor by the end of the day. If not, you will be sorry."

"That is not possible," Tevye said rather timidly. "We couldn't possibly carry all of those bricks upstairs in one day." He didn't see the swing of the stick coming from behind him, but he did feel the pain that knocked him off his feet. More gasps were heard from the group as the leader started lashing out with his whip.

"Get busy. Start moving. Now!"

As prisoners started moving toward the pile of bricks to begin the work, there were more beatings to "motivate" the workers. By the end of the day, Motel-Yosel and Tevye were correct. The brick-carrying task was not achievable and they, as well as many others, were viciously beaten. When Motel-Yosel walked in the door at home, he was exhausted and sore from the work and beatings and went directly to bed.

✡

At the same time in another part of town, Sonja's cousins Sore and Miriam Zelbovich, ages eighteen and sixteen, were part of a crew of six girls taken by Lithuanian partisans to clean toilets in a house. After arriving, Sore asked a German officer for rags to perform the cleaning. After laughing in their faces, he told them, "We won't waste good rags on you. Use your stinking hands to clean out these filthy toilets." None of the girls took a step toward the toilets, so the Lithuanians struck the girls to give them some incentive. Fearing for their lives, they did as they were told. After completing the task, they held out their hands, turned them with the palms facing upwards, motioning for something to clean off their hands.

"Yes," smirked the same officer who refused to give them rags. "You need to wash your hands." Then, in a harsh and malicious voice, he said. "You can use your underwear, but only after you wash the toilets with it." When the girls' faces showed disgust and they didn't respond to the guards, they were beaten again.

After cleaning the toilets with their undergarments as ordered, the girls were forced to put their underwear back on. The complete and total humiliation was just about over when the barbarians came up with another brutal idea. They walked over to Miriam and blocked her path. One of the Lithuanian partisans reached out and slowly stroked her long, beautiful black hair. He quickly grabbed a handful of her hair, twisted it forcibly, and pulled her over to a toilet as she cried out in pain. With a guard on either side of her, they forced her head into the toilet bowl and then flushed the toilet. The cowardly pack of barbarians thought this vile way of washing poor Miriam's hair was the funniest thing they had ever seen, and they were doubled over laughing as the girls ran out of the house hysterical and crying.

✡

That same morning, Berl and Daniel woke up in the storeroom/prison they shared with Lithuanians who were involved in the Soviet administration during their occupation. The first thing they noticed was a Lithuanian prisoner who had hung himself during the night. He was still hanging by his neck in the storehouse. The guards had no desire to take him down as they knew the sight of him hanging would further increase the agony among the prisoners.

To allow a little bit of light inside the room, a small window had been cut into the wall and an armed guard was positioned just outside at the door. When they decided to feed the prisoners, they callously tossed in pieces of bread through the make-shift window opening. After waking the next day, Daniel and Berl believed that they were going to be killed when they were taken into a room filled with armed guards. Two Lithuanians stared at the boys when they were marched into the room. As Daniel was walking past one of the guards, the guard jammed his rifle butt into Daniel's stomach, causing him to wretch and fall face-forward into the ground.

"Why the hell did you do that?" shouted a furious Berl, as he took a step toward the guard.

"Back up and settle down, Jew," demanded the other guard as Berl retreated a step and helped up a stunned Daniel.

"Search them," the leader commanded the other guard. The boys were frisked, and their pockets were emptied.

"Who are you? Where are you from? What are you doing here in Kupreliškis?" The questions were barked in a staccato pattern by the lead guard.

"We were traveling with our parents and we lost them along the way." Berl responded. He was making up a story. He stopped a moment, and said evenly. "We were heading back to Biržai when you arrested us and brought us here."

"You expect us to believe that? What are you guys, thirty years old, and you 'got lost from your parents?.' I should stick my rifle butt in your gut, too, you Jew Communist. I should really kill you, but we know who you are, and we have plans for you. Take these two away."

Much to their surprise, the Lithuanians not only didn't kill them, but they put them on a wagon pulled by two beautiful grey horses with white snouts and white feet. Two Lithuanians with white armbands escorted Berl and Daniel. As the wagon began the journey back to Biržai with two Jews who were unsure of their fate, the leader called out to the two guards. "Hold on to that one tightly. You are transporting an important person."

They were not certain which of them the leader had fingered as the "important person." Their souls were overcome with gloom.

CHAPTER 27:

No Work and No Play

Wednesday July 2, 1941

After the cold wind and snows of winter subside, the warm months of May and June embrace the forests around Biržai and transform the densely populated rural area into thick groves of birch trees covered in white bark enveloped by lush green growth and rolling mounds of earth. It normally was a perfect sanctuary to find solitude, but now it seemed to be a perfect place to hide. This is exactly what Moishe-Shiye Hendler[53] and Dr. Josefas Aptekin thought until they were captured by armed Lithuanians.

Moishe-Shiye Hendler, born in 1872 and approaching seventy years old, was a very popular iron merchant. Dr. Josefas Aptekin was thirty-two years old and married to Ita (nee Orlin). They were captured in the forest and forced to strip down to their underwear. In the process of their apprehension, they were bruised and bloodied from the many blows they received, then cruelly marched barefooted from the forest into the town. The armed Hiwi murderers terrorized the two prominent and respected Jews through the main streets of Biržai, continually beating them. The two men, wearing only their underwear,

---

53   The Hebrew is Movsha-Govshei/Ovshey. Ovshey translates to Shia in English. In Lithuanian documents, his name is given as Mausa, which is Lithuanian for Movsha.

were bleeding from their beatings, and their mangled feet were leaving a bloody trail behind them. The abhorrent scene was made worse by the hostile Lithuanian citizens who were openly cheering the armed men and reveling in the brutality being heaped on the two men.

As the sounds and hateful cries of the mob increased, someone called out to the Hiwi captors, telling them to march Hendler over to the priest's house so his son could see the horrible beating and disgrace his father was enduring. It happened that earlier on the same day, Moishe-Shiye's son, Benzion Hendler, and Moishe's son-in-law, Moishe Luria, a civil engineer who designed the Hasidic synagogue built in 1938, were being forced to pull weeds at the priest's house. The armed men and their frenzied mob paraded Moishe-Shiye Hendler and Dr. Josefas Aptekin to the priest's house. The Hiwis pulled Moishe-Shiye's son and son-in-law out from among the weeds and shot all four of them in front of the cheering mob.

The town was tense following the murders outside the Hendler house but for very different reasons. The Hiwi and their local collaborators were joyful about the murders while the ordinary civilians and the Jewish people were terrified. Sheina and Moishe Magid were on edge. They had not heard any information on the fate of their children who had left Biržai a week earlier. Sheina also knew her friend Khane-Sora Beder's son Motel-Yosel, and Khane's two nieces had begun their forced labor assignments the day before. She decided to visit the Beder house to learn how they fared on their first day.

When Sheina entered the Beder house, she didn't have any expectations of what she would see but she was shocked when she saw Motel-Yosel Beder. The nineteen-year-old boy who she had recently seen now had aged tremendously. He had bruises on his face, he was walking hunched, shuffling his feet and limping, and he was moaning with every short step he took to greet Sheina.

"Oh, no. What happened to you, Motel-Yosel?" Now turning to look at Khane, she asked with fear in her voice, "What happened to him? Who did this to him?"

"Who do you think, Sheina? It was those murderers, those ruthless collaborators who are killing and beating our people. Your kids were the smart ones. They got out of here before all this happened. Lord our God, we need to pray for our children."

"Motel-Yosel, go back to bed." Sheina softly commanded. "You cannot go back to do that work in your condition." Sheina waved off Khane-Sora with a non-verbal sign to indicate she would take Motel-Yosel back to bed. "Rest up, Motel-Yosel. All will be right. God will not forsake us in this time of need." Sheina assisted him onto the bed and returned to sit with Khane, trying to console her over a pot of tea. Once the tea was served, Khane-Sora spoke in a low, sad voice. "Do you remember, Sheina, when you and your family just returned from Kazan, and we sat here in this very kitchen and talked about our lovely shtetl?" Not waiting for an answer, she continued. "It was such a happy moment and things were so simple, calm, and peaceful. Now look at this insanity. The world has gone mad."

As if on cue, there was a loud pounding on the door, and the two Lithuanians who had beaten Motel-Yosel were angrily standing at the doorstep. "Where is he? He is late for work!" one shouted as the other much bigger man barged into the Beder house.

"Where do you think you are going?" Khane-Sora responded firmly as she rose from her chair. "Get some manners and wait until you are invited into to my house."

"Shut your mouth, your Jew wench, before I shut it for you. Now for the last time, where is the boy?"

"He is sick and weak. He cannot do that heavy work today, but he will be there tomorrow. He is in bed and he needs to rest today. Please. What difference can a day make?"

The Hiwis ignored her words and moved toward Motel-Yosel's room. Khane-Sora reached for them, yelling at the same time. "No! Leave him be, don't touch my son." At this, Sheina stood to help Khane-Sora when the smaller man blocked her path, but not before she saw Khane-Sora receive a back-handed slap across her face and get pushed to the ground.

"No! Stay out of my way before you really get hurt," the burly intruder shouted. He stepped over Khane-Sora as she lay sprawled on the floor. He walked into Motel-Yosel's bedroom and dragged him out of his bed. "It's time for work, boy, and you are late. Say goodbye to your mother."

The two Hiwis left the house with Motel-Yosel as Sheina rushed over to check on Khane-Sora who appeared to be more shaken than hurt, though there was a bright-red bruise on her face in the outline of a hand. "I wish it was the Hand of God instead of the hand of a murderer," was Khane's only remark.

✡

A similar scene was repeated at the Zelbovich house. When the sisters had come home from their humiliation of cleaning toilets, their mother, Hene, assured them they were not going back to work in the morning. Just as at the Beder house, the two Lithuanians who struck Khane-Sora and abducted Motel-Yosel were pounding on the door looking for Sore and Miriam. Hene quickly hid her daughters in their beds and covered them with pillows.

"Where are the girls?" barked the first Hiwi. "They are not at work."

"There must be some problem with communication," their mother explained calmly. "You see, a very important German officer came here. He picked up the girls and took them to work. So, if you leave here and go back to that house, you will find them there."

"You are a damn liar," the Hiwi yelled as he began beating the woman. Hene's youngest daughter, Khasele, was nearby and started crying when she heard her mother's screams. Frightened for her mother, she called out, "Ima, Ima, please tell them where they are. Please Ima, before they kill you."

"I knew they were here all the time," the Hiwi said harshly. He cast a mean glance at Khasele and shouted in her face with hatred in his voice, "Stop your stupid crying, you baby." He raised his hand and pushed her away. She fell and struck her head on the floor, splitting her brow open. Bright red blood poured immediately from her head. Alarmed at the sight of the young girl's blood, the two Lithuanians ran out of the house. Hene, who was in a terrible state, screamed at them. "What is wrong with you animals? You brutalize young girls; you arrested my innocent husband; and now you crack open the head of a young girl. You all should burn in Hell!" Slowly rising from the floor, she composed herself and took Khasele to the hospital. It was becoming clearer every day that all of Biržai and the surrounding countryside was under the devil's power.

✡

Berl-David and Daniel were getting closer to returning to Biržai, but not in the manner they had imagined: they were still prisoners of the Lithuanian guards. The ride to Biržai on the wagon went faster than they had hoped. They were not looking forward to learning whether it was true or not that Germans were killing prominent Jewish men. They arrived in a house in Biržai but there was no one around to ask about the killings. The house, which had a cellar, had belonged to local priests before the Russians used it to imprison people. It was now being used by the white arm-banded Lithuanians, servile collaborators of the Nazis, for the same purpose. As the two guards prepared to throw Berl and Daniel down into the cellar, one of the Lithuanians stopped Berl and stuck a knife into his side, enough to get his attention but not hard enough to break the skin. "Now I can do with you whatever I want. I can even shoot you. But I'm not going to do that." He grinned coldly and pushed them both down into the dark and damp cellar. As their feet hit the ground, they lost their balance. Fortunately, their fall was broken, but not by landing on the cellar floor. They landed on other bodies. They realized instantly that were not alone in the cellar.

CHAPTER 28:

An Oasis of Hope

I n the morning, with some light shining through the floorboards, the boys were able to identify several Jews who were already in the cellar. There was Sholem Gordon, a butcher; a neighboring Jew from Anykščiai who had a wine business in Biržai, and many others. Berl was assessing the situation in his head, then he turned to face Daniel. "This is not good." His normal positive view on survival was weakening. "The guards joked about being able to do what they want with us, but it is no longer a joke. They really can do what they want to do. We are easy targets; we need a plan to get out of here." Daniel was about to answer when Itsik Shek appeared. Their neighbor and friend was in an agitated state.

"Where is my brother? He left with you guys a week ago. I don't see him here in this cellar. Did he make it to Russia?"

They were shocked and saddened to see Itsik in the cellar prison with them and to learn Zundel's whereabouts were unknown.

Daniel proceeded to tell Itsik what they knew. "We were hoping Zundel made it home. We last saw him getting on a wagon with the Rotsamer brothers and their families who were heading back to Biržai. Has he not made it home?"

"No, we have not seen him since you all left together last week." Itsik continued, his face lined with worry. "When I saw you from across the cellar, my heart sank because I knew if you didn't make it, it was not a good sign for Zundel."

As they were talking, Sholem Gordon came over and joined the group. Daniel asked them, "How did you come to be in this cellar?"

"The Hiwi came for us," Itsik answered. "Just like when the Russians sent people off to Siberia. They had lists of names. They were looking for specific men to arrest. They were also looking for Zundel, but he was not home. Now I don't know if he is alive or dead."

"And Berl," added Sholem, "there were two Lithuanians who were sent to your house looking for you."

"Well, that doesn't surprise me. They think I am a Communist working for the Russian administration. It's amazing that I am not dead already." Berl-David then asked excitedly, "Is my family all right?"

"Yes. They seem to be targeting the men," Sholem replied. "The Germans encourage the Lithuanians to target any Jew who had loaned them money or with whom they had a quarrel. This seems to be the Germans' way of making many Lithuanians happy and soon these same Lithuanians work closely with the Germans."

Over the next couple of days, more and more Jews were thrown into the cellar, so many that soon there was no place to stand and it was getting harder to breathe. Berl could not help but remember his arrival in a boxcar from Russia twenty years ago. He thought to himself, how can this be happening again? As the day wore on, the number of prisoners increased. He watched three brothers from Vaškai, a small town nearby, brought in with their hands bleeding because they had been tied so tightly with wire; a shoemaker Gershon Belicki, who was also the chief of the Biržai volunteer fire department, was brought in; Eliya Davidov, the watchmaker; Hirsh Becker, the hat maker; and several others were added. Six yeshiva students from Białystok were shoved into the cellar. They were able to hide from the Russians when their colleagues, including Rabbi Levin, were shipped to Siberia, but now their situation was far worse than that of their friends. Certainly, the cellar was not a good place to be, but while Berl, David, and the other Jewish men were prisoners in the cellar, more atrocities were being committed against their fellow Jews of Biržai.

✡

A local lawyer and prominent scholar named David Kirshon who taught economics at the high school, his wife Rachel (nee Luria), and their two daughters Miriam and Golda were given asylum by Lithuanians in Biržai who they considered to be their friends. Sadly, their "friends" changed their minds to protect themselves and they turned the family over to the police. All four members of the family were murdered.

The members of the Zelbovich family who remained at the house were increasingly fearful. Hene was concerned about her husband who was arrested earlier; her daughter Khasele was still in the hospital; and Sore and Miriam were facing yet another day of work with the abusive Lithuanians. As Hene saw the girls about ready to leave the house for forced labor work, she stopped them at the door.

"Where do you think you are going? You don't think I am going to let you go back there after what happened yesterday?"

Sore was the oldest and she answered in a straight-forward manner. "Ima, I don't think we have a choice. They know where we live. They came here yesterday and beat you, and they cracked open our sister's head. What choice do we have? We're afraid that if they come back here looking for us, they will shoot you!"

Though she was not happy with what Sore said to her, Hene realized she was right: the girls were choosing the lesser of two evils. So, the girls left the house and headed back to work knowing what was waiting for them. When they arrived at the house, the two Lithuanians who had "washed" Miriam's hair and beat their mother greeted them at the door.

"Well, well, well," smirked the same guard who hit Hene. "Look who decided to show up for work today. You two think you are so special, taking the day off yesterday. Well, guess what. It is double the work for you today." The other guards laughed as they shoved Miriam and Sore toward the other girls. One of the foulest-looking guards announced to the other guards. "You know what, they should all pay for what these two did yesterday and I know just how we should take our revenge. We've never slept with Jewish girls before, so you girls are going to have sex with all of us."

The look of horror on the girls' faces seemed to excite the villains even more. They began hooting and slapping each other on the back and moved threateningly toward the girls. The young girls trembled as the guards approached them and one of the men got right up into the face of Miriam, just an inch from her nose. "I am going to enjoy screwing you, you sweet little thing. And I'll bet that I am your first, so you will always remember me." He ran his hand through her hair and made a vile gesture with his tongue. Miriam, repulsed by the man touching her, turned her head away from him and said, "You are a pig!" He immediately released his hand from her hair and punched her in the face. Although she was in pain, she refused to show it, using every ounce of her strength to keep from crying. A trickle of blood rolled down from her nose and onto the floor. "Now you've gone and done it, you Jew bitch, you got blood on the floor," whined the guard who hit her. "Now, get to work and we will have our fun later."

The girls spent the entire day in fear, not knowing if and when they would be sexually assaulted. Over the next days, the girls were continually subjected to the abuses of these sadists. The guards' demands grew more vocal and they tormented the girls with death threats and beat them on a daily basis. Their tormentors also made them aware that Jewish men were being arrested and shot in town and if the girls didn't have sex with them they would also be shot. After weeks of abuses and being constantly threatened with a life-or-death option, the girls submitted and all six were raped. The murderers and rapists later boasted to everyone in town about their "successes." In truth, there was no one in Biržai who believed the girls willingly consented. It was plainly known to be a situation of do or die.

✡

All of these atrocities occurred within a week of the Germans arrival in Biržai, and two weeks since Hitler's Operation Barbarossa began against his former ally, Russia. The Jews of Biržai could never have imagined that this would be what life was going to be like under the German regime: under any regime. Beatings, rapes, arrests, and murders were occurring on a regular basis and everyone lived in constant fear for their lives. The biggest surprise, however, was not the behavior of the Germans, which was well documented; but the intense hatred and perverse violence on the part of their non-Jewish neighbors, the local Biržaim.

The random killings of prominent Biržai Jews, led by the Hiwi partisans and the Germans, continued throughout the month of July. In one instance, ten to twelve Jews were taken from the jail at the police station and shot inside the Biržai Jewish cemetery. In another killing, a shokhet[54] was tied with his beard to the tail of a horse and dragged through the streets of Biržai until he was dead.

By the end of the first week, the entire Jewish population, already under tight restrictions from the Germans, was feeling squeezed by the pressure closing in on them. Berl was still imprisoned in the cellar as more and more Jews were added. With pressure increasing throughout the town and real pressure of too many prisoners inside the cellar, something had to give soon. Everyone was at the breaking point.

Another day had passed when a booming voice rang out from above the packed cellar. "Magid. Where is Magid?" Berl was dragged out of the cellar by the guards and led into the front room of the house.

---

54 Shokhet is a Jewish butcher who followed the religious kosher slaughtering laws.

He was apprehensive of being singled out and anxious about what was to happen to him. As he approached the front room, his gloom turned instantly into joy. Standing before him was his sister, Perl. Berl's emotions were elevated skyward as he and his sister embraced tightly for moments, without a word being spoken. He gently separated from Perl and tried to find some words. Sensing his inability to speak, Perl began the conversation. She spoke softly, almost in a whisper.

"Our parents discovered you were back in Biržai and found out where you were being held. They negotiated with the authorities to allow me to visit with you. On one hand I am so happy to see you, but on the other it fills me with sadness to meet you like this."

Berl was speechless and could only nod to Perl to acknowledge he knew exactly what she meant. He secretly wished this meeting was not happening because that would mean he had escaped. He then explained to Perl what he experienced trying to make it to the Russian border. After he completed telling her his stories, he looked into Perl's eyes and held her shoulders tightly.

"Perl, listen closely. I have some news to tell you. Do you remember the family that Sore-Libe and Rivka Bass left with to escape Biržai?"

"Yes, of course," her face lit up, now anxious to hear their fate. "Please, tell me what you know."

"The cellar they keep us in is packed with Jews from town. They bring in more and more every day. Sometimes they bring news. Yesterday, they brought in the husband from the family that Sore-Libe and Rivka traveled with. The good news is they both made it to Russia. They have been spared this insanity and hopefully they will be safe and survive this war."

Perl smiled for the first time, then asked, "What about the father? It can't be a good thing that he is back here in Biržai?"

"That is true. They were forced to come back and soon found their home was robbed. The husband was separated from the rest of the family and he is imprisoned here with me. It is probably not good news for them, but he did confirm the others made it to Russia. You must tell Ima and Abba and also tell Taube Bass about the fate of her daughter."

"Of course, I will, Berl." Then she produced a sack filled with food and some homemade wine concealed in a dark bottle so that no one would know what was inside. "Here, Ima prepared a package for you." Berl and his sister enjoyed a peaceful moment, celebrating the joy that their sister had made it to Russia. They spent the little remaining time together drinking some wine and talking about the family. Their brief oasis of joy ended abruptly when the guard re-entered the room and told Perl it was time for her to leave.

"I love you, Perl." Berl whispered to his sister while he held back his tears. "Please be safe and tell Ima and Abba I love them. I really hope this has a happy ending." They briefly embraced one last time. Perl's tears flowed freely as she was escorted out of the room. Berl was returned to the cellar to join Daniel and the other prisoners where they would all wait together to find out their fate.

CHAPTER 29:

Pain Partners

Week of Thursday July 10, 1941

It had been a terrifying number of days for the Jews of Biržai, including for the Beder family. Sonja had seen her brother excessively worked and beaten nearly to death, her mother beaten in front of her in her own house, and numerous other Jews beaten and murdered in town. One evening, the Beder family was in the kitchen cleaning up from dinner when they heard noises outside on the street. Motel-Yosel walked over to the window and spread the shade just ever so slightly so he could look outside. Motel-Yosel was still very sore from the continued grueling work and beatings, but he someone managed to summon up a reserve of energy he didn't know he had and ran back into the kitchen.

"Ima. Abba. They are here," he yelled. The entire household including his parents, grandmother, sister, and brother were now immediately on edge. "There is a group of men walking toward our house and they have guns." Berel Beder got up from the table and starting walking toward the door to meet the men.

"Abba, what are you going to do?" asked Motel-Yosel.

"I don't really have a plan, son, but I'm not letting them do any harm to my family," he said, as the men began banging on the door. Upon opening the door, Berel Beder was confronted with a group of

Hiwi men. Gathering courage in the face of the mob, he challenged them. "What is the meaning of this? What do you want?"

A man purporting to be the leader of this group told him exactly what they want. "We are here to search your house for weapons."

"Weapons? What makes you think we have weapons? I am a businessman and if I had a weapon, trust me, I would have used it already on some of your kind." Berel realized too late it was not a good idea to antagonize these men, as the butt of a rifle connected with his stomach and he doubled over in pain. The household let out an audible gasp and Sonja moved forward toward her father.

"Stop. Don't take another step," exclaimed the leader, pointing the rifle toward the frightened family. He motioned toward his men to begin searching the house and the grounds around it. "While searching your house," he sneered inches away from Sonja's face, "we will take any other treasures we find here from you rich Jews. And don't get in our way or there will be more of this," he said, pointing to Berel who was still writhing in pain on the floor. The men begin to ransack the Beder house looking for weapons that didn't exist. Sonja rejoined the huddled group of family members as they helped and comforted Berel.

The part of the house where they were standing looked like it was damaged by a tornado with their possessions strewn across the room. The sounds of breaking glass and of drawers being dumped on the floor from upstairs was upsetting to the family.

"Hey, look at this, I've never seen one of those, it must be very valuable," said one of the vandals. "Stick that in your pocket, my friend, it is definitely worth something, and it is yours now." Berel and Khane-Sora looked at each other, they couldn't believe their family heirlooms were being stolen right in front of them.

Seeing the look of dread on her parents' faces, Sonja leaned in toward her parents and whispered. "Abba, remember last week when you caught me coming back into the house late that night?" Berel nodded affirmatively, but the look on her mother's face meant that he never told her. Sonja continued. "Well, I didn't think you would approve, so I never told you where I was." She paused, building up her courage and also the curiosity of the family. "I went through the house and I took all of our jewelry and valuables and I hid them."

Shocked, though happily stunned, her father whispered in an inquisitive tone, "You did what? How? Where?" Still speaking very softly, Sonja explained what she did that evening and shared her frightening experiences at Hela Savitzky's house.

"Don't worry," her father assured her, "anything these barbarians take from here isn't anything of value." Her parents embraced Sonja and wept softly with temporary joy, as the boots on the steps above them indicated the bandits were returning downstairs to meet the family.

Without saying a word, two bandits walked over to the huddled family and grabbed Motel-Yosel and Berel. "You are both coming with us," ordered the leader and directed his men and his two prisoners to proceed out the front door.

"Wait, what are you doing?" Berel asked, as he resisted the order to move. "You came here for weapons and obviously you found none, as I told you we had no weapons. What are we being arrested for?"

"I don't have to explain myself to you Jews," the leader replied angrily. "I have my orders. Now go!" Immediately several men shoved the father and son out into the street. As they stepped into the street, they saw their neighbor Itzik Mas was also arrested and being held prisoner. The Beder family, all of them now out in the street, watched the terrorists escort Motel-Yosel, Berel, and Itzik Mas off into the distance. In only minutes, they were gone.

Khane, Sonja, Chackelis, and the grandmother returned to the disheveled house. The looters had left the family in ruins, both physically and emotionally. What were they to do? How could they carry on not knowing the fate of Motel-Yosel and Berel? Realizing they weren't going to find out any information that night, they cleaned up the mess and went to bed.

After the long night ended and morning arrived, they agreed Sonja would go to the prison to get information on her father and brother. When she arrived at the formal prison, the German guards told her they were not on their list but there was a house that once belonged to local priests where they are also keeping prisoners. Sonja arrived at the priests' house where the Jews were being kept in the cellar. She was surprised to see so many people outside the house trying to find information on family members or asking to visit the prisoners. She saw a lone guard and approached him.

"I am looking for my father, Berel Beder, and my brother, Motel-Yosel Beder. Are they here?"

The guard looked through his list and shook his head no. Sonja had now heard the same thing at two separate prisons and she was getting frustrated. "What do you mean they are not here," she said in a raised voice. "Where are they? I demand answers."

"Calm down," the guard advised her. Then he offered her a piece of information. "Some of the prisoners have been taken to a concentration camp in Radviliškis." In the next moment, his demeanor changed as if he realized kindness was dangerous in this place. "Go," he ordered her gruffly, "leave here now or I will arrest you." Sonja sensed the danger in that instant and walked away from the guard, but she did not move too far from the house. She began to call out for her father at her normal speaking voice. "Abba. Abba, can you hear me? I am looking for Berel Beder. Can anyone tell me where Berel and Motel-Yosel Beder are?" She continued to call out for her father and her brother, her voice rising progressively louder and louder and people started noticing her. Her actions were beginning to create a scene, and the crowd and guards were getting agitated.

At that moment inside the cellar, Berl Magid's head twisted toward the window. He listened carefully and turned to Daniel. "Did you just hear that? Do you hear a woman's voice calling for Motel-Yosel Beder?"

Trying to get the men in the cellar to be silent, Daniel heard Sonja calling out. "Yes, I hear it. She must be outside, and she sounds frantic." Berl-David walked over to the corner of the cellar where her voice was the strongest. He waved his hands up and down, signaling to the men to remain quiet.

He recognized Sonja's voice. "Sonja." He called out loudly, then once again. "Sonja, can you hear me?" Berl's voice was very loud in the close quarters of the cellar, igniting very dirty looks from some of his fellow prisoners trapped with him.

Hearing her name the second time, Sonja replied excitedly "Berl? Berl Magid, is that you?" She called out again, "where are you?" then she listened carefully in order to locate where his voice was coming from.

"Yes, it's me Sonja." Berl's words were rushed, there was so much to say before he might be stopped. "We are being held as prisoners in the cellar below with many other Jews from Biržai. It is so good to hear your voice. What happened to your father and brother? I heard you calling for them."

Inching closer toward the rear of the house where Berl's voice seemed louder, she answered his questions. "They were arrested and taken from our house last night. I have been trying to find them all morning and I am not getting any information from the Lithuanian or German guards. I am worried and losing my patience. Are they down there with you?"

"I don't want to dampen your spirits, but they are not here." Trying to avoid dwelling on that bad news, he asked her another question. "How is your mother and the rest of your family, are they still safe at home?"

"They are home, but I don't know how much longer any of us will be safe." With frustration and fear rising in her voice, Sonja said aloud what every Jew in Biržai was thinking to themselves. "There has to be some way to get help; someone from outside of Biržai needs to know what is going on here and help us. What should we do?"

"Sonja, listen to me. Daniel and I tried to flee Biržai, but we were captured. It is terrible everywhere in the villages. There are Germans and Lithuanians with guns arresting and killing people. You know that, you have seen it yourself. You need to get help. Maybe it is not so bad in other towns. You worked for an engineer in Kaunas, maybe he can come to Biržai and try to save your mother and your brother."

"Maybe." Sonja admitted. "It's a good idea. But what will happen to you? Oh, Berl, I am so scared."

"Don't worry about me, you must protect yourself and those family members who are still with you. Go home now. Tell your mother you are going for help, then you need to leave. It may be too late for your father and brother but it's not too late for you and the rest of your family. Hurry, and please be careful."

Sonja said goodbye, turned away from the priests' house and began to walk home. A short distance from the prison house, a Lithuanian woman, Mrs. Baltziunis, approached her and told Sonja the same thing happened last night to her husband. The murderers came to their house and arrested Mr. Baltziunis because he was a former member of the Communist party.

"I have bad news to tell you," the woman began as Sonja's body stiffened in anticipation of hearing unimaginable words. "My husband and the people you are searching for are dead. They were all shot last night at the edge of the lake. Your people were shot because they were Jewish and my husband because he was in the Communist party." The woman, still speaking, collapsed in Sonja's arms; she was now crying and barely mumbled her last sentence of sympathy for Sonja, "I am very sorry for your loss." Sonja's legs weakened but she recovered to hold the woman closely, knowing they now shared a common bond of having their innocent family members murdered for no reason other than hate fed by deep-rooted prejudices and lies held by the newest occupiers of Biržai. This time it was the German army.

Sonja sat the Lithuanian woman on a nearby bench. She softly said goodbye and turned away slowly, then ran home. Berl was correct. She needed to get help and leave Biržai.

CHAPTER 30:

New Places

Sonja wasted no time in planning her journey to Kaunas. It was difficult because the normal ways to travel were now off limits to her: to all Jews. During the journey, she was hopeful Antanas Ratziukaitis, the engineer who had shown interest in her, would be willing to help her and her family.

She arrived in Kaunas, went to his home, and knocked on his door. Antanas, who was not expecting her, opened the door and was about to say something when he recognized Sonja; his face lit up and he instantly reached out and embraced her. He held onto her very tightly. She didn't realize how much she needed that close contact; she made no attempt to move away from him. The last time Sonja was in Kaunas, Antanas frequently asked her out which made her uncomfortable because at that time he was also her boss. Antanas finally released her and held her by the shoulders, looking at her for what seemed like minutes before finally speaking.

"What a sight for sore eyes you are, my dear. How did you get to Kaunas? What brings you here? Please come in. Come in. I have so many questions." Antanas led Sonja to a sitting room and made her comfortable. Sonja was pleased and greatly relieved at the warm welcome.

"Thank you, Antanas," she said with great charm. "I apologize for the sudden intrusion. I was hoping you would be receptive to my unannounced visit."

Obviously, Antanas had a special place in his heart for Sonja, so it was never going to be a problem for him. Sonja caught him up on the troubles that were occurring in Biržai. He was very compassionate and listened closely to her. At the end of her stories, she asked him if the same things were happening here in Kaunas.

"Yes, Sonja, I am sorry to say, but the same things you told me are occurring in Biržai are also occurring here in Kaunas. I realize you probably have not been following the news, but did you hear about the massacre at Lietūkis garage?" Sonja indicated she did not, and Antanas continued. "It was horrible. Shortly after the Germans arrived, the same day as they arrived in Biržai, they arrested fifty to sixty men, and beat and tortured them in front of a crowd of cheering Lithuanians. They were all killed with shovels or iron bars. When it was over, the Hiwi leader climbed on top of the pile of dead bodies and played the Lithuanian national anthem with an accordion." Hearing this and thinking about her father and brother, Sonja started to cry. Antanas comforted her and she was able to calm down. A few quiet minutes passed between them. Surprisingly, although Sonja came to Kaunas to get help from Antanas, it was he who was the first one to mention the idea.

"Sonja, I just thought of something. Let's get married. You know how I feel about you and marrying a Lithuanian will save your life, especially if you convert to Christianity."

Sonja lifted her face quickly and looked deeply into Antanas' eyes. "What, convert to Christianity?" She paused, took a breath, and continued, "My people and my family are being killed because they are Jewish, and you want me to give it all up and abandon them?" Shaking her head vigorously, she declared, "No, I can't do that."

"Do you want to survive?" her suitor inquired. "I don't think you are very religious. Am I wrong? This conversion could save your life."

"You are right, I am not very religious, but I am Jewish, a member of the Jewish people, and we are all being persecuted. I will not abandon them."

"OK." was his final comment in accepting the firmness of her words. He retreated from his proposal of conversion. "But what about my first idea? Let's get married." Then, leaning closer to her, and almost pleading with her, he said gently, "Sonja, will you marry me and become my wife?"

Sonja was eighteen and Antanas was forty-four years old. She had come to him for help, but now her head was spinning from talk of conversion to Christianity and marriage. She needed time to digest and think about of this. Marrying a Christian was not something that happens very often in the shtetl, let alone converting to another religion. She told Antanas she needed some time to think, and he was very gracious to have her stay in his house with him until she decided. But before the conversation ended, he had one more important idea he thought might get her to change her mind.

"Sonja, I want you to know how so sorry I am to hear about your father and brother. After we get married, we can look for ways to save your mother, brother, and grandmother. Don't you want me to help you save your family?"

There was so much to digest for Sonja, so young and frightened. She came to Kaunas seeking help from Antanas and he graciously offered to help her and her family, but at what cost. She had only known him for two months, he was not Jewish, and she was unsure of her feelings for him. It would not be a marriage of true love, but one of convenience. She needed to do some serious soul searching on what to do next and she was just eighteen, all alone in Kaunas with no one to help her decide. Sonja wished she could speak with Berl Magid; he was always so easy to talk to and so helpful. But Berl-David was in the middle of a worse situation in Biržai.

✡

The cellar of imprisoned Jews had become so jam-packed it was impossible to add anyone else. The door to the cellar opened and above them stood a German that the prisoners hadn't seen before.

"Juden, raus!" Berl didn't understand much German, but the commanding tone of the order and the backward waving of the hand convinced him they were all going to be moving. To alleviate any doubt, the Lithuanian leader of the guards bellowed to the prisoners.

"You, damned Juden. You world criminals. Your end will yet come. But for now, we are moving you to the train depot. Let's go." And with that, the prisoners from the cellar were marched through the streets of Biržai to the train depot at the Biržai train station escorted by armed Germans and Lithuanians.

Figure 22. In Vilnius, a Lithuanian soldier with a group of Jews ready to march to the assigned job. All Jews have a "J" on their chest and back on a white background to indicate their race. While this photo is not from Biržai, similar scenes would have occurred in Biržai. Attribution: Bundesarchiv, Bild 183-B10160 / CC-BY-SA 3.0.

When they arrived at the station, the prisoners found a large number of arrested Lithuanians and Soviet war prisoners already in the train depot prison. The guards told the newly arriving Jewish prisoners not to talk to them. Berl smirked at Daniel and asked sarcastically, "Why on earth would we want to chat with the Russians? We have our own worries."

The Jewish prisoners were all tormented by their thoughts of what would become of them. Would death be the outcome for them? The Germans and Lithuanian guards continued to bring in Jews from the surrounding villages including those who unsuccessfully tried to flee to Russia. Like Berl and the other Jews in the cellar prison, many of these men were arrested on the roads before they could return to Biržai or other nearby towns and villages.

Once again, the memory of the gypsy with the tarot cards with her prediction of him 'hanging between life and death' was replaying over and over in Berl's mind.

CHAPTER 31:

An Empty Train, Truck, and Promise

Saturday July 19, 1941

It was Saturday in Biržai, and this Shabbat was not the usual joyful celebration. In fact, there was no celebrating at all by the Jews in Biržai. Three and half weeks had passed since the Germans arrived and transformed the town from a peaceful shtetl into a nightmarish prison for the Jews. The town physically looked the same but that is where the normalcy ended. Religious life, family businesses, and a sense of community were replaced with rapes, murders, and innocents being imprisoned. All of this was happening to the victims just because they were Jewish which the Germans considered an offense against humanity. For the second time while Berl-David was imprisoned, his family was able to find where he was being held captive. On a normal Friday, Sheina would have prepared an evening meal for the family to enjoy on Shabbat after spending the day praying at the synagogue. On this particular Friday, she did prepare a meal, but it was for a different purpose.

Moishe, Sheina, Perl, and Zelda all arrived at the train depot to visit Berl where he and other prisoners were being held. He was escorted by the prison guards and brought to see his family. The Magid family shared a long embrace in front of the guards' watchful eyes. While it had not been a very long time on the calendar, it seemed like much more time had passed since they all were last together. Berl was aware of some of the events because of the continual stream of new prisoners into the prison and also because of his previous meetings with Sonja and Perl. He thought his parents had aged a few years right before his eyes due to the stress of their situation. Sensing the concern of his parents and the effect of that on his younger sisters, he attempted to lighten the mood a bit.

"Thanks for coming to my party," he playfully boasted. "You didn't have to bring me gifts but since I see you did, thank you so much. What do you have in the bag?" His playfulness was successful, and the family shared a much needed laugh.

Sheina handed Berl a canvas bag. "These aren't exactly presents, but a few things I think you will need. First of all, I'm sure you aren't eating enough so I made you a roasted chicken and included a couple bottles of homemade wine. Shabbat shalom." That brought a smile even to the face of the mildly religious Berl, who realized it was Shabbat. Sheina continued speaking as she pinched her nose together. "I am sensing you aren't bathing much so I brought you a change of underwear and some clean socks; there is also a small cushion in there for when you sleep." Berl thanked his mother and showed the bag and the contents to the guards who nodded. "You should keep the bag," his mother added. "You never know when you might need it. It could be useful."

Moishe appreciated the playful exchange, but as the family patriarch he grew serious and approached Berl, taking him off to the side. "Son, what is going on here? Why are all of you here in prison? What are their plans for all of you? This is a very scary situation. Your mother and I hear horrible things and we are frightened for you."

"Abba, I don't know. But I do think that if they wanted me and all of my 'friends' killed," Berl said pointing to the other prisoners, "we would all be dead already. I think they have plans for us, but I am not sure what they are. For you and everyone else in town, I hope the killings of the past few weeks were just to scare everyone and they will end. I really think you all will be fine."

"I hope you are right, son, and I wish I shared your optimism. I want to let you know that if it doesn't work out the way you outlined, that…" But Berl cut him off before he could finish, not wanting his father to feel embarrassed if he should cry in front of his son.

"Abba, I don't want you to say what I think you are going to say. I have been working on a plan. There are a few of us who think we can escape from here."

"And then do what?" his father asked. "The Germans and the Lithuanians are everywhere in town and they have guns. What are you going to do against them? Berl, listen to me. Your plan might work for your escape, but then what? Where will you go, what will you do? If they capture you after escaping, you will surely be killed."

Sheina, Perl, and Zelda moved closer to their father and brother when they noticed Moishe and Berl were involved in an animated conversation. At this time, the guards also gave non-verbal signs that it was time to end this family reunion. Everyone expressed their love for each other, hoped they all would be safe, and said goodbye as Berl was escorted back to join the other prisoners.

Shortly after Berl returned, he called over Sholem Gordon, Hirsh Becker, Itsik Shek, and the two Portnoy brothers. "Listen," he said to his fellow Biržai prisoners. "When I was visiting with my family, I saw a lot of activity from the guards. Something is going to happen, and I think it is today." Berl's instinct was frightfully correct.

The prisoners were still huddled together talking when they were suddenly all told to line up for an inspection. A group of Hiwi wearing their white armbands came into the depot led by a Lithuanian in uniform. The Lithuanian had been an undercover policeman in Kaunas under the previous Lithuanian regime. During the year of Soviet control, the policeman hid in Biržai because it was his wife's hometown. Now this opportunist was the chief of the local collaborators

209

who served the Nazis and murdered Jews. One other person carried a clipboard with a list of the names of the prisoners. He walked up and down the line of men making sure they were all present and accounted for.

The Lithuanian leader spoke next. "When I call your name, move over there," he said, and pointed to a spot a short distance away from the where the main group of prisoners were standing.

"Belicki."

"Davidov."

The reading of specific names continued and joining Gershon Belicki and Eliya Davidov were others who were assembled away from the group. When the reading of names was finished, those men were escorted out of the train depot. Berl asked one of the guards where those men were being taken and he was told they were being released. That was the first piece of good news he had heard in days.

The leader then selected thirty other Jews and separated them from the main group of prisoners. Among them were the six yeshiva students from Białystok, Itsik and Berl Fisher, Daniel Segal, Yoske Moskevich, Avram-Leyb's son Shmuelkeh, Yankl from Anykščiai, who had a wine business in Biržai, Shmuel, the butcher, one of the Portnoy brothers, the shingle maker's son, a couple of Jews from Vaškai, and also unfamiliar Jews from other small towns who happened to be in Biržai at the time.

Thinking they were also being released, Berl walked over to the second Portnoy brother. "Go with your brother." But the remaining brother told Berl "no", and that he would find his brother later wherever he would end up. The thirty Jews who had been selected, along with Soviet war prisoners, were escorted out of the depot and put on a train.

Sholem Gordon, Hirsh Becker, Itsik Shek, the remaining Portnoy brother, and Berl Magid were shocked they still remained in the train depot. All of the other Biržai Jews were either released earlier or sent on the train. Why were they being kept here, and what was the plan for them? Berl-David shared his roasted chicken and wine with his friends as they continued to try to figure out what their next step would be.

Two hours later the train returned empty. It was understood all the "passengers" on the train were murdered. It was fortunate for the second Portnoy brother that he did not take Berl's ill-fated advice.

✡

A few days later, in a small village about seventy miles south of Biržai, Regina Batvinytė's Aunt Ona was working outside her house in Braškių, near the Užušiliai forest, when she saw four men in the back of a truck being driven by five guards. She called out to them and asked if they all needed a drink. The guards stopped, drank their full and also allowed the prisoners to have a drink of water. Since her sister was from Biržai and she had been in Biržai many times, she recognized one of the prisoners.

"Excuse me, aren't you the head of the Biržai fire brigade, Gershon Belicki? Why are you a prisoner and what are you doing out here in this forest? Who are the others with you?"

Gershon looked up, accepted the drink, and replied, "We are being taken to interrogation. We were released from prison a few days ago and they just want to talk to us." Pointing to the person next to him, he told Ona, "This man is Hertz Sherman, he is a shoemaker in Biržai." Returning the drained cup, he bowed his head politely and said, "Thank you for the water." The truck soon continued on its way with its prisoners.

In less than ten minutes, gunshots were heard from the nearby forest. Ona shrieked, fell to her knees, scrambled to her feet, and sprinted into her house. She was still shaking as the truck, now empty, drove past her house.

Around the same time and about the same distance away in Kaunas, Sonja agreed to marry Antanas. She was adamant that she would not convert to Christianity and her future husband agreed to allow her to remain Jewish. They soon married with both of them mindful of Antanas' added nuptial promise to help save her surviving family members.

CHAPTER 32:

Think Outside the Box

Friday July 25, 1941

The tension all along the eastern front reached new heights on July 22 when Hitler ordered the German Luftwaffe to bomb Moscow, Russia's capital city. Fear and despair peaked in Lithuania as the German Einsatzgruppen (SS forces) raced swiftly into the recently conquered towns and villages where they safely embedded themselves behind the front lines and setup interim administrations supported by local security forces. This planned systematic humiliation of Jews, the forced relocation of Jewish families into ghetto communities, and the increasing reports of mass executions spread horror across the country. All of this was reflected in the fewer lights illuminated on Friday nights as Shabbat approached.

Previously, losing electrical power in Biržai was unusual—and it was never deliberate. Now, even that changed. Regina Batvinytė and her parents, non-Jewish Lithuanians, were home listening to the radio in the evening, trying to stay current on events of the war, when their lights and radio cut out. The room became eerily quiet and dark when the sounds on the radio ceased. The silence was short-lived, interrupted by a knock on the door. Startled by the knocking, Kazys Batvinis looked at his wife, Marijona, cocked his head slightly to the side and asked, "Are you expecting anyone?" She shook her head no. Kazys went to the door and asked lowly, "Who is it?"

"We are the ones who ask the questions. Open the door," a loud and fierce voice responded. Kazys could hear other voices outside the door. Though reluctant to do so, he decided he had no choice but to open the door. When he did, there were two Hiwis standing at his doorway. The leader was looking down at a list of names on a sheet of paper but raised his head to look up when Kazys opened the door. Holding up the paper, the leader pointed at a row on the sheet of paper. "Look here and verify this is the correct house on Apaščios street and this is your name." Seeing his name and house number were on the paper, Kazys confirmed it was correct.

"Great," the leader said, satisfied with himself that his list was in order. "Now get out. You and your family must leave immediately."

Standing in his own doorway, dazed by the man's words, Kazys questioned the shocking orders. "What do you mean, leave? This is our house. Where are we supposed to go?"

"Look, I don't really care where you go, but this house is going be given to Jews. I will give you tonight to pack but if you don't leave here by tomorrow morning, you will be treated just like them. Is that what you want?"

Kazys tried to explain to the leader. "We have lived side by side with the Jews all the time and there were never any conflicts or disagreements. They are no different than us. They don't harm us, and we don't harm them. Why are you doing this?"

"Well, do as you wish," the leader conceded. "But it will not be good for you and your family if you are here when we come back tomorrow."

The shocked and startled Batvinytė family lit candles and huddled together, planning how best to deal with this sudden turn of events.

Saturday July 26, 1941

Every day in the month of July under the Germans occupation started out the same for many of the Jews of Biržai. Those who were forced labor workers left their houses and went to their work assignments.

On this day, many were not aware of the actions that happened to the Batvinytė and other families the previous night.

In the morning, Hena Raize Shapira (nee Eting), a Jewish dentist who lived a couple blocks away near the bridge on Basanavičiaus Street, visited Marijona Vinclavaitė-Batvinienė. Safely seated inside the house, Hena spoke very quickly, her words hurried and disjointed.

"Marijona, we don't have time. We need to move fast. But will it all fit? I don't see how we can do it so quickly." Hena's sentences were piling one on top of the other. "What do you think?"

Marijona hadn't yet registered everything Hena had said. "Slow down, Hena. I think I know you are talking about my unwelcome visitors last night, but you are not making sense."

"Oh, OK. I'm sorry. There's just so little time to act." Hena paused, then started again. This time more slowly.

"The Nazis are creating a ghetto in Biržai. They have identified the streets that all of the Jews must move to by the end of today. Marijona, your house is inside the ghetto so you must move out so Jewish families can move inside the ghetto. My house is outside the ghetto, so as a Jew, I must move to a house inside on one of the approved streets."

"This is crazy. It is not right." Marijona protested. "My husband went to work this morning like so many others and no one will have time when they get home to find proper accommodations for their families."

"That is what the Germans and their dupes want." Hene said to her friend. "The Jews are getting no notice and the non-Jews are being put in a dreadful position. I have a suggestion that I think might work." She proceeded to explain her plan to Marijona, telling her that her house is large and can fit multiple families.

"We have a lot of people in the house. My father, a dental technician, and my grandmother both live with us. We also have my husband, who as you know is also a dental technician, and my daughter Riva, who is in the eighth grade, and my son Grisha, who is twelve. We have space for a few families as everyone I just mentioned has their own rooms, plus we run our dental practice from the house. We just can't move," insisted Hena.

But move they did. Following the non-negotiable rules instituted by the Germans, the Shapira family moved into the Batvinytė's house. The Batvinytė family, the Krikščiūnienė family, and Judeikienė and her son, moved into the larger Shapira house. There was no time or space to move the furniture from the Batvinytė house to the Shapira's, so they left the furniture behind.

✡

Sore and Miriam Zelbovich were on their way home from another humiliating and grueling day of forced labor when they noticed a frenetic amount of activity in and around the shtetl. Everyone was ignoring the restrictions of movement posted by the occupiers and the shtetl streets were filled with people. The disturbed looks on everyone's faces frightened the two girls. One woman was crying and walking briskly with some items in her hand. Sore stopped the woman and asked her what was happening.

"This. This is what is happening." The woman handed Sore a folded newspaper and a flyer. Sore and Miriam opened the newspaper and immediately saw an article circled in pen. Sore read the article to Miriam.

> *"The Lithuanian nation must be cleansed of minorities. The minority question in Lithuania was relevant before June 15, 1940, as well, but at the time it was not properly dealt with. Today this matter has taken on a new phase. The question of minorities has been decided and all that is left is to properly deal with it."*

"'Properly deal with it'," Miriam was puzzled. "What does that mean? Who would write such an article?"

Sore pointed at the bottom of the newspaper. "It says here it was published by the Lithuanian Activist Front, Biržai Chapter." With fear nearly choking her words, Sore looked dejected as she said, "I guess it is official now. The Nazis have allies in Lithuania."

"What's that flyer say?" Miriam asked. "The last flyer sent around town wasn't good for us."

Sore read the flyer out loud to her sister.

"By the order of the mayor of Biržai (G. Galvanauskas): from July 28, 1941, 8 p.m., all Jews living in Biržai are ordered to move to the following district of the city: Vilniaus Street from Rinkos Square to Dvareckienės Street, Rinkos, Dagilio, Karaimų, Lintupio Streets and Apaščios Street to the river. Lithuanians living in that area are allowed to exchange real estate with Jews by free agreement. It is forbidden to walk in the area from 8 p.m. until 6 a.m. The police officers will by force evict into the ghetto those Jews who did not move themselves from their apartments."

Miriam, frightened and desolated, looked at her sister Sore and said with much sadness, "We'd better hurry up and get home and find Ima." As they were walking down the street approaching the center of the shtetl, they rounded the corner and stopped dead in their tracks. Staring back at them was an approximately seven-foot-high fence topped with barbed wire. Standing in front of the fence were numerous Lithuanians with white armbands and rifles patrolling the ghetto, the new home for the Jews of Biržai.

In less than a day, and for many persons with less than an hour's notice, the Jews of Biržai were herded into the ghetto, bringing with them only what they could carry. As a result, there were limited quantities of money, medicine, clean clothes, adequate shoes, and soap. After making their home in the town between two rivers for two hundred years, a nightmare of nightmares had engulfed them. They could only pray God would not abandon them further.

CHAPTER 33:

Angels Among Devils

Week of Sunday July 27, 1941

The Biržai ghetto was truly a locked box from multiple perspectives. Three sides of the ghetto were defined by the three streets of Biržai the Germans had selected and promptly fenced in. The fourth side was the Apaščia River, which provided a natural barrier to easily control entry and, most importantly, prevent exit from the ghetto. The largest trauma imposed on the Jewish population in the new living quarters was the single gate the Germans erected inside the ghetto. This gate physically locked the Jews in at night and left them hopeless with no chance of escape. The degradation of this confinement was embittered by having local civilians who wore white armbands on their left arms, some of them former neighbors, guard the gates twenty-four hours each day. The guards patrolled the area all the time. The single entry was closely guarded. It was impossible to enter or leave the ghetto without permission or paperwork. The leader of the guards was a German soldier who was accompanied by a local Lithuanian who translated orders from the German to the other guards.

It didn't take very long for things to become miserable in the ghetto. People were forced into unfamiliar living spaces in poorly equipped homes crowded with strangers. The overcrowding immediately threatened the health and sanitation of many people in the ghetto. The old sewer system, barely adequate for this poorer neighborhood even before the war, was quickly overwhelmed due to the sudden increase of people. Most of the houses cordoned-off inside the ghetto had only outdoor toilets originally intended for a much smaller population. The water supply was equally inadequate for the large number of people now forced to live in the confined space in the ghetto. These factors made personal hygiene exceedingly difficult to maintain.

The Germans purposely made things worse. Few resources were allowed into the ghetto, especially food, and a limited amount of refuse was allowed out. Proper garbage removal and even burials were extremely limited, and residences became soiled with excrement; garbage cans quickly overflowed, sometimes piling as high as the second-story windows, threatening serious impact on both the physical and mental health of the people.

Some families already living inside the defined borders of the ghetto were able to remain in their houses, but many families forced inside the ghetto had to find new places to live. Everyone had additional families living with them. The Beders, Sandlers, and Nankins who had lived outside the restricted area, moved into the ghetto and were forced to live with strangers in unfamiliar accommodations.

The Batvinytė family was distraught with the formation of the ghetto in their hometown, but it was not because of their own situation. They were very concerned for their Jewish friends and neighbors who were forced into the ghetto. Kazys and Marijona realized if nothing was allowed to enter into the ghetto, their friends would soon face starvation. They couldn't sit back and do nothing, so Kazys devised a plan to help feed their friends.

"No, I don't like it, it is too risky," Marijona said firmly to her husband. "I like the idea of helping them, but Regina cannot be involved. What will they do to her if she gets caught? No. I have a better plan." The original plan had Regina delivering the food, but her mother disagreed.

"What do you suggest, Marijona?" her husband asked as he nervously stroked his chin.

"Me. I will be the one," was his wife's swift reply. "I will deliver the food. The guards will pay less attention to me."

Kazys listened to the rest of the plan, thought silently for several moments, then he agreed she was right. The plan was a good one and now they had to make it happen. Orka's family, who had eight children, were once neighbors of Kazys and Marijona before they were all relocated. Looking out from the Shapira house where the Batvinytė family now lived, they could see the home where the Orka family was living.

"Are you ready, my dear?" asked Kazys. Marijona nodded yes.

At that moment, Regina walked in from the kitchen with a basket. "Mom, I loaded the basket with potatoes, making sure that there are enough for their whole family, and a few extras. I didn't want to make it too heavy for you to carry."

"Oh, Regina, you are so very kind. Thank you for helping our friends." Marijona gave her daughter a quick hug, then took the basket full of potatoes from Regina and steadied herself. She stepped outside and walked down Apaščios Street toward their former house. She took a long look around to make certain there were no guards in sight. Once she determined it was safe, she walked a short distance to the river. She knelt down, looked around once more to be sure she hadn't been noticed, and emptied the potatoes into a shallow spot in the river. She stood up, stepped backwards, turned, and headed in a normal stride back toward the Shapira house with the empty basket. When Regina saw her mother walking home, she waved her arms out of the window toward Orka. It was the signal all agreed to use once the potatoes had been delivered. Since the river was the border on this side of the ghetto, Orka was free to walk toward the river with his own basket, a basket filled with rags so if the guards were watching, it would appear he was going to wash up. He then removed his rags, dipped his basket into the water, and filled the basket with the potatoes while he was washing his hands and face. He dried himself with the rags, placed them on top of the basket of potatoes and returned back to his home. Later that week, Marijona and Regina were walking along the border fence of the ghetto and saw Orka. He waved to them and they met at the fence.

"Orka, how great to see you," Marijona said warmly. "How are you and your family holding up?"

Bowing his head politely, Orka answered with a smile. "Thanks to you and your family, we are surviving. Your food baskets are a lifeline for us and for some others here in the ghetto." His smile faded quickly into a more serious look and his voice trailed off. "So many people are starving; it is very difficult inside." Orka coughed a few times, looked down at the ground, and winced in pain.

"Orka, your cough sounds horrible." Marijona exclaimed. "Are you hurt? Sick? Can we do anything for you?"

Appreciating his friends' concern for his health, Orka regained his spirit. "You have already done plenty for our family. You were smart enough to plan this food drop in the river. It is genius." He hesitated for a moment, then said, "If I can impose upon you, I do have one more request."

"Of course," Marijona told him. She would do whatever she could, and asked him what he needed.

"My little one is sick, like a lot of people inside. There was a grandmother sitting on her shop windowsill selling apples. I looked around carefully to make sure no guards were looking because we are not allowed to buy food from anyone. I walked over to the woman to buy apples for my kids and out of nowhere a young man charged at me and kicked me in the chest. He kicked me so hard that I fell down. I have been in pain and I've had trouble breathing ever since. I couldn't buy any apples for my sick child and I'm in agony."

Marijona and Regina were heartbroken hearing Orka's story. Before he was able to ask, they promised him they would include some apples from their garden with their next food drop in the river.

They stayed a little while longer talking to Orka, comforting him as best they could through the fence. Just before leaving, Marijona asked Orka if there was anything else he needed or wished to tell them.

"I want to tell you this amazing story. I saw a Lithuanian officer, in full uniform, walking in the ghetto holding hands with a woman who was dressed and smelled as miserable as us. So, I walked up to him and asked him what was he is doing in the ghetto with this girl. You know what he said? He told me that she was his wife and if she had to live in the ghetto, then he was going with her. That's a new one. He's not going to die because he is Jewish, but because he married a Jew."

✡

Later that evening, Eduardas Valintėlis' horse and wagon pulled up in front of the guard gate and Eduardas dismounted from the wagon. He carried a basket in his hand and as he approached, one of the guards repositioned his rifle from resting on his shoulder to pointing in Eduardas' direction.

"Stop!" commanded the guard. "What is your business here?" A second guard took several steps toward Eduardas.

Eduardas stopped immediately and put down the basket. Slowly, fearing he might get shot, he reached down into the basket and slowly pulled out two bottles of vodka. He stretched his arms straight out so the guards could see he was holding the bottles by their necks, then he smiled and held the bottles in the air. Both guards hesitated, then the guard closest to him returned his rifle back onto his shoulders and accepted the two bottles of vodka. The first guard continued holding his rifle pointed forward and formerly inquired, "What do you want?"

Eduardas picked up the basket full of food and handed it to the same guard who accepted the bottles, then answered calmly. "I want you to please deliver this basket to Shmuel Liberman. Please make sure that he and his family get this, I'm sure they really need it." Adding in a clear voice. "The bottles are for you."

"Who should I say sent this?" the armed guard asked. But Eduardas had already begun walking back to his wagon. He climbed up into the seat. Still not answering the guard's question, Eduardas took hold of the reins and prepared to move away from the gate when he heard the click of a rifle being cocked. He turned his head quickly to see a rifle pointed at him.

"I'm only going to ask one more time. Who are you?" shouted the first guard with his finger on the trigger.

"An angel." He answered. And with that, he was gone, disappearing into a cloud of dust.

CHAPTER 34:

We Are All Hasidic Now

Tuesday August 5, 1941

Not one day living in a ghetto can ever be considered normal but this morning was noisier than usual and there was much activity. There were more guards than usual inside the ghetto; they all had their rifles and bayonets pointing at people as they yelled curses and commands, both in German and Lithuanian. All of the people seemed to be heading in the same direction: toward the fourth side of the rectangle, the river side of the ghetto.

The Bass, Magid, and Khait families all resided in one very cramped house in the ghetto. Taube Bass was very anxious about all of the activity outside their front door in the streets. She decided to send her son, Aaron, to go outside to see what was causing the commotion.

"Aaron, find out what is going on. It looks like people are on the move again."

"OK, I will be back shortly." But before Aaron could get his shoes on, there was a loud banging on the door.

"Juden raus. Juden raus," a single German soldier yelled over and over again as he went from door to door on their street. Using the butt of his rifle, he slammed it into each door and continued his chant. His Lithuanian Hiwi underling was doing the same on the other side of the street yelling, "Jews out. Jews out."

Aaron and Yehudah opened the door and walked outside to talk to the Lithuanian collaborator. "What is happening here? Where is everyone going?" asked Aaron.

"Get your family together and go to the Hasidic synagogue. Now!" The soldier demanded. "We have an announcement for everyone. Hurry up and go."

"What is the reason?" asked Yehudah, who was now standing alongside Aaron. "We aren't going anywhere until you tell us what is going on."

"This is what is going on," said the Lithuanian. In the same instant, the German soldier crept up behind Yehudah and hit him with full force square in the back with the butt of his rifle. Yehudah fell with a hard thud into the street and Aaron rushed over to assist his brother. At the same time, the soldier raised his rifle with the bayonet pointed outward, ready to spear him, when the Lithuanian stopped the soldier.

"No, not now," he said to the German. "We have our orders." Looking now at Aaron and Yehudah, he contorted his face into a hateful grimace and said, "Go get your filthy family and head to the synagogue or I will let this šunų gaudytojas[55] deal with you." The German looked as though he was irritated at the Lithuanian and asked if he just called him a dog catcher. They both shared a hearty laugh as they walked away from the Bass brothers who realized they were both fortunate to still be alive.

As ordered, the Bass, Magid, and Khait families left their house and joined the rest of the ghetto occupants who were heading to the synagogue. The Hasidic synagogue was converted from a wooden structure to a modernist neo-classic structure designed by Biržai resident Moishe Luria, who was killed in one of the first attacks a month ago. The new synagogue was a two-story building with a hipped roof, and four sloping sides. It was taller than the surrounding buildings. This was intentional to allow the place of worship to be visually

---

55 Šunų gaudytojas means dog catcher in Lithuanian.

distinctive from everything else in the shtetl. The building was rectangular, and the windows were recessed in a symmetrical arched vertical pillar. The magnificent exterior included ornate detailing on the façade of the building, a complementary colored molded cornice just below the slightly overhung roofline, and pastel earth-toned materials.

Figure 23. The new Synagogue of Habad Hasidim on Dagilio Street. Built in 1938 by the architect Moishe Luria. Reproduced by permission of Biržai Region Museum Sėla.

The interior was also spectacular. The Jews of Biržai were proud of their synagogue and of young Moishe Luria, the Biržai resident who designed it. Upon entering into the vestibule and lobby there were two heated rooms, the first-floor women's area, the main prayer hall, and a staircase leading to the second-floor women's area. Twelve windows filled the main prayer hall with light and illuminated the chandelier, a stained-glass Star of David was configured in the ceiling, and all this was complemented by the ornate detail of the multiple two-story columns. The bimah[56] stood in the center of the prayer hall

---

56 Bimah means platform in Hebrew. It is the podium in a synagogue from which the Torah is read.

between two rectangular pillars and the Torah ark was situated in the middle of the wall facing the congregation. The floor had symmetric tiles with keystones at the four corners of each square. The pews were shiny dark wood facing the bimah, and there were multiple candelabras and Judaica making the Biržai synagogue a great place to worship God.

But when Moishe Magid entered the synagogue, he barely made it across the entrance threshold before he stopped dead in his tracks. He couldn't tell what was more shocking to him, the intense heat emanating from the building or the amount of people packed into it. He saw Nazi soldiers and their Hiwi and Lithuanian collaborators carrying rifles, corralling close to 3,000 frightened and confused men, women, and children into this sacred space. But stopping was not acceptable to his captors. He was crudely shoved in the back and told to keep moving. When he moved into main prayer hall he was able to take in the entire scene. The community's beloved place of worship was jammed with people, including people on the second floor packed up against the railings and looking down to the first floor. There were so many people packed into the building on this hot summer day that it seemed difficult to draw a fresh breath of air.

Moishe, who was a very spiritual man, was disturbed by the contradiction of this mystical and holy place now filled with evil and vile monsters. A German soldier stood on the raised platform situated in front of the ark where the Torah was kept. The soldier was in full uniform with a Nazi swastika on his sleeve, a rifle and bayonet on his shoulder, and a Stahlhelm on his head with the chinstrap dangling casually, showing everyone that he had no fear of these innocent Jews in the synagogue.

Moishe was the most internally tormented he had ever been in his life. His vigor of belief and divine strength was being ripped apart by the contradiction of the sights and sounds he was experiencing at this moment in his synagogue. This beautiful place of worship, where one strengthened their convictions and faith in God and all things good, was now becoming just the opposite. It was becoming a place of despair and lost hope, a revolting place filled with living demons, breaking down and weakening the congregation: a now-desecrated holy place filled with all things evil. He had never been one to question God, but he couldn't help to think why, why was this happening to them. As he was deep in thought and prayer with the conflicts and contradictions in his head, a wild shriek brought him back to reality.

"Achtung! Achtung!" shouted a soldier. When the crowd didn't come to an immediate silence, the soldier slammed his rifle onto the floor, breaking one of the tiles and getting everyone's attention. A Lithuanian guard stood next to the German, ready to translate for him.

"Sie werden alle in den jüdischen Staat umgesiedelt," the Nazi declared, then looked at the Hiwi, who translated the soldier's words.

"You will all be resettled to the Jewish state." There was a loud buzz in the room, which irritated the German.

"Halt deinen Mund!" he screamed. After telling everyone to shut up, the Nazi leader communicated that all the able-bodied men were needed for a special work project and they should head out of the synagogue now. As the approximately 500 men walked out the door, including Aaron and Yehudah, they were all handed a shovel or a spade and told to stay in line and follow the group out of the ghetto. There were many townspeople who continued going about their business with expressionless faces as they watched this procession of prisoners march out of the ghetto and through the village.

After the men were removed from the synagogue, there was much more space for the women, children, and older men to spread out. But before they could get settled in, a group of drunken Lithuanians carrying rifles and large sticks remained in the synagogue. Aware the German leader and the Hiwis were gone, these opportunists began to take advantage of the elderly, the women, and the children.

The man who appeared to be the ring leader of these bullies spoke out loudly. "I see some of you brought bags with you for your journey. We know you are protecting your money, gold, and silver, so hand it over. You won't be needing it where you are going. Bring it here, now!" When there was no movement, the leader repeated "Now" in a much louder and more menacing tone. He randomly swung the large stick he was carrying at the group, connecting with a woman who screamed out in pain as her blood sprayed across the wall, landing on people standing near her. The screams and cries increased as people rushed forward to give the requested possessions to the guards.

✡

In the evening, the men returned weary and exhausted from their special work project. There was now a frenetic level of activity as families reconnected with their loved ones, seeking to find out any more information they could from the returning men. Aaron and Yehudah huddled with their mother Taube, their sister, and the Magid, Khait, and Beder families. Taube had seen her sons tired from a hard day's work in the past, but she could not believe the appearance of her sons now. She looked at them and started crying, thinking of what they must have gone through. Yehudah, who was beaten earlier in the day outside his house, was in tremendous discomfort and too exhausted to speak. After they laid him down and tried to make him comfortable, Aaron started to explain about the day the men spent in the woods.

"They marched us about two miles out of town to the Astrava Grove in the Pakamponys Forest. Fresh trees had been cut down which created a path to a large clearing in the forest. The Lithuanian police and the guards with the white armbands divided us into two groups. Each group was instructed to dig a large pit. They kept yelling and threatening us and beat anyone who slowed down even for a second. We had no machinery to help us, just a shovel. Some men were passing out from the heat and exhaustion. Look at my hands," Aaron turned over his hands, so that his palms were now facing upwards toward the ceiling. His mother gasped. His hands and fingers were covered with red sores, some just puffy and raised, and others with layers of skin removed. They were red and raw. Of course, there were no ointments or bandages available to treat their wounds and certainly no gloves were provided to the workers.

"Why are they making you dig these pits? What are they going to use them for?" Taube asked.

"Ima, I don't know," Aaron said. "We were never told, and we never even had a moment to think about it. There were also some Lithuanians digging with us. We didn't know what that was all about. Maybe they are prisoners of some sort or just helpers. What I do know is the work out there isn't done; we will be heading back out there tomorrow. Now, I really need to rest. I am exhausted."

While her boys slept, Taube decided she was not letting her boys go back to dig without doing something to protect their hands. She took the sweat-soaked shirt Yehudah took off before he laid down. She ripped off the sleeves and fashioned the removed sleeves into makeshift gloves, with the bulk of the material formed into pads around the palm and below the finger joints. This wasn't perfect but it provided some much-needed protection for them. She went around the synagogue and told as many families as she could about the idea for gloves before the men headed out tomorrow. As she made her rounds, she saw Moishe Magid standing in front of the Holy Ark. He was silently praying. She stood next to him and their sorrowful eyes briefly met. In silence, they slowly shook their heads and prayed amid this incomprehensible situation.

Wednesday August 6, 1941

In the early morning, the guards handed the men their shovels and spades and marched them back to Astrava Grove. The men knew what their day was going to be like, but many were now better prepared with homemade gloves, thanks to Taube's quick thinking. Sadly, after the men left the synagogue, the remaining guards once again took the opportunity to exploit and shakedown the remaining prisoners in the synagogue.

✡

In Kaunas, Sonja and Antanas were having breakfast in a café discussing ways to help her family back in Biržai. Their discussion hadn't gone on too long before Sonja recognized two men who walked into the cafe. She stood and waved to the men to come over to their table. The two men smiled at Sonja as they approached the table.

Sonja spoke first, "Hi, Shlepetis and Lapenas. It is so great to see some friendly faces from Biržai." She turned to Antanas who also stood up. He acknowledged both men and shook hands with them.

"Antanas," Sonja said warmly, "I want you to meet my two drivers who previously brought me back and forth to Kaunas from Biržai." With a beaming smile, she introduced Antanas. "Shlepetis and Lapenas, this is my husband Antanas. We were just married a little less than three weeks ago."

"It is very nice to meet you, Antanas, and congratulations on your wedding, or should we say mazel tov?" It was Shlepetis who spoke for both of the drivers.

"It is fine to say congratulations," Sonja answered and added, "Thanks for asking." Quickly changing the subject, Sonja continued. "So, what is happening in Biržai? Antanas and I were just discussing how we could help my family, so we are very interested to hear any news that you have."

Shlepetis looked at Lapenas in a way that clearly communicated to Sonja that neither of them wanted to say anything. The look on her face and the joviality that she had displayed only moments ago was instantly replaced with deep concern.

"What? What is it?" Sonja's heart was beating rapidly. "You must tell me right now. Has anything happened to my family?"

"Let us all be seated," suggested Shlepetis. "Please sit down."

When everyone was seated, Sonja reached across the table and held Shlepetis by the sleeve of his shirt. Startled at the sudden force of her movement, his eyes opened very wide. She immediately apologized to him and urged him to tell her everything he knew about what was happening in Biržai.

"As far as I know, your family is fine. But the Germans created a fenced off area with barbed wire and guards around the area closest to the synagogue and they moved all the Jews in there. There are now multiple families living in single houses and the conditions, including lack of food, are not good. We don't know what the German plans are or what happens next, but this was the situation when we left Biržai last week."

Sonja leaped up, "Come, Antanas, we need to travel to Biržai and help my family." At the same time, she addressed her friend. "Thank you for the information, Shlepetis. Will you be able to take us to Biržai?"

Shlepetis regretfully informed Sonja they could not take them to Biržai due to other commitments and also mentioned that traveling anywhere around Lithuania was now very difficult. With a quick goodbye, Sonja reached her hand out to Antanas and repeated with even more urgency, "Come on. We need to go now."

Antanas did not rise from the table and made no attempt to stop eating.

Sonja stared at her husband. "Why are you not getting up, we need to get moving?"

"I can't just get up and leave town on a moment's notice. I am an engineer and people expect me to deliver on my commitments. Plus, what are we going to be able to do anyway? They are in a guarded ghetto."

Sonja looked at him incredulously. "What? What did you just say? Are you kidding me? Europe is at war, my father and brother have already been killed, the rest of my family is in trouble, and you are only concerned about your work."

"Sonja, you must understand. I have a house, bills to pay, and…" but before he could finish his sentence, Sonja was walking away from the table.

"Please, come back and let's talk about this, together," Antanas pleaded, but his words dissipated into thin air. No one heard them.

Sonja stopped, looked back at him, and said her goodbye. "You bastard. You lied to me. I can't believe I married you. I was unwise to think you were ever going to help me. You tricked me and what a fool I was."

And she was gone.

CHAPTER 35:

All Together Now

Thursday August 7, 1941

For the third morning in a row, the guards lined up the 500 Jewish men in the synagogue to be forcibly paraded back to the forest where they would work another long day under the blazing sun to complete digging a long line of ditches. As they prepared to leave, Berl's mother, Sheina Magid, bravely approached one of the Lithuanian guards.

"Why are you taking the men to the forest to dig these ditches? What are you doing out there in the middle of nowhere? Will we be relocated to new buildings away from town?"

The surly guard resented her boldness and raised his hand to strike her, but stopped just as he remembered the orders from the German leader to keep the Jews placated to avoid resistance. Striking a woman, he knew, would surely arouse the men's anger, so he slowly lowered his hand.

"Don't worry," he said flatly. "Tomorrow morning the Germans are bringing gasoline tanks to be used to supply their vehicles and we will bury the tanks underground. The gasoline is needed to be closer for the German army." Sheina walked backed to her family, believing what she was told. She told the others what the guard said.

The conditions for the Jews of Biržai slowly worsened every day since Operation Barbarossa, the Germans' invasion of Russia, had begun. Now conditions were deteriorating dramatically. Everyone who was not able to dig trenches was sitting on the floor of the synagogue weeping. They were all exhausted and starving. Shortly after the men were escorted out to complete their work, a drunken gang of Lithuanian guards randomly entered the synagogue, abusing and intimidating everyone until the criminals had taken all their money, gold, and silver. The Jews were depressed and hopeless and many gave up their possessions hoping to gain mercy from their oppressors to stop the beatings. Later things momentarily quieted down, enough for Lina Birger (nee Fridlender) and her sister-in-law Tirca Fridlender (nee Kravitz) to sit down for a conversation.

"I wonder if my sister Mina made it out," Lina wondered aloud, recalling the last time she saw her sister on the big truck headed out of Biržai. "She was so excited about joining the Russian army to fight against the Germans. I can't believe it was only a month ago, so much has happened since then. What do you think, did she make it?"

"Your sister is strong and tough," Tirca answered. "Praise God, she will make it."

"How are they doing?" Lina asked Tirca, pointing to Tirca's three daughters Henia, Miriam, and Reiza Sara.

Lina didn't realize how absurd that question was in these circumstances until she heard Tirca's reply.

"How are they doing? Really. Are you wondering how my family is handling being locked into our synagogue, deprived of food and treated like animals, while my husband Chaim, their father, is sent out every day like a slave?" Shaking her head, sadly, side to side, she said in desperation, "We are not doing so good, not at all, just like every one of us trapped in here."

"I am sorry to upset you, Tirca, in fact, my intention was just the opposite. I came over here to talk about planning for the upcoming Shabbat. If things were normal, and they certainly are not, we would all be at the marketplace today buying food and preparing for the beginning of Shabbat tomorrow night. I thought that maybe if we can get people to start thinking about Shabbat, it will help a little."

Tirca appreciated Lina's gesture but she realized that without food, candles, and potentially enough able-bodied men to form a minyan,[57] a Shabbat service in their synagogue was looking very unlikely.

✡

After Sonja blistered Antanas for his cowardice, she made her way back to Biržai in an attempt to help her family. She was in a bad emotional state. She was heavily burdened with the knowledge of the atrocities in her town, the murder of her father and brother, and the betrayal of her husband who did not fulfill his marital promise to her. She was left on her own to negotiate the treacherous roads filled with Germans and their collaborators who were out searching for Jews on the run. Her anxiety continued to rise as she hurried to Biržai; she constantly replayed scenes in her mind of her family imprisoned in a ghetto. Walking alone in the woods and obsessing about her situation, she started talking out loud. "I'm so stupid, how could I have been such an idiot. God forgive me. How could I marry that deceitful man? What was I thinking? How could I have fallen for his lies. 'I can help your family' was such rubbish. No," she shouted to the empty sky, "Only I can help my family." In her frustration and self-condemnation, she reached to the ground, picked up a fallen stick and smashed it against a tree. Exhausted with grief, she fell hopelessly to her knees onto the wooded trail and wept uncontrollably.

Once her tears were emptied from her and with her eyes still closed, she called out almost unconsciously, "Berl, where are you? I need your help. Somebody, please help me." In an instant there was

---

57 Minyan means number in Hebrew. It is a quorum of ten Jewish adult males required for religious obligations.

a rustle of trampled leaves. Looking up, she saw her father standing before her.

"Abba, oh Abba," Sonja gasped. "We need to help Ima." She rose quickly to reach for her father, but he was gone. Confused and dazed, and not knowing what to make of this, she continued on her way to Biržai. As she approached her home, she felt excited to be able to see her family again. She hurried up the street, bounded through the courtyard, and entered her house through the front door.

"Who are you and what are you doing in my house?" cried out a shocked and surprised Lithuanian peasant woman who now lived in Sonja's family home.

The shocked woman told Sonja to leave. "This is my house now and everything inside is also mine. You and your family no longer live here, and you don't own this house anymore. Now get out before I call the Germans."

Stunned, Sonja questioned the woman. "What are you talking about? This is my house. Where is my family? What have you done with them?"

"I've done nothing with them. The Germans moved all the Jews to that synagogue and that is where you should be. Now get out of my house."

Without saying another word, Sonja left the house. Her head was spinning after hearing the news from the peasant. Her only thought now was of the safety of her family. She ran down the street to the synagogue.

✡

Regina was looking all over her "new" house for her puppy. She asked her mother and father if they had seen it, but they both said no. "Mom, if he got out, he might have gone to the old house, so I am going out to look for him." Regina walked to her old house which was now inside the ghetto. As she approached the ghetto, she noticed that there were no longer any people in the ghetto. She continued to search for her dog and spotted him further away, outside the synagogue, where she walked over and picked him up. As she was hugging and kissing her puppy, she spotted her friend Anna from school standing by the synagogue. She walked over to her and introduced Anna to her puppy.

"Hi Regina, your puppy is very cute. But aren't you afraid to take your dog for a walk through the ghetto?" asked Anna.

"Yes, but I wasn't walking him here. He got away from my new house again and he went back to our old house inside the ghetto." As she was saying that she realized she could have ended up like the Jews, because if there had been a guard on duty, she would not have been able to leave the ghetto. The thought scared her very much and she grew quiet. Anna sensed something was suddenly bothering Regina.

"Are you OK, Regina? You seem deep in thought."

Regina explained her unease to Anna. "What is going on here?" she asked her friend. "I see hundreds of men leaving the synagogue the last few days without their jackets, just in pants and their under-shirts. They have shovels and digging tools and when they walk past my house and return to the synagogue, they looked tired and sweaty. They can barely walk. What are they doing out in the forest?"

Speaking low, Anna told Regina what she knew. "My dad is also helping with the digging. They are digging pits. Big ones."

"What for? What are they doing way out of town digging pits?"

"I don't know but I did overhear my parents talking. Dad said the Lithuanians who are digging, including him, are scared. They don't know if the pits they are digging are for themselves or for the Jews."

"I don't understand. What does that mean?" Regina asked as she pet her puppy who was now sitting comfortably in her arms.

"I don't understand either. But I do know my parents are scared. Look, we're just thirteen but I can tell you something is wrong here."

Regina and Anna finished their conversation just as Regina noticed a young woman moving very quickly in their direction, heading for the synagogue. Regina recognized the woman as Sonja Beder. She watched Sonja, now out of breath, distraught, and looking disheveled, approach the guards in front of the synagogue.

Sonja was alarmed to see so many Lithuanians from town guarding the synagogue with weapons in their hands. She recognized one of the guards as a man who worked for her father for many years. This made her even angrier. One of the guards approached Sonja with a smile on his face but his intention was evil.

"I've been looking for you for a long time. It's a shame you weren't here earlier. Your polished fingernails would have cleaned out all of the garbage cans in town." The guards grabbed her and forced her into the synagogue. She was flung rudely through the doors, turning the heads of the Jews inside. She stood there frozen in complete shock and disbelief. She saw thousands of people crammed into this once holy place of worship that was now turned into an anteroom of death. She could never have imagined the scene she witnessed.

A group of Sonja's friends and family, led by her mother Khane-Sora and her grandmother Sheyne-Rive, approached her with great sadness that presented itself as anger.

"No, no, no!" cried out her mother. "Why did you come to this God-forsaken place?" She dropped to her knees and pounded her fists on the floor. "No, no, no!"

Adding to the noisy reunion, Sonja's grandmother Sheyne-Rive started wailing and crying. "You were our hope for life. You were the one chosen to survive, but you entered here to die with us. I can't go on any longer." Then as the old woman started to tear her hair out, shrieking in pain as she did, she called out, "Take me now God, take me now." As if on cue, Sonja's mother, still on her knees and crying, began to also tear at her hair. The chaos was too much for Sonja to endure in her frazzled state of mind and she called out for help.

"Berl, please make them stop. Help, I can't take this." Hearing his son's name called out, Moishe Magid's head spun around toward the women and the sights and sounds filled with turmoil and confusion.

Aaron Bass reached over to take Khane-Sora by the wrists and wrapped his arms around her. His brother, Yehudah, took similar actions to comfort Sheyne. There was much crying and emotion in the room as Sonja seated herself on the floor, crossed her legs, and began rocking. She saw Berl helping her mother and grandmother and muttered softly and then loud enough to be heard. "Thank you Berl, thank you for saving my family. Thank you. Thank you. Thank you."

Moishe walked over to Sonja, lifted her up, and hugged her. She finally relaxed in Moishe's tight embrace. "Thank you. I think I was about to lose my mind. This is a nightmare." Aaron and Yehudah joined the hug and the three men eventually walked Sonja away from the synagogue door. As they walked, Sonja saw Dr. Levin's widow and son, Tzirke Milner who is very pregnant, and many others from town. The four of them and the many other numerous sorrowful souls in the synagogue stopped and prayed in silence to the Holy Ark.

✡

Shortly after Sonja was able to calm down and rest, a drunken Lithuanian who graduated from the Biržai school with many of the boys from the shtetl burst into the synagogue and again demanded all the Jews surrender all of their valuables or they would be shot on the spot. If there was anything left from the previous robberies, the Jews now surrendered everything they owned. As Moishe walked back from the altar to find his wife, he saw his friend Shmuel Tabakin sitting on the floor, looking dejected with his back against the wall. Moishe knelt down, put his arm around his friend, and asked Shmuel how he was doing.

"How do you think I am doing?" his friend answered gruffly. "Not good. We are in a horrible situation and we are doing nothing about it."

"What can we do, Shmuel?" Moishe said, his face shadowed in grief. "They have guns. They are soulless brutes. They are beating and killing us, and we are all innocent prisoners."

"Let me tell you a story, Mr. Magid. You know how families always have the same stories they tell at family gatherings?" Moishe nodded his agreement.

"I want to tell you this legendary story my family tells all the time. The story is about an older pious man named Berchick from the village of Anglininkai. He was my uncle. It was a very cold and windy Shabbat afternoon with the wind creating heavy snow drifts and it was still snowing and sleeting. The wind was blowing the snow sideways and it was best to just stay home by a warm fire. Berchick, who had been enjoying a Shabbat meal with us, stood up and wrapped himself up in his tallit[58], put on his large winter fur coat, snuggly put on his hat, and zipped up his collar all the way to his chin. The bewildered family looked at him and asked him where he was going."

"Tonight starts Purim," he said. "I am going to the synagogue in Biržai to hear the Story of Esther." His family was shocked because the weather conditions were very bad and Biržai was six miles away. They exhort him not to go, telling him the journey in these conditions would be dangerous.

Berchick explained that it was very important, and it was a tradition for every Jew to hear the Story of Esther read in the synagogue. He further explained he was an ordinary Jew and missing the reading would be extraordinary. He continued to describe that our forefathers had listened to the Story of Esther for hundreds of years and he would not be breaking that tradition tonight. 'Feh, it's just a few flakes,' Berchick declared, dismissively.

Shmuel paused for a breath and continued the folklore of Berchick. "The snow and wind were blowing in his face as he walked to find the synagogue. It was getting dark and there was not a soul on the roads due to the Shabbat and the storm. Berchick did not know if he was going to make it to the reading in time and wearing a watch

---

58   Tallit is a fringed shawl traditionally worn by Jewish men during prayers.

was not permitted on Shabbat. This ordinary man kept on walking through the darkness still concerned he would miss the service, when suddenly he noticed a flicker of light in the distance. With his spirits energized, his pace quickened as he followed the single ray of light. Finally, after the multiple-hour journey, he arrived at the door of the synagogue." Shmuel wisely paused for effect, stepped out of the story and said, "He was probably at this synagogue we are in now. This once beautiful Hasidic synagogue where my uncle risked his life to hear the Story of Esther is now our prison."

Then Shmuel continued, "The synagogue on that night was brightly lit up, filled with people dressed for services, and everyone was in a festive mood. Berchick opened the door of the synagogue and let in the cold snowy air. The cozy congregation was startled, everyone swung their heads to the doorway. The sight before the congregations' eyes was incredible. Standing before them was a man completely covered from head to toe in snow. There was nothing visible to them except for the two small openings of his eyes. He looked like an upright polar bear. His clothes, jacket, hat, and beard were completely snow covered. Fearing frostbite, the congregation immediately ran over to help him. The rabbi approached the frozen figure and asked him if he was all right." Once again, Shmuel paused for affect. "The rabbi who tried to help my Uncle Berchick was Rabbi Bernshtein. The same rabbi who was brutally murdered by these monsters a few weeks ago. May God give him peace."

Shmuel resumed his story. "Berchick wiped the snow from his face and beard, removed his hat, and unbuttoned his coat leaving a few inches of snow on the floor. 'It's Berchick!' said one of the congregants, now recognizing him. "What happened to you? Why are you in such a state? Quickly, get him some hot tea. Can we help you?"

"No, no, I am fine," he said weakly, waving his hand in the air. "I came to listen to the Story of Esther. I did not come to tell my story. Was I too late?"

Shmuel ended his story by saying, "That is my Uncle Berchick, an ordinary Jew. He risked his life to attend services. He did not want help from anyone. He was only concerned about missing the reading and potentially disrupting the service."

Shmuel and Moishe sat in silence for a few moments before Shmuel spoke again. "Mr. Magid, this is what I am talking about. My Uncle Berchick had his religious convictions, and he risked his life to honor them. He willed himself to get to this synagogue, to hear a Purim prayer delivered by this rabbi," Shmuel said as he pointed to the Holy Ark, "and Berchick made it happen. What are we doing here other than waiting for death?" The air above them stood motionless as his words rested on Moishe.

"Shmuel," Moishe began. "As you know, I am a very devout and pious man. Admittedly, my faith is being challenged. I understand the pain as well as everyone else does in this dreadful situation. But the story you told me is different in one very key aspect. It is not about our will or our desire to survive; we all have that, just like Berchick. The difference is that Berchick's battle was his own against the elements and his personal will to make it to the synagogue. He was a good man fighting a personal battle for his principles with nobody trying to stop him. While we all have the will, the battle we face is not on an individual level. Ours is a universal struggle of good versus evil. The evil forces around us are incomprehensible and they are actively trying to stop all of us. Children, women, and men have been brutalized and locked in this holy building. I can't believe the same holy building that Berchick risked his life to enter will become our graveyard. I pray every waking moment for God to remove us. I pray every day for our Exodus 'Red Sea' moment when God will deliver us from this place. We, as innocent and unarmed civilians, do not stand a chance against these armed and vicious captors that imprison us in this once beautiful, and still, holy place."

"I know you are right, my friend, but I feel so helpless. I feel we should be doing something."

"What you should be doing is praying. My advice, Shmuel, is to leave it in the hands of God; he will judge all and determine everyone's fate for all of eternity."

On this third night in the synagogue, no one could sleep as they were all consumed with dread and despair. Fathers, husbands, sons, and brothers, although exhausted from digging all day, found it difficult to close their eyes and rest their worrisome minds, all of them were wondering what would come in the morning. What should they do? No leader had stepped forward. After being driven like slaves in the sun all day, there was no energy to plan or act against the guns pointed at them: guns they knew the guards would gladly use to kill anyone who resisted. Where would help come from, or when would it come was what occupied their thoughts and prayers. They believed God's hand in this trial would yet rise and save them. This was their common prayer. Others silently welcomed the continued labor of digging ditches, believing as long as there was no end to their digging, there would be hope for survival.

CHAPTER 36:

What For?

Friday August 8, 1941

The Jews of Biržai had been isolated and held captive in the ghetto for nearly two weeks. The last three days found them all crowded inside the synagogue with newer persons being added every day. Typically, Biržai summers were not oppressively hot but the August days were long, averaging sixteen to eighteen hours of daylight. It was often wet through July and August with thunderstorms and showers scattered midday. The temperatures dropped lower in the evenings, but there was little relief as the air was humid and hung heavy in the packed synagogue. Looking at Biržai from afar, one would see a peaceful town. However, nothing was peaceful or normal in Biržai in August 1941. For the Jews of Biržai, all of their lives are about to change forever.

✡

In the morning, unbeknownst to those inside the synagogue, a detachment of German security police and Lithuanian collaborators quietly surrounded the ghetto. A Gestapo officer arrived at dawn with a brigade of Einsatzgruppen. None of these uniformed men looked familiar to the men of Biržai. This was because they were a separate paramilitary gang of murderers trained by the Nazi SS to specifically kill the unarmed civilian enemies of Nazi Germany, real and imagined. They were not German army soldiers, they were mobile killing units who followed the German Army into Soviet territory, descending upon defenseless cities, towns, and villages now behind the front battle lines. They were in Biržai for only one purpose—to murder civilians, primarily Jewish men, women, and children.

9:00 AM

The men in the synagogue were informed by the Gestapo guards there would be no ditches to dig but they would instead be sent to Latvia to work.

The men dropped their heads and faced their loved ones with woeful looks. They did not believe the Germans. They did not believe they would see Latvia today or any day. They were quickly separated from the women and children, then aggressively pushed through the crowd by the guards who were prepared to lead them out of the synagogue.

With the men removed, the white arm-banded collaborators walked one last time among the women and children to take all of the remaining money, precious jewelry, and anything of value they found among those in the building.

10:00 AM

The process of moving Jews out of the synagogue was performed orderly, obviously a product of the German sense of precision, practiced and performed earlier in similar towns and villages.

In an eerily quiet manner, the captives were ordered to remove their shoes and socks before they were organized into three large groups of equal formation, roughly ten columns with five men in each row, for a forced march to Astrava Grove.

At a loud command, the white armbanders motioned the first group of prisoners out of the synagogue onto the street. The bright morning sun blinded the prisoners momentarily and they stumbled clumsily into one another. Once they adjusted their eyes to the outside light, they saw German security police, Lithuanian collaborators, and fearsome attack dogs lining the streets.

All along the journey to the Astrava forest, the Jews were tormented and beaten while they were held at gun point with rifles bayonet-ready.

11:00 AM

The white armbanders marched the columns of men into the woods where they awaited orders to move 100-200 men at a time to the Astrava Grove, to the pits dug on the previous three days by these same prisoners: the pits or trenches roughly measured 65-100 feet long, 5 feet wide, and 8 feet deep.

Here the men were ordered to strip naked and place their clothes onto a pile.

They were forced to kneel by the edge of the pit. Those who resisted were beaten with rifles and bayoneted.

The murderers initially started killing Jews in groups of ten.

Pasirengusi. *Ready.*

Tikslas. *Aim.*

Ugnis. *Fire.*

Ready, aim, fire. These were the last words the Jews of Biržai heard.

The gunfire could be heard throughout the forest, followed immediately by the agonizing screams and moans of the wounded.

The massacre was supervised by Gestapo officers. German security police, white armbanders, and local Lithuanian collaborators and policemen, all who shot on command.

Dr. Avram Levin's son, Eliyahu, was killed in the forest.

Women and children were now walking on the same path to the woods. Some of them wore heavy winter jackets in the heat still believing they would be sent to Latvia, to someplace away from death. Some brought their belongings they took into the synagogue.

As they left the synagogue and walked into the woods, they could hear the gunshots. The gunshots were clear because there were no birds singing, there were no sounds of animals rustling nearby. The animals had abandoned this place of death.

The women, children, and older people were drawn in a long line.

The Lithuanian women of Biržai stood on the town sidewalks and they said goodbye, waving or bowing their heads with their acquaintances, including Hena Raize Shapira, the Racemor family, and other neighbors.

Regina watched speechlessly as she saw two grandmothers fall and watched a Nazi collaborator cross the street, break off a board from a wooden fence, and use it to beat them. Two younger women helped to escort the bleeding grandmothers to their feet and away from the crazed sadist. It was unspeakably difficult for the young people to witness the brutality.

Sonja Beder asked Perl Magid if she had seen her brother Berl. Sonja told Perl that she saw Berl at the synagogue. Perl said she last saw him at the train depot.

12:00 PM

Elvyra Valintėlytė and her mother Akvilina were riding in a horse-drawn wagon from Parovėja to Biržai on J. Basanaviciaus Street. Before they reached the turn to Astrava Street, they saw an approaching crowd. Zelma Liberman's son broke away from the shuffling crowd to meet them. He grabbed the yellow stallion by the reins to stop the horse. Zelma tried to give her baby grandson to Elvyra, but a German soldier ran over and thrust a bayonet into Mrs. Liberman's back. She cried out and was pushed back into the crowd.

Sonja, who was walking in the long line with her mother, brother, and grandmother, witnessed the stabbing and spontaneously called out again for Berl to help them.

On later recollections, Biržai townsfolk reported it was said of the doomed prisoners, "They all kept going—they slogged like mummies, without bending their legs…it is impossible to forget that."

1:00 PM

A mere two hours into the all-day slaughter and without even waiting for the end of the executions, the Belicki house was robbed by a local Lithuanian mother and son. This triggered a copycat run by other neighbors who dragged things from the ghetto houses with sacks and bags thrown over their shoulders.

The large macabre parade of marchers was halted at a holding area located several hundred yards away from the trenches. From this holding area, a long grove of trees obstructed the marchers' view of the trenches. Here, the Jews were separated into smaller groups and beaten into submission by the guards who escorted the doomed on their final steps to the pits. Once they were positioned at the edge of the pits, the shooters fired mercilessly upon them; smoke mixed with blood rose from the falling bodies. Many of the shooters were aroused to a frenzy to participate in the blood feast: taking turns, sharing rifles, resting only long enough to drink themselves drunk on vodka.

The Germans, fearing the killing squads were working too slowly and the task would fall behind their timetable, ordered the shooters to increase the number of prisoners to be shot at one time from ten to sixteen. Though consuming gluttonous amounts of vodka, the squads kept pace with their German masters' demands to increase the pace of killing Jews.

In the midst of the calamity and chaos, a group of women among the mix of families, toddlers, teens, and young adults sang the *Hatikvah*.[59] There were thousands of silent tears shed within the throng of marchers and among the dear friends and neighbors. They watched the horror with broken hearts and saw the act of courage and steadfast faith of the doomed marchers to sing such words as "our hope is not yet lost."

---

59 Hatikvah is a 19th-century Jewish poem and the national anthem of Israel.

251

2:00 PM

Elvyra Valintėlytė and her mother, Akvilina, arrived home to tell Eduardas everything. Motel Levitan happened to be working in the forest when they returned. Eduardas rushed through the woods to find Motel to tell his father and tell him what was happening in town. Motel Levitan was ten miles away from Biržai at the Valintėlis's farm. Upon hearing the horrifying news, he returned to Biržai to be with his family.

The Germans sometimes waited until all members of a family were together before taking them to Astrava.

Once Motel was reunited with his family, they were all marched together out to the grove.

The Lithuanian officer who married the Jewish girl and went to the ghetto with her was murdered alongside his wife at the pit.

3:00 PM

The afternoon became chaotic.

Women threw themselves at the feet of the murderers, begging them not to shoot their children.

Some children were thrown in the pit alive. Some babies were shot in their mother's arms.

When there was resistance from some of the executioners to kill babies, the German officers stepped in to complete the killings. Many women at the pit asked for nothing more but a quick death.

Older children were killed with rifle butts or wooden boards.

4:00 PM

Tzirke Milner, who was pregnant, was shot at the pit and gave birth.

Mixed in with the terrible screams of the wounded and dying Jews in the pit, were the cries of a newborn baby.

The killing was still going too slowly for the German overseers, so they increased the killing groups from sixteen to twenty-five at a time.

One of the guards recognized Aaron and Yehudah and told them boastfully he was now their "žydušaulys'" or "Jew shooter."

5:00 PM

The entire Lifshitz family was killed by one shooter, except Yitzhok Lifshitz. The shooter went to school with Yitzhok and he couldn't pull the trigger. A different drunken murderer briskly pivoted and shot Yitzhok dead.

"What for?" was one last haunting call heard from a victim at the edge of the pit.

6:00 PM

One group of patients was taken from the hospital and driven to the forest by truck. The patients were still in their pajamas, including Khase Zelbovitz.

Anna waved to her Jewish friends from the side of the street having no notion of what was about to happen to them. She may have believed they were going to Latvia.

The Beder family arrived at Astrava. They were stripped totally naked and forced to walk to the pits. They inched ever so slowly forward until the horrific site came into view and where they were able to witness the executions and know that within minutes they would suffer the same horrible fate. The screams and cries of the begging, pleading, and dying was overwhelming.

Chackelis Beder kissed his murderer's boots, pleading not to be shot. The murderer struck Chackelis in the head with his rifle butt and crushed his skull.

Sonja Beder, her mother Khane-Sora, and her grandmother Sheyne-Rive, witnessed the murder of Chackelis as they inched closer toward the pit. Sonja's mother wept bitterly and wildly and begged her daughter to run away. "You are young. You can make it."

Sonja was physically and mentally exhausted from all the events she had experienced and witnessed over the past few days. She told the guards about the gold and valuables she hid at Hela Savitzky's house, thinking it could save them.

Just as Sonja was pulled away from the lineup, her mother and grandmother were killed in front of her eyes; their final screams flooding her head and breaking her heart. She was suddenly pushed into the woods and escorted by a drunk Lithuanian to get the treasure at the Savitzky house.

Sonja dressed herself quickly by grabbing articles from the large pile of clothes next to the pits which had been formed when she and her neighbors had been forced to undress.

Motel Levitan and his family now lined up at the pit in a group three rows deep. Motel stood in the front row closest to what was once a pit, but which was now a mountain of dead bodies. The entire group was shot.

Motel fell first onto the pile of corpses and all the others fell on top of him.

7:00 PM

One Lithuanian shooter started going through the valuables of the murdered Jews. He was told to stop by a fellow shooter because that was a German soldier's job. When he didn't stop, they shot him and threw him in the pit with the Jews.

Somewhere in the woods, with Sonja walking in front of her armed escort, the drunken guard paused to straighten his pants and boots. Sonja remembered her mother's words, "you can make it," and she started to run. The guard pursued her, but he was too drunk to fire his rifle and he was unable to catch her.

Sonja escaped.

The shooting stopped.

8:00 PM

Like a witch's cauldron, the pits overflowed with bubbling blood in all directions. In the pits, a bloody mass of humanity lay exposed. Limbs stirred randomly, and the sounds of those dying rose from beneath.

The Germans ordered the pits doused with bleach, lime, and sawdust. But that would not be done until the next day. The stench of death spread across the forest and likely beyond it. The soft, bloody, moving earth now offered this concrete memory to eyewitnesses: "a foamy sea of blood."

The shooters left Astrava Grove and sang on their way back to Biržai. They spent the rest of the evening—Gestapo, Eisengruppen, Hiwi, Lithuanian collaborators, and German security police, murderers all—drinking and laughing. All of them were enjoying their "victory" after the massacre of 2,400 Jews.

Dusk approached, yet the lingering sun stubbornly revealed the ruthless efficiency that primal evil has when armed with bullets, power, and blind obedience. The sun itself was soon ashamed of the images it was forced to show. As the sun set and the Shabbat arrived, there was nobody alive to celebrate it. Just as the last trace of smoke escaping from the barrel of the murderer's rifle announced that the lives of the Biržai Jews had been extinguished, so did the final smolder from the Shabbat candles this night proclaim the end of a once vibrant Jewish community.

The Jews of Biržai were silenced, echoed by a hallowed quiet.

It was the last Sabbath for the Jews of Biržai.

✡

The massacre at Biržai lasted eight hours, from 11 a.m. to 7 p.m.

It is recorded that 2,400 Jews of Biržai were killed that summer day. Their tears will be long remembered after their blood stopped bubbling, their limbs stopped moving, and their hymns of praise were silenced.

900 Jewish children under 14 years of age
780 Jewish women
720 Jewish men
90 Lithuanians

CHAPTER 37:

Not Even a Scratch

Friday August 8, 1941
9:00 PM

Darkness mercifully hid for some few hours the horrid deed that hate and bloodlust had visited upon all humanity this day. Bodies in the pits were positioned in unnatural angles. The heat permeating through the cord-tight bodies rose like an eerie, warm fog climbing from a cool, breezeless lake. Air in the damp trench was in short supply and drifted away unused. Any sign of movement had long since stopped. Some families were entwined together, embracing their loved ones in one final act of battling fear, and locked in the same huddled unmoving positions. Other sons and daughters were barely separated by inches from their parents; yet they were an eternally insurmountable distance apart from rejoining them in those final moments. Even the few moans and cries for help reached no one.

Suddenly, one feeble sound signaled hope, disturbing the unnatural silence. An indescribable smell so vile and nauseating provoked a seemingly dead person to be brought back to life, forcing a sensation in his mind as though his nose was on fire. On awakening, it was impossible for him to move enough to wipe away that sensation. Slowly, this once-dead man recalled now where he was, and how he got there. Laying there he recalled the ordeal, the noise, the cries for mercy, and the blood and tears! How was it possible he could survive this? Though this nightmare continued, his eyes slowly opened. It was dark but he was not looking at death. Though his perceptions told him he must be dead, he was a survivor. What had become of his wife and children? With his eyes open now, he realized he was surrounded by bodies. But he could not move. There was a body—no, multiple bodies—sprawled on, around, and above him. Movement was impossible. First, he was able to wiggle his fingers. Voiceless, he tried to speak but the forming of words was futile. His lips were dry, tightly closed as if they were glued shut. He inhaled what little air there was through his nose. With effort, he freed one arm from beneath the knotted pile of limbs and placed his freed hand on the bodies beneath him and braced himself as he struggled to lift himself up. Listening for groans of resistance, he heard nothing. He listened harder for moans or faint whispers from his wife and children. He gingerly pushed himself away from one body, then another. The lack of a response, or movement, or any sound from the bodies he touched filled him with dread.

As he rose toward the dark sky dimly lit by the unfeeling moon, he heard faded moans and the indistinct sounds of subtle movements amplified in the black silence. He was not the only one that was alive. Another had survived. Again, he tried to call out, to make a sound, but speaking was a task too difficult to complete. He was relieved when there was enough space for his chest to rise and fall, and air to fill it.

"Help," he was finally able to say, but there was no reply. With increased effort, he repeated the word, and once again called out a muffled "help." He was laboring to breathe and knew he must get out of the trench before he suffocated. Move. He must move. Freeing his other arm, he was able to start moving some of the dirt around him. He soon created a cocoon of space for himself. He began to untangle his legs, and with his legs freed, he propelled himself upwards, making slow progress in extricating himself from the pit. He continued to have difficulty breathing and he needed to move fast. Faster.

Using all of his strength to push bodies aside, he extended his legs, and bracing himself by using the dead bodies as macabre steps, he moved steadily upwards.

He was fortunate he was in one of the final groups to be shot because he spent less time in the pit and had fewer bodies to crawl over. Finally, he reached his hand upwards and there was no resistance. He felt the cool night air on his outstretched arm. With a last pull and push, his head was fully extended into the fresh night air. Dirt and blood covered his head, face, nose, and eyes. He appeared as a demon freed from hell. In truth he was resurrected. He used his free arm to wipe the gore out of his eyes and he took the deepest breath of his life to fill his lungs with air and spoke with humble praise, "Thank you, God."

Motel Levitan was alive.

10:00 PM

Smerel Nankin had a similar experience to Motel and he also survived the shootings. He was able to free himself from the pit. Naked, covered in the blood of others, and in a frazzled state, he looked around and tried to size up the situation. It was dark, still, and quiet. Thinking it was now safe to move, he walked slowly through the forest. He followed the north side of Lake Širvėna and headed toward town. As he approached Rinkuškiai village, just two miles away from the Astrava Grove, he spotted a house with lights on. Momentarily excited and in a state of euphoria, he ran up to the window, cupped his hands on his face to shield the glare, and peeked into the house, hoping someone was at home and willing to help. Instead, his spirits were dashed as he witnessed the second-worst sight of his life. Staring back at him from inside the house were the killers who were celebrating the massacre. He had just made the cruelest decision of his life. Before he could escape, the killers ran outside and grabbed him before he could flee. They shoved him into their truck, and drove away with him.

11:00 PM

Motel opened his eyes, blinking them repeatedly to adjust to the darkness. He had survived, but he knew he was not out of danger. He crouched close to the ground in between the trenches, turning his head every way looking for guards, trying to be sure it was safe to move around. As he worked to free his other arm, he saw the headlights before he heard the engine. Driving down the newly created path toward the pits was a truck traveling at a high rate of speed. It was moving directly toward him. He froze. He was crushed; he couldn't believe they discovered him so quickly. Unable to move and still mostly buried in the pit, he stood helpless, awaiting certain death, again. As the truck drew closer, he saw it was filled with many men. The truck stopped near the edge of the pits a short distance from him and the men got out, all except for one. One man reached back and pulled out the naked Smerel Nankin. The men armed with rifles pushed Smerel to the edge of the pit. Smerel was standing just a few yards from Motel who now laid back among the bodies. The men were loud and raucous and not as organized as they were a few hours earlier. They yelled obscenities and started shooting wildly at their naked target, hitting Smerel several times, with other bullets wildly dispersed all over the pits. One bullet came within inches of Motel's exposed head and he gasped at the shock of the near miss. Finally, Smerel's dead body fell onto the top of the mountain of bodies. The vodka-soaked assassins continued to shoot wildly at the pile of bodies and more bullets came within inches of Motel. The men were extremely drunk and did not see Motel who blended into the pile of bodies surrounding him. The drunken men returned to their truck and left the same way they arrived, except with one less passenger.

Motel waited for what seemed an eternity, then extricated himself from the pit and laid still in the bushes for some time, making sure it was safe before moving on. He knew he could not go back to Biržai, and why would he—his family was wiped out by the murderers in

Biržai. Staying low, he crawled across the road, disappeared into the woods and headed away from Astrava.

At the end of this horrible day, Motel Levitan and Sonja Beder were out of the pit and into the woods running for their lives. They were the only Jews of Biržai to survive the massacre at the Astrava Grove where 900 children, 780 women, and 720 men were murdered on Aug 8, 1941, because they were Jewish.

✡

Saturday August 9, 1941

Sonja spent the night in the woods, not really sleeping, but behaving like prey being stalked by a hunter. She closed her eyes and slept fitfully. When she moved, she moved farther away from the pits. During her time in the woods, she occasionally hallucinated and called out to Berl. In the morning with the sunrise, she made it back to Biržai and was given refuge in a church.

Also early that morning, Motel made it to a farmhouse and was received by a Lithuanian farmer who gave Motel clean clothes and allowed him to wash up. Motel thanked the farmer and continued on his way.

Eduardas and Akvilina Valintėlis were working in the field loading hay that morning when Akvilina stopped, stuck her pitchfork into a pile of hay, and pointed into the woods.

"Look," she said pointing toward the forest. "There is someone coming out of the woods."

"That is odd at this time of day." Eduardas remarked. "I should go check it out, maybe someone needs help."

"No," Akvilina cautioned him. "It's not safe. With all the craziness that went on yesterday, what I witnessed yesterday, and what our daughter witnessed." She lowered her voice, shook her head, and said, "We need to be safe."

Eduardas picked up the pitchfork and approached the person emerging from the woods. As they each closed in on each other, Eduardas realized the person coming out of the woods was Motel. They both picked up their pace a bit and then embraced each other. Eduardas looked at Motel, stared deeply into his eyes, and saw Motel had changed. Concerned, he stepped back and asked him if he was all right.

"Help me. Let me survive," answered a weary and broken man.

CHAPTER 38:

The Aftermath

Second Half of August 1941

Biržai did not return to normal following the mass execution of the Jewish population. The townspeople were eyewitnesses to the marching and beating of Jewish prisoners through their streets prior to their execution at Astrava. Some townspeople participated in the extermination of their Jewish neighbors; others were there and had first-hand eyewitness accounts of the execution. The townspeople went to second story windows in an attempt to see the beatings and executions but only heard the gunfire echoing from the forest. The townspeople's ears were witnesses to hearing the crackle of gunfire all day long; the stench of death permeated the air for days and was noticed miles away.

Regina Batvinytė and her parents Kazys and Marijona were among many Lithuanian families who were displaced from their homes. Now they returned to their "new" home, which was the former home of the Shapira family. The Lithuanians were threatened by the Hiwis and their collaborators to take nothing that belonged to the Jews or they would meet the Jews' same fate. Arriving at the Shapira house, they realized the Germans had already collected all the valuable things. The house was ransacked, damaged, and disheveled. The guards took what they wanted, leaving anything they didn't in a piled mess. They left behind all types of Jewish pottery, religious objects like shofars[60], and books. Kazys did not want to leave these objects behind so he piled them into a cart and took it all to their house. When they arrived back at their house, it looked much like the Shapira house. Their furniture and the furniture of the Jewish inhabitants was gone. All of their clothes were also taken. But their furniture and clothing were nothing in comparison to the beautiful Jewish objects that remained untouched. There were many books written in Hebrew that were in great condition, and pottery and shofars on the shelves. Regina noticed an odd item she had never seen before. She pointed to it and shrugged her shoulders.

"Dad, what is that Jewish thing with the shaft and two handles, one on each end of the shaft?"

Kazys had seen one before but never this close up. "I think they call it a Torah and I believe it is their bible."

"What are we going to do with it?" Regina asked.

"I think we should save all of these religious items," Her father answered. However, feeling apprehensive about keeping any Jewish religious articles in the house, he added pensively, "I'm just not sure where to put them."

After a family discussion, they agreed the items could not be left in the house because peasants and other Lithuanians were moving into the former houses of the Jews. Just across the street, peasants from the village had already moved into the Orka and Racemor family homes. They wanted these religious items to be saved so maybe one day they could be rescued. They decided to bury these items along the riverbed. Later, while digging into the soft ground and burying these beautiful religious objects, Regina was overwhelmed with emotion and began crying, mourning the loss of her neighbors and the end of civility all around her.

60　Shofar is an instrument made from the horn of a ram which it traditionally is blown at the Jewish New Year morning service.

✡

A short distance away, at the farmhouse in Dvaroniškis, Motel and the Valintėlis family were making adjustments to life. People in the area were aware families who hid Jews were risking their own lives. Their entire family could be shot if someone discovered they were hiding Jews. In addition to Motel, the Valintėlis family was also helping two Armenians: Abramian Apetnak and Makar Sarkisian who escaped from the Šiauliai ghetto. Because Motel was in constant fear and afraid of everything, he always stayed close to the farmstead or remained in the farmhouse, barn, or other buildings. The children knew what the secret meant and how costly it could be if anyone found out, but they were very committed to helping their boarders who had no place else to go. The neighbors of the Pamiškė farmsteads knew what was happening. They also helped the Jews even though the discovery of these strangers on their land could be fatal for all the families.

Motel was fed in the house and he mostly stayed inside. The Valintėlis family had worked out a system for feeding the Armenians and others who were hiding in the forest. The elder children of Valintėliai carried the food prepared by their parents to a designated spot in the forest where there were deep reed-covered ditches. Grass was loaded on top of the basket to conceal the food and Eduardas told them which bush to hide the food under.

One day, Eduardas and Akvilina left the farm for a funeral in Kupreliškis and the children were left on guard. Motel happened to be in one of the rooms of the house when the children noticed a group of Hiwis coming to the farmstead. Panic immediately set in as the children not only feared for the safety of Motel but feared for their own safety as well. Elvyra, who was just ten years old and the oldest, sprang into action.

"Motel, we have to hide you quickly," Elvyra told the older man.

"Where? How? There isn't any time!" exclaimed Motel. His fear was rising as fast as his heart was beating.

"In the kitchen, follow me," Elvyra whispered firmly as she moved swiftly into the next room.

Looking out of the front window, six-year-old Regina called out to her sister, "Look El, there are some strangers coming to our house."

"Don't open the door, yet," Elvyra responded calmly to her young sister as she directed Motel into a corner of the kitchen. In the kitchen, the central focus of the home, the bread had already been baked for the day and they had the good fortune that the oven had already cooled down.

"Get in!" was Elvyra's clear command.

Motel looked at the oven and then back at Elvyra, incredulously. "You want me to get in the oven? Are you crazy?"

"If you want to live, just do it!" she said curtly, as she pushed the bigger adult into the oven.

As the murderers approached the front door and were about to enter the house, Motel was still only halfway inside the oven with his buttocks sticking out into the kitchen.

"Regina," Elvyra called out. "Get away from the front door. Come here, quick."

Regina ran into the kitchen and laughed out loud when she saw Motel's rear-end sticking out of the oven. This broke the tension in the air but for only a fleeting second. Showing Regina what she was doing, she motioned for her to help. "Motel is stuck, we need to hurry. Quick, push. We need to get him in there."

As the two young girls pushed Motel into the oven, a thunderous bang rattled the front door. The children jumped at the sound, but somehow they managed with a final push to move the rest of Motel's body into the oven and Elvyra drew the sink curtain across the front of the stove. Profusely sweating, Motel was moaning softly in the cramped quarters of the oven. Fearing the sounds would give him away, Elvyra, with her incredible presence of mind, had a great idea.

"Open the door immediately!" shouted a raspy voice from outside the front of the house.

Elvyra told Regina to open the door and at once a group of armed men bolted into the house. The men saw Regina, then noticed Elvyra but not before Elvyra grabbed a laundry basket full of goose feather-filled pillowcases. Motel, who was having difficulty breathing in the oven, tried to speak to Elvyra. She firmly shushed him just as the men noticed her in the kitchen.

"Who are you talking to, girl? Are you hiding Jews in here?" A leader demanded.

"What? I am not talking to anyone. I am just trying to get these pillowcases washed before my father and mother get home." She continued to wash the pillowcases, alongside the oven, making as much noise as possible to hopefully cover any sounds Motel might make.

"Let us be the judge of that. Boys, go search this place. Every room."

As they searched the house, Regina and Elvyra prayed Motel wouldn't make a sound. The girls continued to wash the pillowcases, louder and longer than they had ever washed them before.

The men came back into the kitchen. "Lucky for you." The leader announced. "We didn't find anybody else in the house. I hope you know what we will do to you and your family if we ever do?"

With her knees shaking, Elvyra said they knew. The murderers left the house. As soon as the door was shut, the girls pulled Motel out of the oven. His entire body was covered in sweat, his face was red, and he was breathing very heavily. But he was alive, and so were they. Finally, after air filled his lungs, he was able to speak.

"You two little girls are amazing. You saved my life and risked your own lives. I can never thank you enough." All three shared a long hug. It was bravery and courage like this that helped to save Motel's life and other Jewish lives.

✡

Back in town, many people became rich from collecting the jewels of the murdered Jews, and some people left Biržai to go abroad after collecting such stolen property. Much of the property not kept by the Germans was sent to the Ausra gymnasium. The effort to transport the property was coordinated and organized by the collaborators. Everyone that had a horse and wagon was commandeered to help. A few days after the Biržai massacre, much of the property was sold at the gymnasium to the locals. The clothes—high-quality suits, skirts, and dresses—were thrown out of a second-floor window by the Germans, and the people below were frantically competing to catch their "new" clothes. There was a woman who was verbally attacked by another for wearing the clothes from their dead Jewish neighbors. She was scolded by some residents who told her it was wrong to buy clothes and property from their Jewish neighbors who were recently murdered.

A few days after the massacre, the pits were guarded by the collaborators. At that time, about ninety Lithuanians were shot and tossed into the same mass grave for allegedly collaborating with the Soviets. Prisoners from the Geidžiūnai forced labor camp were brought in to bury the additional bodies. The prisoners were ordered to dig in the pits to look for gold, to remove teeth with gold fillings from the corpses, and to go through the pile of clothes looking for valuables.

✡

After leaving the church, Sonja fled about five miles to Pabiržė where the Lithuanian police recognized her and arrested her. She was then taken to Pasvalys by truck. On the way, they stopped for a drink and the driver shot the Lithuanian murderer who was guarding Sonja and took her to Telšiai, about 100 miles west of Biržai. In Telšiai, Sonja was able to locate Antanas, and they lived as husband and wife for over two months.

One day, an engineer from Kaunas who was working in Telšiai discovered Sonja was Jewish and he turned her in to the Gestapo. She was able to escape again and stayed for several days with a neighboring peasant, until she spoke Yiddish in her sleep one night and she was again handed over to the Gestapo. She was taken to a barn in Geruliai with thirty women who were all scheduled to be shot. One of the Lithuanian murderers from Telšiai recognized her as Antanas' wife and let her escape from Geruliai. She fled from there to Tryškiai where she hid in a warehouse for a few days. From the warehouse, she was once again captured, and she was taken away immediately to be shot. Fortunately, on the way to her death, they ran into a German officer and Sonja showed him documents she had obtained in Telšiai. The German took her to the police station, left the two Lithuanians behind, and took her by car to Šiauliai. Somehow, Antanas found out what had happened, and he moved all of his furniture and other possessions there. They lived together again in Šiauliai.

✡

A few weeks following the massacre Regina Batvinytė was walking her dog along the sidewalk in town when she met her classmate Vanda Stiklerytė. She noticed Vanda looked very pale and she asked her classmate if she was sick.

"No, I am not sick." Her young friend replied. "I just feel very sad by what happened in our own town. The killing was horrible and when they started throwing the clothes of the Jews out the windows, everyone started pushing, cursing, trying to catch the clothes, and stuffing them into their potato sacks. I felt terribly sick. I had to run home. For the last two weeks, I have not eaten well, or moved from my bed, and I have terrible headaches. I cannot believe what I saw and heard. How could people do that? My parents were appalled, and I am glad there is not one thing of the Jews in our house."

"I agree with you, Vanda. We also do not have any property of the Jews. In fact, we hid some religious items left in our house."

"That is so nice your family did that, Regina." Standing on the sidewalk under the August sun, Vanda continued to pour out from her heart words normally spoken by adults four times her age. "My mother and father couldn't understand how it was possible for anyone to live with those things; how it was possible to use them and not cry for their real owners and not feel a deep sense of guilt for what happened to them." Holding back her own tears, she said, "My mother is still crying."

For a long moment, Regina and Vanda stood in silence trying to make sense of what happened in their town. It was too much violence, brutality, and malice for young people to fully understand. Having a friend to share their experiences with, Vanda continued telling her story.

"I was so scared when the shooting started. We had no idea what was happening. You know we live on the other side of town, but we heard the shooting very clearly. We couldn't stay outdoors, couldn't bear the sound, so we went inside to try to block it out. Our neighbor told us the Jews were being killed and we were so scared. We asked each other, "When will it be our turn?""

Up to that moment, Regina hadn't thought she might be killed. She was concerned for her friends. "I can't help but think about some of our Jewish classmates who were killed. It is just so sad." She proceeded to tell Vanda about their classmate, Chait.

"I can't get our classmate Chait out of my mind. He was tiny, small, and a very good kid. He was always smiling, even when the taller boys picked on him. When the war started, I met him, and he was very sad because his family was being forced from their homes to the ghetto. I will always remember him as a nice kid." She paused, and a sadness settled across her youthful face. "I can't help but think of the deep, large, sad eyes of Chait. And now he is gone."

The girls started to cry and suddenly embraced each other tightly, knowing their lives would never be the same again.

✡

Weeks after the murderous events in the forest, the town and surrounding area was quiet, but a constant threat of betrayal and death smothered social exchange between the residents. There was an unspoken rule to return to normal living after the Germans had purged Biržai of its biggest perceived threat to the Nazi's new Germany.

As the final days of August approached, Algimantas Gureckas, a recent high school graduate who was not from Biržai, was invited to attend a wedding of his friend in Biržai. Following the celebration, his friend, who was a Biržai native, insisted on taking Algimantas for a tour to see both the girls and the village where he grew up. On their stroll through the town an older man riding a bicycle pedalled up to them and stopped.

"Do you know?" was all the man said to the two friends.

"Do we know, what?" asked Algimantas.

"The Biržai Jews have all been killed," the man said without emotion.

In disbelief and shock, the high school friends looked at each and both mouthed the word "what." Algimantas gathered his voice and asked, "What are you talking about, what do you mean?"

The man on the bicycle told the boys about the ghetto and the shootings of all the Jews at Astrava. "All." He emphasized.

Again, the boys looked at each other, unable and unwilling to believe their own ears.

"Children and babies?" Algimantas' friend asked defensively, expecting the man to correct himself. "Do you mean they shot babies?"

"Everyone." The man replied. He described the German officers shooting babies in their mothers' arms, and described in graphic detail how the Germans and Lithuanians killed the Jews of Biržai. He also mentioned he "resigned" from the Lithuanian auxiliary police after the killing of babies. In Algimantas' mind, he felt the man resigned one day too late.

Algimantas returned to his hometown of Panevėžys to tell others about Biržai, but he soon discovered this murderous and genocidal purge was happening all across Lithuania and Latvia. Through the middle of August, Germany's Einsatzkommando 3 forces and the

Lithuanian police carried out five separate large Aktions in Panevėžys: on July 21 and 28, and on August 4, 11, and 23, in which they murdered more than 1,220 innocent and defenseless Jews.

In September 1941, Einsatzgruppe A reported that Kreis Birsen[61] was judenrein.

"Cleansed of Jews."

---

61 Kreis Birsen means Biržai district in German.

CHAPTER 39:

Ghosts Reprise

December 1942

For fourteen months, Sonja continued living in hiding with Antanas in Šiauliai. He would often leave Šiauliai without providing food for her, and because she was unable to venture safely outside, she frequently suffered from hunger. As time went on, Sonja grew increasingly annoyed with this arrangement. One morning things finally reached a breaking point in the bedroom of their apartment.

"You say you love me, but you are often away, and I am left here alone. Why do you continue to treat me this way?" she questioned him, sternly. "I am your wife and sometimes you treat me like a slave."

"Sonja dear," he responded softly while standing in front of his dresser bureau, "You know things are difficult all over and I am doing the best that I can for us. I need to do what I can to make money for us so we can survive."

"Yes, Antanas, I understand but you leave me here alone with no food which forces me to venture outside, and you know how dangerous that is for me." With frustration overcoming her emotions, she appealed to him almost in tears. "Don't you care at all about me and my safety?"

Abruptly, and with a considerably raised volume in his voice, he moved to her side of the bed. "Enough! Stop your incessant badgering with this nonsense. I have done everything I can to help you and your family and this is how you re-pay me?"

"What? What have you done?" she demanded. "You wouldn't even go with me to Biržai to help my family when they were all put in the ghetto. I had to travel alone, at considerable risk, to try to save them."

Antanas seemed to intentionally dismiss these last words and slowly approached Sonja. He loved her but only as it suited him, and it suited him now. He stood above Sonja as she remained seated on the edge of the bed with her elbows on her knees and her face in her hands, gently crying.

"Sonja, Sonja, darling," his words were wrapped sweetly with practiced tenderness. "It is all going to work out just fine. Now be a love, take your clothes off and perform your wifely duties."

The educated engineer, who Sonja had a certain respect for up until now, finally showed his true colors. Based upon his courting and his persistent pursuits of her back in Kaunas, she felt he was truly in love with her. She now realized exactly how calculating he had been all along. "What? What kind of animal are you? You want to make love? I don't want you to ever touch me again. I thought you treated me like a slave, but now I realize it is much worse, you treat me like your whore." A flood of hate and fury was aroused in her heart. She realized she had been insulted, mocked, and exploited in a very under-handed way. She felt like a complete fool and now the flood gates of tears rolled across her face. Her heart was pounding with anger at this so called "good Lithuanian" who exposed his true feelings about "his love" for her. Nonetheless, her awakened feelings mattered little to her husband; he was focused only on his one desire. He ignored comforting or responding to his hysterical wife, repeating again his instructions for her to disrobe for him.

Sonja stood up and slid quickly away from him and the bed. She looked at her husband with complete disgust and cursed him. As she walked to the door to leave, she stopped, turned back to face him, and said without tears in her eyes. "If I survive, I will take my revenge on all the Lithuanian murderers. And especially you."

So, once again, she left him. She had no idea where to go. She was hungry and decided to go to a local store to purchase food with the small amount of money she had in her pocket. While standing in line, a Lithuanian who worked for the Gestapo and knew about her situation with Antanas from other Lithuanians arrested her. At Gestapo headquarters, she was interrogated and beaten. The interrogators were interested in finding out who shot the collaborator when she was being escorted between Pabiržė and to Telšiai. Though Sonja knew who it was, she lied and told the Gestapo that she and other women had escaped from the pits at Pasvalys. For the present, they seemed satisfied with her explanation and sent her to the Šiauliai ghetto.

The Šiauliai ghetto was one of the larger ghettos in Lithuania. Unlike the smaller ghettos the Germans created as temporary holding areas prior to mass executions, the larger ghettos were more organized and established with a Judenrat 62 and Jewish police force. The Judenrat comprised influential Jews whose primary responsibility was to direct ghetto life while also interfacing with the German and Lithuanian officials. The three main ghettos in Lithuania—Vilnius, Kaunas, and Šiauliai—functioned in this manner through 1943 and supplied a forced labor workforce to German projects outside the ghetto.

When Sonja arrived at the ghetto, she was reticent to speak Yiddish because she had spoken only Lithuanian for so long. The Jewish police at the ghetto didn't understand why a Jewish girl, who said she was from Biržai, could not communicate with them in Yiddish. The police were aware there were other Jews from Biržai in the ghetto, so they

---

62 Judenrat means Jewish council in German. These were formed in larger ghettos representing the Jewish community.

275

sent for one of them to help them clear up this matter. Sonja sat in a chair in the police office, still very sore from her beatings by the Gestapo, and also emotionally distraught from her recent confrontation with Antanas. She cried continuously with her face buried in her hands, her elbows resting on the arms of the chair. She was oblivious to the activity in the room as several men arrived to sort out this matter with the police. She had survived two ghettos, a massacre, was captured several times, and escaped an equal number of times. Now she was back again in a German ghetto. There was no place to run. No place to be safe. She sat in the chair, hearing and feeling nothing. She knew it was over. She would die today.

"Sonja Beder, is that you?"

It must be a dream. Her name was so pronounced so clearly to her and the voice was so sweet and welcoming to her ears. She was fearful to move. To even take a breath. Still resting her elbows on the chair with her face buried in her hands, hopelessly exhausted and ready to ask her God for entry into a more welcoming place far, far away, she managed to draw remarkable strength from within herself. She tilted her head ever so slowly to the side in the direction where the sound of her name was spoken in a voice so familiar to her. She readied herself to peek, then opened her eyes.

There standing in front of her was Berl-David Magid.

End Notes

"What did a happy ending even mean
in real life, anyway? In stories you simply
said, 'They lived happily ever after,' and that
was it. But in real life people had to keep
on living, day after day, year after year."

Scott Westerfeld, Author

Epilogue

Morris Dishler – Emigrated from Biržai to Philadelphia, Pennsylvania, USA, in 1899. He died in June 1945 and is buried at Mt. Lebanon Cemetery.

Isaac Khait – Emigrated from Biržai to Amsterdam in 1905 and arrived in Philadelphia, Pennsylvania, USA, in 1910. He married Rose Dishler in 1910 and they had five children: Joseph, Hilda, Reba, my grandmother, Harold, and Lillian. Isaac died in Philadelphia in March 1968, just three months after Rose, saying he wouldn't make it to Passover, and he didn't. He died of a broken heart at the passing of his dear, beloved Rose. They are buried together at Mt. Lebanon Cemetery, outside of Philadelphia, PA.

Samuel Khait – Immigrated to America in 1910, arrived in Brooklyn, New York, USA, and ultimately settled in Boston, Massachusetts. He married Dora Waranofski in 1917 and they had three children: Harold, Theodore, and Louise.

Sholem Gordon, Hirsh Becker, Itsik Shek, and the Portnoy brothers – The last time these four were mentioned in Berl-David Magid's memoir was when they were with Berl in the Biržai basement prison. They are with Berl when he left Biržai as a prisoner bound for Šiauliai. The author is unsure if they survived or not.

Sore-Libe Magid – Survived by making her way to Russia. She married Zev Bagranski in Vilnius in 1955. Together they immigrated to Israel.

Naftali Magid – The long road to survival brought Naftali together with his brother, Berl. After the war, Naftali married Rivka Hofenberg in Munich in 1946. He fulfilled his lifelong dream when they immigrated to Ramat-Gan, Israel. They had a daughter named Yaffe. Naftali and his sister Sore-Libe met later in Israel.

Rivka Bass – Survived the war by escaping to Russia. Worked at a factory somewhere in the Ural Mountains of Russia. After the war, she married Eliyahu Kaplan in 1948 in Vilnius. They had a daughter named Yona, who was born in Vilnius in 1952. They immigrated to Israel. Yona married Yakov Shochat, they gave birth to Erez and Aya, and they moved to Brooklyn, NY, USA.

Figure 24. Left: Rivka Kaplan (nee Bass) and Eliyahu Kaplan.
Right: Rivka Kaplan (nee Bass) and Yona Kaplan in 1956.
Reproduced by permission of Yona Shochat (nee Kaplan).

Rabbi Levin – He lived in Biržai at the Magid house and then he was deported to Siberia in June 1941. He was able to survive the deportation and he immigrated to America, settling in Brooklyn, NY, USA.

Rabbi Shapiro – The head of the Białystok Yeshiva, a vibrant Jewish community in Poland. He lived in Biržai at the Magid house and then he immigrated to America, by way of China.

Motel Levitan –Saved by a virtuous, righteous Lithuanian family. Following the end of the war, Motel initially lived in Biržai. He met Dora after the war. During the war, Dora was in hiding with her son Boris Abel in Kupreliškis and Vabalninkas Motel and Dora were married and later gave birth to a daughter, Golda. The family moved to Kaunas, where they lived out the rest of their lives. They are buried in Kaunas. Their children immigrated to Israel around 1970. A photo of Motel Levitan and his wife Dora can be found on the Biržai Region Museum Sėla website: https://www.birzumuziejus.lt/zydai/.

The Valintėliai Family – The Lithuanian family who rescued and hid Motel Levitan. Eduardas and Akvilina Valintėliai, and their daughters Elvyra and Regina, were awarded the Cross of Salvation. The award was presented to them by Motel and Dora's relatives in Israel by Marti Malka Levitan and an Israeli citizen Mosque Dribin. They also were awarded The Life Saving Cross. It is a Lithuanian state award, presented by the decree of the President of the Republic of Lithuania to people who, despite the imminent threat to their lives, rescued people that were in real danger.

The Jievaltai Family – The Lithuanian family who rescued Dora (Dvora) Levitan. Elzė and Romas Jievaltai, were awarded The Life Saving Cross in 2016.

The Balčiūnai Family – The family who rescued Abel Levitan, Kazimiera and Kazimieras Balčiūnai, and their daughter Genovaitė Balčiūnaitė-Grubinskienė, were awarded The Life Saving Cross in 2016.

Samuel Evans – Sam continued to communicate with Jadviga Šušytė-Pančkauskienė throughout his entire life. When there was no hope of re-uniting, he eventually moved on with his life and married Lillian Berstan, having a son Allan. Sadly, Lillian died when Allan was only eight. Sam introduced Allan to Jadviga, and they cultivated a friendship. Sam and Allan continued to communicate with Jadviga. Allan was able to visit Jadviga one time in Biržai, before she died at the age of 104 in 2018. Allan Evans died in 2020.

Jadviga Šušytė-Pančkauskienė– A Lithuanian woman, who was born (1914), lived, and died (2018) in Biržai. She was an English language teacher. During World War II, she studied in Kaunas and in numerous ways helped the Jews who were imprisoned in the Kaunas Ghetto. She was honored by the Biržai Jewish Culture and History Society, with a tree planted at Remembrance Square, which preserves the location of the former Biržai ghetto. On June 16, 2019, the Square was formally dedicated and commemorates the courageous Biržai citizens who—in the face of death—aided and rescued Jews from the German war machine.

Gendler Family – One of the families deported to Russia in June 1941. Mauša and Lėja Gendler, and their children Nathan and Elchonon. Mauša and Lėja died in Russia, but the children Nathan and Elchonon survived and emigrated to Texas. Nathan and his wife Rokhel Kayla adopted their niece Ruth Vinn, who immigrated from Biržai. This branch of the Gendler family, changed their surname to Hendler.

Sonja Beder – She survived the Holocaust and was liberated by American troops while on a death march from the Dachau concentration camp. Sonja immigrated to America and married Sam Kohm.

Sheftel Melamed – Although he was not mentioned in the narrative, I did want to mention Sheftel. When Operation Barbarossa began on June 22, 1941, his older brother was serving in the Red Army. When they fled Biržai, his brother pulled Shetfel into their truck and they escaped. While Sheftel's brother fought in the Lithuanian 16th Division of the Red Army, Sheftel, who was sixteen at the time, worked in a Russian factory and later he also joined the Russian army. He survived and returned to Biržai after the war and became known as "The Last Jew in Biržai." He frequently gave tours to visitors until he passed away in 2015.

Acknowledgments

Teresa "Tisa" Bien: I would be nowhere without your eternal love, support, patience, and kindness. We are completely committed partners in everything we do in life, including working together on this book project. I have called you my muse on this project, but you have always been my source of inspiration in every aspect of our lives together. The amount of time we spent on this project is incalculable, but spending it together is what made it so rewarding. I can't thank you enough for being the best wife, mother to our children, friend, muse, and comedian. 51.

Robert McLaughlin: You've taught me that the book won't write itself and I needed to have my "butt in chair." Thank you for giving me tools and critiquing the muddle I made with these tools. I also concur that ~~edt, editting,~~ editing never ends until it goes to print. As you remind me, there can always be a next edition. You also exceeded expectations and stepped into the breach to become the most generous copyeditor. Words cannot express how thankful I am for all that you did for me and for the memory of the 2,400 lost souls. It never would have been completed without you, there is no doubt.

The Deliberate Page: An important addition to the success of the book is Chris Knight, a literal stranger, that I found through a posting for a proofreader on the Editorial Freelancers Association's website.

She was easy to work with, delivered exactly to my timelines, and was the Sherlock Holmes of reviewers. She went from stranger to trusted advisor in a short amount of time. She then introduced me her business partner, Tamara Cribley. Tamara provided the clean and well integrated interior design that I could never have accomplished on my own. Thank you Chris and Tamara for your help in making this book smoother to read and better to view.

JoAnn Barnes: Nothing could have prepared me for the brilliant book cover artwork you produced. You took my images and vague concepts and delivered covers that evoked the emotional impact I had hoped. Thank you for perfectly weaving all of the elements together. I believe it is safe to say you can "judge this book by its cover."

Ted Kirsch and Leo Laventhal: These two are a package deal. My Uncle, Ted Kirsch, the son of Reba Kirsch, was the second-most interested person in the genealogy of the family. Berl Magid's memoir, written in Yiddish, needed to be translated. Ted, the best at working a network, serendipitously made the connection to Leo. Leo was teaching himself to read Yiddish, and he cheerfully accepted the mission. Between October 2011 and May 2013, Leo steadily translated sixty-eight installments of Berl Magid's memoir, *What I Have To Tell: Pages From A Life* from him. Yes, Leo, it may not be perfect, but you were the Rosetta Stone to the *Jews of Biržai*. Sadly, Ted passed away and never saw the completion of the book, but I know he is smiling down on us and loving every word.

Abel and Glenda Levitt: Living Legends. There would have been no Chait-Kirsch family genealogy without Reba, no protagonist without Leo's translation, and no memorial wall and tour without Glenda and Abel Levitt. They not only wrote the foreword, but they truly are inspirational leaders. They conceived and breathed life into the memorial in Biržai and they made it a reality.

Veronica Belling: A sheynem dank.[63] Thank you for your contacts and the many translations you provided, from faded words above the door of the synagogue to letters and documents.

Jonathan Dorfan: Professor, you were the right person for the right job at the right time. The second large deliverable of this Biržai book project was the database. Our self-imposed remit was a listing of every possible Jewish resident who could have been alive in Biržai in June of 1941. As the list swelled to over 6,000 souls, I cemented an appreciation for the rigor you devoted to memorializing our kinsmen. Thank you for showing, teaching, supporting and validating as we combed the data and added names to the memorial wall (2021-2022).

Merūnas Jukonis: You are the epitome of a father and son team. The work that you and your father Vidmantas did resurrecting the Jewish cemetery in Biržai is without compare. The continuation of your efforts partnering with the "Biržai Jewish Culture and History Society" to provide education and awareness in Lithuania is remarkable. The work you have completed is tremendous. However, the joy of meeting you and spending time with you and your father was even better. Jūs esate puikus žmogus[64]. You are a mensch.

Sheryl Silberg: Thank you for introducing me to the Beder family and for spending time with me and your sister Lynn in Biržai. One of the fondest memories of the June 2019 tour was the time we hung out by the Apaščia River in the heart of the former shtetl. Our scene is recreated in Chapter 9 as we spent reliving how our ancestors experienced the village. Appreciation goes to your cousin Greg, too, for taking care of Sonja in Los Angeles. Thank you for the efforts that

---

63 A sheynem dank means thank you very much in Yiddish.

64 Jūs esate puikus žmogus means you are a great person in Lithuanian.

you both made recording her and transcribing the information onto paper to be shared and included in my book. She was a very strong young lady and I am was eager to portray her fortitude and bravery.

Cyril Ferber: I am grateful that you willingly provided me with stories about your family, pictures, and the letter from your Uncle Samuel. I was so touched and honored to participate with you and other members of the tour in the first minyan in Biržai in over eighty years at your father's grave.

Adena Greenberg, Doris Greenberg, Rachel Greenberg: I will never forget walking the three kilometers from the heart of the shtetl to the massacre site at Astrava Grove with you and your family. Singing together the songs that many Jews sang together as they faced their death march was hauntingly surreal. Also, a big thank you for providing me with the connection to the pivotal and inspiring story about Motel Levitan and the righteous Valintėliai family.

Allan Evans: We had grandiose plans to create a virtual Biržai shtetl, but sadly your illness took you way too soon. With fondness I will always remember the time we spent together before the 2019 tour. Thank you for the information and photographs you provided me about life in Biržai. You opened your home, heart, and the breathaking Samuel Evans-Jadviga love story with us. Ahhh those eyes. You would have loved this book, especially the parts about your father and Jadviga.

Yona Shochat: My number one champion. Though Biržai is a dark place for you, as a daughter of the only Chait survivor, you are light and joy in my life. You are a great love, our little dove, we hope this book reflects back to you a little solace. Deep is my gratitude for Reba and Uncle Hookie Chait for reaching out to you - oh so many years ago. That connection brought you, me, and Berl Magid together.

Florence and Joseph Levin: To my cousins who were open to receiving that cold call many years ago. You listened. I am grateful you accepted the documents we provided you to confirm the family linkage. Thank you for taking the leap of faith by meeting us in that Manhattan synagogue honoring Lithuanian Jewish Holocaust victims. Your warmth and care to help me curate our Biržai family history has been helpful and touching. You've been very generous to me and this project.

Jacob Hogan: To my nephew and Godson, I am grateful that you expressed an interest in the family history and for making the journey to Biržai with me. Thank you for carrying the torch for the next generation who will remember our relatives and never forget what happened in 1941. Our "Shtetl stroll" and the time we spent with the Silberg sisters sitting by the river in the shtetl are events that I will always cherish.

James Williams: Thank you for teaching us two small words that made a world of difference to 6,000 rows in our spreadsheet: pivot table. That transformed and compressed a large volume of individual pieces of data into smaller comprehendible pieces of information for what happened to my family.

Lisa Shiroff (Tasfil Publishing): Thank you for believing in this engineer turned budding author and for the help you provided me initially shaping the book. Thank you for convincing me there was a worthy story to tell, and an eager audience for the Biržai memoir. I am deeply grateful for your coaching and advice as the book took shape. I was relieved when you said it was not a "vomit draft." I hope that you like the finished product.

Greta Barnes: More than my first editor, dear future daughter-in-law, you taught me many writing techniques. You did not hold back, yet shared your opinions with "grace and style". Amazing confidence to tell your future father-in-law that his stuff isn't as good as he thought it was. Your bravery and insights are very much appreciated, it made for a better read.

Reviewers: There were many people who reviewed the various incarnations of the manuscript. I was able to incorporate the full gamut of feedback, ranging from a simple nugget to wholesale changes. Thank you to my anonymous reviewers, previous mentioned reviewers, and Elizabeth Hendler, Florence Levin, Dolores Eagan, Pat McNichol, Melissa Brokalakis, and Glenda Levitt.

Alfred Platschka: Thank you for taking my son Kolbe and I on a private spectacular personal tour of concentration camps in the Munich, Germany area in June 2019. The information and your tour will always be remembered and could be very helpful in the future.

JewishGen.org: Thank you to all of the volunteers who spent many hours translating old Russian and Lithuanian documents in many languages, converting them to electronic records, and making them available for the many professional and amateur genealogists.

Emilija Raibužytė-Kalninienė and Edita Lansbergiene: Thanks to the amazing curators at the Biržai Region Museum "Sela." Whatever I asked you for, you provided me, and more. Labai ačiū.[65]

Thank you to the friends, family members, and strangers, identified on the images, who granted me permissions to use the images in the book.

The most profound thanks goes to Berl-David Magid, Sonja Beder, and Motel Levitan, the three survivors who told their stories. By the

---

65 Labai ačiū means thank you very much in Lithuanian.

Grace of God, against the most unlikely odds and despite both insane and inexplicable circumstances they survived. They are my heroes. I have studied these three young adults for two years; they are locked in my heart. Thank you to the survivors and witnesses who documented their experiences for the rest of the world to understand what happened to the Jews in towns across Europe.

Thank you to the righteous Lithuanians who proved that people can still do the right thing when everyone and everything around them has gone sideways. Thanks to Regina Batvinytė and the Drevinskienė and Valintėlis families for being mensches.

Author's Notes

Boxcar Transportation (Chapter 1): The Magid family did return from Kazan to Biržai, and probably by train. The description of the Magid return was based on research of people in a similar circumstance. These stories shared similar conditions including being packed into boxcars and the treatment they received, both in their homeland and foreign destinations.

Shtetl Life (Chapter 2): The source of information that I communicated in the Magid-Beder meetings was shared by Sonja Beder's cousin Sheryl Silberg, to which I am very grateful. Sonja made recordings that provided important examples of everyday life in Biržai. Sheryl only knew of her cousin as Sonja, which is how I referred to her in the book, although she found out later that she was also referred to as Sheina/Sheine. I do not know if the Magid and the Beder families knew of each other or if they socialized together to exchange information about life in the shtetl. I am not sure if Gersh Zundelevitch gave the kids candy.

Shmuel the Security Guard (Chapter 3): The eighty-year-old guard, Shmuel, existed at the Biržai marketplace; however, his name is unknown to me. I named him for my great-great-grandfather, Samuel Bien. The stories about this person's role of providing security, collecting money, and his clock obsession were all true. The interaction between "Shmuel" and Berl were of my creation; the two men may not have ever met.

Teacher's Nicknames (Chapter 6): The religious education teachers and their nicknames were mentioned in Berl Magid's memoir.

Name Changes (Chapter 7): Tame Bencelovicius Khait and Leib Khait did indeed come to America. Their trip took place between 1910 and 1926. Family lore reports they didn't like the American culture and returned to Biržai. Tame, her brother Bennet, and his wife, Anna, were born in Biržai. Bennet changed his surname to Atkins when he immigrated to America.

Gravestones (Chapter 7): Tame and Leib Khait are buried in the Biržai Jewish cemetery. In June 2019, I was able to visit their grave sites and recite the Mourner's Kaddish, a prayer that honors the deceased.

Figure 25. L-R: Tame Khait's tombstone, died 1926, and Leib Khait's tombstone, died 1927, in the Biržai cemetery. Photo by author.

Berl Joins the Army (Chapter 8): Berl did enlist in the Lithuanian army in 1931. The enlistment year is approximate based on the enlistment age of eighteen and his birth year which was 1913. He served for one-and-a-half years in Panevėžys. He experienced anti-Semitism in the service, but I didn't discuss it in the book.

High School Boys (Chapter 8): The two high school boys who are introduced at Berl Magid's 1931 military sendoff were probably not as yet Lithuanian nationalists. The two high school students were friends with the Jews and with Daniel Segal. When Berl and Daniel were on the run in 1941, they met the high school students again, but this time they were nationalized, carrying rifles, capturing Jews, and they captured Berl and Daniel. I added that they wanted to learn how to shoot a rifle as an ironic twist and a bit of foreshadowing.

Berl Magid and Motel Levitan (Chapter 9): I do not know if Berl and his friends met or knew Motel Levitan and his family, however I wanted to introduce Motel before his story was unveiled later in the book.

Moishe and Berl Magid and Regina Batvinytė (Chapter 9): Berl and Moishe Magid may not have met Regina, however I wanted to introduce her to the reader before incorporating her eyewitness testimony later in the story. She was born as Regina Batvinytė on January 2, 1927 in Braškiai village in Biržai county. Her parents were Kazys Batvinis and Marijona Vinclavaitė-Batvinienė. She married Juozapas Drevinskas in 1955 and they had a daughter Asta Drevinskaitė-Vaitiekūnienė in 1960. They lived on Apaščios Street in 1939. The street name was later changed to Zemaites.

Figure 26. Regina Drevinskas (nee Batvinytė) in 1955. Reproduced by permission of Biržai Region Museum Sėla.

Weddings (Chapter 9): I used the wedding of Abram and Jenta Alzutski (nee Shtein) as a device to bring folks together to talk about Biržai weddings, marriages, and ultimately for the reader to meet the famous Rabbi Lintup.

Shtein Family (Chapter 9): The Shtein family does indeed have several daughters, including Jenta and Reiza. Reiza was born in 1913 and was the same age as Berl and his friends. At the 1932 wedding of Jenta Shtein, Reize was unmarried. However, the boys at Abram and Jenta Alzutski's wedding missed their chance as Reize did get married to Zundel Tkach in 1937.

Neshomes Recipe (Chapter 9): The neshomes described are indeed a real recipe that Samuel Evans received from Leah Glas, a friend of his father from Biržai. The recipe is listed below:

NESHOMES
(Matzah Balls with Souls)

Ingredients:
- 6 eggs, separated
- 1 cup matzah meal
- 1 teaspoon fat
- 1 teaspoon salt
- A pinch of pepper

Stuffing:
- 3 tablespoons chicken fat
- 2 large onions, chopped

Beat egg yolks until creamy and beat the whites until a foam rises.

Combine and add the matzah meal, chicken fat, salt and pepper. Refrigerate for several hours. Half an hour before cooking, remove and shape into balls. Sauté the onions in the chicken fat and place a teaspoon of mixture inside the center of each ball. Drop into boiling soup and cook, covered for 30-45 minutes. Yields 12-14 matzah balls.

Sam and Jadviga, a Love Story (Chapter 9): While some of the data about Sam and Jadviga is from the Sam Evans newspaper article, "Hearts Be Broken, Souls Survive," I did meet with Allan Evans, Sam's son. Allan told me of the long love affair between Sam and Jadviga, which was both spectacularly romantic and a truly sad, heart-breaking story.

Samuel Ferber (Chapter 10): He was one of eight children who were born to Abraham and Vita Eida Ferber. Eta Zelda, Chana, Israel Zelig (US), and Lamech (Argentina) survived, but Batia Rachel Shuster (nee Ferber), Orel Aron Arzik, Sara Leia Sorrel (nee Ferber), including Samuel Ferber were murdered. This family lived at 50 Pasvalio Street, close to the Magid family. I was able to meet Sam's nephew Cyril Ferber, from South Africa, during the Biržai Memorial trip in June 2019. Cyril provided me with a letter that Sam wrote from his home in Biržai to his family in South Africa, inviting them to attend his bar mitzvah in Biržai in 1933 and seeking their help in emigrating to South Africa. Sadly Sam, age twenty-one, was killed in the Astrava Grove.

Figure 27. Avraham & Vita Ferber (nee Kremer), with children Bessie, Orel Aron Arzik, Samuel, and Eta or Chana. Reproduced by permission of Cyril Ferber.

Pinkhus Girshovich, The Engineer (Chapter 10): The engineer who lived with the Magid family was never given a first name in Berl's memoir. However, when Berl was later in the Šiauliai ghetto he meets a Hadassah Levin (nee Girshovich). She shares with Berl Magid that her husband was a rabbi in Telzh, Lithuania. She was the sister of the religious engineer who lived with them in Biržai. I found her maiden name was Girshovich, born in 1912, and she had three brothers named Pinkhus (1906), Abram (1908), and Izrael (1911). I couldn't determine which brother was the engineer, so I selected Pinkhus because he was the oldest and he would have had sufficient time to become a respected engineer, relative to Berl's age (1913).

Khatseh-Maneh Magid (Chapter 10): He had immigrated to South Africa in 1929. He did send money, British pounds, to his family in Biržai. When Berl was housed in the displaced persons camps in Munich in 1945, Khatseh-Maneh did send him paperwork to immigrate to South Africa, but Berl decided to go to America instead. I included the immigration papers that accompanied the letter to the family at the get together in 1938.

Figure 28. Khatseh-Maneh Magid. Source: Berl-David Magid, What I Have To Tell: Pages From a Life (Peretz Publishing, 1992).

The Last Immigration Ticket to America from Lithuania in 1938 (Chapter 10): The story of Sam Evans receiving his visa was described in the newspaper article that I have previously referenced, and it was also explained to me by Allan Evans. Sam made multiple attempts to have Jadviga emigrate from Lithuania to America. Approved by US immigration, but was declined by the Russian authorities who said that she would have no trouble finding a suitable husband in Lithuania. I was shown a picture of a very sad Sam and Jadviga at the Biržai train station when he departed for America. Berl was able to visit Sam both in the US and later in Israel. Allan has multiple pictures of the two lifelong friends: Sam and Berl.

Berl, Naftali, and a Pregnant Miriam Magid (Chapter 11): Berl did indeed go to Ramėnai at the behest of his brother and work at the sanatorium. I am unsure how Berl and Naftali would have communicated following the Memel annexation in 1939, but I had them meet in-person to discuss their future plans. I have not been able to find out when Naftali Magid and Miriam Oppenheimer met, and where or when they married. However, in Berl's memoir, he mentioned that he found out while he was in the Šiauliai ghetto that Miriam was in Biržai during the German occupation and she was killed on August 8, 1941. There is also Yad Vashem testimony submitted by Miriam's sister that documents her murder. Miriam was meeting with her in-laws and was pregnant at the time.

Speculation about Soviet Sympathizers (Chapter 12): Eyewitness Algimantas Gurekas speculated there might have been more Jewish sympathizers, percentage wise, than Lithuanians in Panevėžys. I applied these percentages in the discussion to Biržai.

The Nanny's Comments (Chapter 12): The foreshadowing by the Ukrainian girl with her comments about planning to go to Siberia did occur.

Russian Nationalization: (Chapter 12): Although there is no hard evidence of the neighboring Lithuanians moving out of their space and into the homes of the Jews of Biržai after the Soviets arrived, this type of occupation likely happened. This house swapping occurred in Panevėžys, about forty miles from Biržai. I chose to include this detail in the *Jews of Biržai*.

I included some of the Russian nationalization activities that were detailed in Algimantas Gureckas's testimony as if they occurred in Biržai.

The Yeshiva Students (Chapter 13): Besides Berl's memoir, there are a couple references that mention the Yeshiva students in Biržai, but not with much detail. The fact that they stayed with the Magids is an amazing coincidence, but not unexpected due to the reputation, integrity, and devoutness of the Magid family.

Brandy for Wood (Chapter 14): When Berl exchanged the bottles for wood, he actually called it *eau de vie*. In French, that literally translates to "water of life" with the most common meaning being brandy.

Berl and Sonja Discuss Kaunas (Chapter 14): Berl and Sonja probably didn't meet at the castle to discuss Kaunas though it certainly was possible. Since Berl had been to Kaunas before, he shared information with Sonja and she communicate to the reader she was heading to Kaunas for a job.

Russian Deportations: June 14-15, 1941 (Chapter 16): When the Russians deported select Jewish and Lithuanian townspeople from Biržai on June 14-15, 1941, it was a surprise to all residents. The Russians did use trucks to transport people to the Biržai train station. They did start the process on the night of June 13, 1941. It is true that the Beker and Gendler families were deported to Russia. What is not known is how they were transported to the train and if the Magid family saw them on a transport truck, as I portrayed in the scene. In June 2020, the Lithuanian government released a list of deported Lithuanians. The list contained over 190,000 names, which included

344 names from Biržai. Of the 344 names, there were approximately 30 Jewish family names, including Beker, Fridman, Gendler, Lipshitz, and others. Icikas Chaimas Beker was born in 1927, so he was approximately thirteen when he and his family were deported to Siberia.

Deportation Drawing (Chapter 17): Much of the description on the railway station platform was pulled from a drawing of the deportation scene in Biržai, located in Biržai Region Museum Sėla. There are similar pictures from other towns.

Mitzvah66 (Chapter 17): Berl does discuss in his memoir about walking to the station and his father delivering goods to the Yeshiva students at dawn on Sunday.

The Fundraiser (Chapter 18): This event for the Biržai families deported to Russia from Biržai is fictional. However, based on the character of the Magid family, their history of helping others, and their adherence to scriptures and tzedakah it is not a big stretch. I wrote this story to transition between the deportations and the German invasion, which occurred just one week later.

Operation Barbarossa (Chapter 18): This event is well documented about the build-up and launch on the early hours of June 22, 1941. I researched but I have not been able to find eyewitness accounts of the German invasion in Biržai. I chose to include data from an account that occurred at Panevėžys. The store that was robbed and owned by Elijah Nankin was in Panevėžys, but I am confident that many of those same incidents happened in Biržai.

Berl and Batvinytė Family (Chapter 19): Berl and his friends spending the day with the Batvinytė family was my creation. I had introduced

---

66 Mitzvah means commandment in Hebrew. Tradition is doing good deeds.

the readers to Regina earlier, so I was able to continue including Regina as a means to communicate future events. This meeting was the vehicle to introduce the Molotov speech broadcast on Russian radio.

German Date of Arrival (Chapter 20): Sonja Beder stated that the Germans arrived in Biržai on June 25. She was emphatic that they were definitely there by June 26, 1941. The German army arrived and occupied nearby towns on the following dates:

- Joniškis: June 24, 1941
- Pasvalys: June 26, 1941
- Vabalninkas: June 27, 1941
- Pandėlys: June 26–27, 1941
- Linkuva: June 28, 1941

These occupation dates align and support the timeframe that Sonja reported as the day the Germans arrived in Biržai.

Biržai Jews Join the Russian Army (Chapter 20): Mina Fridlender (also spelled Fridlander), and about ten young men and women, did leave in a truck and fled from Biržai on June 25, 1941. They got as far as Jėkabplis, Latvia, when their truck ran out of gas. After sneaking onto a military train, they arrived in Gorki, Russia, about a month later. After Mina received a telegram from her brother Kalman Fridlender, a lieutenant in the 249th Brigade, she went to Balakhna, Russia to join his Russian Brigade to fight against the Germans.

Mina and her brother Kalman survived the Holocaust, and he attained the rank of captain. She moved to Be'er Sheva, Israel. Pictures of Mina Fridlender, Kalman Fridlender, and Reuven Shein can be found on pages 155-156 of the book *Road to Victory: Jewish Soldiers of the 16th Lithuanian Division 1942-1945*, Leivers, Dorothy.

Mina's brother Chaim Fridlender, his wife Tirca, their three daughters Henia, Miriam, and Reiza Sara, and Mina's sister Lina Birger died in Astrava and they are listed on the Memorial Wall.

Many Lithuanian Jews joined the Russian army, including some serving from Biržai:

- Peretz Glazer was killed in battle.

- Faivel Glazer survived and moved to Israel. Both Peretz and Faivel Glazer served in the 249th Brigade.

- Meir Shakas served in the 249th Brigade and died in combat.

- Reuven Zelikovitz served in the 249th Brigade and died in combat.

- Yakov Chasid served in the 156th Brigade. He was killed near Alekseyevka, Russia.

- Mendel Moroz served in the 167th Brigade and died in the battle to liberate Klaipėda, Lithuania.

- Sheftel Melamed, according to his daughter Leta.

Meeting with Dr. Levin (Chapter 21): Berl does meet Dr. Levin on the morning of June 26, 1941, based on Berl's memoir. There are no details of the conversation. Berl reported that Dr Levin's daughter Ester called home to say she was in transit travelling on a troop train to Russia. I have confirmation that she survived because she was out of town in her last year of medical school studies at Vytautas University in Kaunas, Lithuania. I combined the two facts in Berl's meeting with the Levin family at their home and Ester's call home. There were also conflicting reports of when Dr. Levin's son Eliyahu died. I received confirmation that he died at Astrava, not at the synagogue.

Two Lithuanian Brothers (Chapter 21): On the streets of Biržai after leaving Dr Levin's house the brothers tell him it is not safe to be outside. All of the other information communicated about the Wehrmarcht, Einsatzgruppen, and new policies was a way to get that information into the narrative. I am not sure if the Germans would have printed posters or leaflets with the new rules, but it is possible.

Hiding Jewels and Valuables (Chapter 22): Sonja did hide the family jewelry at Hela Savitzky's house based on Sonja's testimony. A safe assumption is this happened around the time the Germans arrived yet prior to the ghetto being formed.

Mrs. Levin's Discovery of Dr. Levin's Murder (Chapter 24): I have not found a source that reveals how Sore Levin discovered her husband had been murdered the previous evening, so I invented a plausible narrative. The 1926 Lithuanian Internal Passport data listed Shmuel and Muse Drumlevich (nee Lipshits), and their children Riva, Yankel, Ida, and Rose living next door to the Levin family at 3 Vytauto Street. I chose to remember another Biržai family by having Muse inform Sore of the tragic news.

There are multiple accounts and testimonies of how the local Lithuanians lured Dr. Levin out of his house the night that they killed him, how he was killed, and the timing of his murder. I pieced together the encounter as best as possible melding all of the data. Most of the accounts are relatively consistent, but none of them were a complete accounting. My intent is both to honor the life of Dr. Levin and to stay true to the facts of his tragic murder. There is one core set of facts that are consistent and verifiable: a well-respected physician and innocent man was pulled from his house and murdered by local Biržai Lithuanians. The exact dates are unknown, but it happened in the last week of June 1941, most likely June 25-28, 1941. The Lithuanians eventually permitted Dr. Levin to be buried in the Jewish Cemetery in Biržai.

Thirty Buried in the Biržai Jewish Cemetery Between June 22 and Aug 8, 1941: There were approximately thirty Jews that perished during the June 22 and August 8, 1941 massacre and were buried in the Biržai Jewish Cemetery. There is a memorial in the cemetery with a Yiddish inscription that translates as: "*In memory of about thirty civilian Jews who were killed by the Nazis and their local allies here in 1941.*"

Figure 29. Memorial in the Biržai cemetery remembering the thirty Jewish civilians that were killed between June 22 and August 8, 1941. Reproduced by permission of Merūnas Jukonis.

Rabbi Bernshtein Killed (Chapter 25): The day after Dr. Levin was murdered, Rabbi Bernshtein was killed. He was one of the thirty Jews that were buried in the Jewish Cemetery. The multiple survivor testimonies and sources are all consistent with the timing and how he was murdered. His wife, Liba Sheina (nee Dverovich), was murdered on August 8, 1941 at the Astrava Grove.

Moishe Hendler's Death (Chapter 27): The details of his death are included in Sonja Beder's eyewitness testimony. He was indeed hiding in the forest.

Dr. Aptekin's Death (Chapter 27): There are no testimonial details of Dr. Aptekin's death, other than he was captured in the forest and killed. I included him in the same scene in which Moishe Hendler was killed instead of telling two killing episodes.

Fate of Khasele Zebovich (Chapter 27): After her head injury, Khasele Zebovich remained at the Biržai Hospital illegally until August 8. It is probable that she was killed when the Germans came and took the hospital patients to Astrava, as part of the last wave of executions.

Kirshon Family Living in Biržai or Pasvalys (Chapter 28): David Kirshon had a law office in Biržai. The Kirshon family also had ties to Pasvalys. Data indicates they may have had a residence there. A Yad Vashem testimony from his cousin Rachel Safra stated he was killed in Biržai. However, there is separate testimony that states he was killed in Pasvalys. Jonathan Dorfan, who conducted research for the Biržai memorial wall project, concluded that the family was killed in Biržai. I concur with his assessment. David and his wife Rachel were remembered on the memorial wall in 2019. Their daughters Miriam and Golda were added in 2021.

The Rotsamer Brothers (Chapter 28): Berl, Zundel, and Daniel did meet the Rotsamer families when returning to Biržai. The actual details of their experiences are unknown, but the Rotsamer brothers were turned away from Russia and they returned back to Biržai. There is no further mention of them in Berl's memoir about their outcome.

Sonja at the Prison (Chapter 29): Sonja Beder did indeed go to the prison looking for her father and brother after they were captured. She met a Lithuanian woman named Mrs. Baltziunis who told Sonja the fate of Motel-Yosel and Berl Beder. Not knowing the location of where Berl Magid was held captive, I placed Sonja at the makeshift jail where Berl Magid was imprisoned.

Picture of Lithuanian Hiwi Guarding Biržai Jews (Chapter 30): Although I was not able to include, for copyright reasons, a picture of Lithuanian collaborators escorting Jews through the streets of Biržai, I substituted a similar copyright compliant German photo. A rare photograph of Lithuanian Hiwi guarding Biržai Jews can be found here: https://pirkis.lt/home/menas-kolekcijos-antikvaria-tas/3591-senos-foto-nuotraukos/15982853-foto-birzai-zydu-trage-dija-1941-07-07-reta.html.

Daniel Segal Outcome (Chapter 31): Berl Magid's memoir stops mentioning Daniel Segal after they were captured and imprisoned in the Biržai cellar. There are two options: Daniel was either released with Gershon Belicki, Eliya Davidov, and the others, or he was sent on the train. I have not been able to find any records of Daniel Segal in Yad Vashem or any other proof of his status, so I put him on the train to provide closure, but his fate is unknown.

Gershon Belicki Murder Site (Chapter 31): The village where Regina Batvinytė's aunt Ona Vyanslovene lived was named Брашкес in Russian. With help from Jonathan Dorfan, I was able to locate the town named Braškių and the Užušiliai forest. This forest that she mentioned where the four or five men were murdered, including Belicki, is about six miles south of Biržai. According to testimony from Pola Elpern, Hertz Sherman and Gershon Belicki were murdered the same week, so I placed them together at Užušiliai forest. Others released from the train depot where Berl was kept, could have been with Belicki when he was shot, including Eliya Davidov.

Berl's Last Appearance in Biržai (Chapter 31): The last time that Berl-David Magid appeared in this book prior to Chapter 39 was on Saturday July 19, 1941 (Chapter 31), when he meets with his family at the train depot in Biržai before he boarded a train to an unknown destination. Following the release of Gershon Belicki, Eliya Davidov, and others, Berl is loaded onto a train with Sholem Gordon, Hirsh Becker, Itsik Shek, one of the Portnoy brothers, and sent to Šiauliai. Upon arrival in Šiauliai, these men were imprisoned, were freed, and then were rounded up and put into the Šiauliai ghetto. David Shokhet, Rakhmiel Eben, Yankele Shuster, Shloyme Bik, and Sonja Beder all were from Biržai and were mentioned in Berl's memoir as having arrived in the Šiauliai ghetto prior to December 1942.

Flyers and Posters (Chapter 32): There may or may not have been flyers posted or passed around Biržai about the pending formation of a ghetto. However, the text that I included in the flyer was verbatim from the Biržai newspaper, Naujosios Biržų Žinios, that was published by the LAF on August 2, 1941.

Conditions in the Ghetto (Chapter 33): Some of the details about the conditions of the Biržai ghetto, including the sanitation, was culled from an article about the Vilnius ghetto, which was created in September 1941.

Transporting Food Into the Ghetto (Chapter 33): The Batviniai family did feed Orka by dropping the basket into the river. Orka was kicked in the chest when purchasing apples for his child. These two stories are in Regina Batvinytė's Biržai testimony.

The story about Eduardas Valintėlis bringing food for the Liberman family is fictional, but I wanted to show that the guards could be bribed with vodka, which was included in the testimony of Algimantas Gureckas. Jadviga Šušytė-Pančkauskienė, the girlfriend of Samuel Evans, also delivered food to the ghetto, but she had already moved to Kaunas. I transferred her righteousness and I applied it to another righteous Lithuanian, Eduardas Valintėlis.

Housing in the Ghetto (Chapter 34): I did not discover sources that discussed the housing arrangements inside the ghetto. The Magid,

Bass, and Khait families, although related, may or may not have been able to reside together. I put them together as a combination of wishful thinking and a way to provide narration to some of the events that were happening in the ghetto.

The Hasidic Synagogue (Chapter 34): It is described very well in the book titled *Synagogues in Lithuania* (Narkiss) from an architectural perspective, however the book does not describe the interior with much detail. I used my 2019 visit to the Peitav-Shul in Riga, Latvia, as the model for describing the exterior and interior detail. That Riga synagogue was classified as art nouveau, similar to the neoclassicalism style that classified the Biržai Hasidic synagogue. The Peitav-Shul was constructed in 1905 and it survived World War II due its protected location in the Old City.

The Nazis Lies (Chapter 35): The Nazis and their collaborators frequently lied to their Jewish prisoners in order to keep them calm. They would talk of resettling to a city or evacuating them, which unfortunately meant sending them to concentration camps or killing them. There were at least two references when the Biržai Jews believed they were going to the Latvian border to work or they were going to Palestine. I used the "Jewish state" option initially because it is not specifically Israel or Palestine. Later, I used the "Latvian border work" reference to show the lies and inconsistencies of their captors.

Underground Gas Tanks—Two Pits (Chapter 35): According to sources, this story was actually what a German SS sergeant told a woman in the Vilkaviškis ghetto. The Germans lied to the Jews about the pits and their intentions at Astrava to keep them calm and to prevent them from uprising. The woman in Vilkaviškis, and most likely in Biržai, believed there was some truth and logic in what they had heard. Here I wrote that a Lithuanian guard divulged this story to Sheina Magid.

Sonja's Hallucinations (Chapter 35): From her testimony, Sonja Beder's hallucinations started when she arrived at the church following the August 8 massacre. I took some liberties and started them just a couple days earlier to bring Berl-David back into the story, who had been sent to the Šiauliai ghetto prior to August 8. Berl being a part of her hallucinations was fabricated by me. My purpose for weaving in Berl into her hallucinations was to give the illusion that Berl was still in the Biržai ghetto. My attempt was for the reader to believe Berl was still in Biržai, even though he was not since Saturday July 19, 1941.

Regina's Puppy and Schoolmate Anna (Chapter 35): Regina Batvinytė did go looking for her lost puppy. The Anna character and meeting were created so Anna could meet Regina in front of the ghetto. Anna communicated testimony provided by a Lithuanian named Teodoras Valotka who lived about sixty miles from Biržai. Regina communicated to Anna parts of her testimony.

Sonja Beder Returns to Biržai (Chapter 35): I do not know exactly when Sonja returned from Kaunas, but it must have been somewhere around the time I computed, June 24, 1941. Sonja returned from her two-month assignment in time to witness the events that occurred in the first week of the German occupation of Biržai and communicate those events to the reader. It also provided a way to discuss some of the potential reasons why the Lithuanians were so eager to collaborate.

Berchick, the Snowman (Chapter 35): In his book *Only Two Remained*, Biržai native Henry Tabakin tells a story about Berchick from Agenishak, a large estate near Biržai. Although only six miles from Biržai, I could not find that exact town. I selected Anglininkai, which was a similar distance away. The *OpenStreetMap* website suggests it could be walked in about two hours. Berchick probably took longer in such intense snowy weather conditions.

August 8, 1941 Massacre (Chapter 36): The timings, facts and dialogue of the August 8 massacre were pieced together from eyewitness testimonies and published articles. Again, I knitted together these accounts, similar to what I had done with the murder of Dr. Levin. These testimonies are fragments of the whole story. One account states the shooting occurred between 11:00 a.m. and 7:00 p.m. I surmised that the start time for organizing and the initial corralling of the prisoners out of the synagogue and then the marching them to Astrava must have occurred two hours before 11:00 a.m. There are many accounts of the Einsatzgruppen process and the same things happened in Biržai. I used other accounts and the Einsatzgruppen operations to fill in the details the Biržai testimonials lack. Many of the descriptions and sentences in this chapter are directly from eyewitness testimonies. Some of the meanings may be slightly altered from human and electronic translations, back and forth from Lithuanian, Russian, Hebrew, Yiddish, and eventually to English. However, the gist of what happened is clear and not debatable. The change in my writing style for August 8 was purposeful to highlight the freneticism and insanity of the day.

Smerel Nankin (Chapter 37): There is a survivor who crawled out of the pit and headed to Rinkuškiai village, which is just two miles away from Astrava. There are two references that suggest this person may have been a Nankin, maybe Smerel Nankin. This survivor did have the unfortunate luck of picking the wrong house to ask for help and he was taken back to the pits and killed the next day. I made his murder occur on the same evening to build up the suspense of the shooters returning to Astrava while Motel Levitan was trying to crawl out from the pit.

The killing of children and babies had sporadically happened throughout Lithuania before August 8, 1941. According to research performed by Alex J. Kay, the first German commando group, Einsatzkommando E2, Einsatzgruppe A, to systematically kill of children grievously started on August 8, 1941 in Biržai.

Burying of Religious Items in the Riverbank (Chapter 38): The Batvinis family buried the religious items of Jewish families in the river to save them. Apparently, the water level in the river was low when the items were buried. During the winter the ice and the water level would rise. In the spring, when the ice melted, the water reached the back of their house and it would be right next to their door. Unfortunately, and notwithstanding their best of intentions, the water ultimately destroyed everything that they had buried.

Vanda and Regina (Chapter 38): The meeting between Vanda Stiklerytė and Regina Batvinytė was a fabricated conversation among two scared Biržai girls. It served the purpose of disclosing to the reader different perspectives on the Biržai Aktion throughout July and August 1941. The source of the Vanda story came from Vanda's published story fifty-five years later. Around the year 2000, Vanda heard on the radio about a Franciscan priest, Father Julius Sasnauskas, who was asking listeners to submit stories about the Holocaust. Vanda's stories were broadcast on the radio. Her daughter, Jūratė Baranova, edited and retitled her mother's story, *The Sad Eyes of Chait*, as a supplement in her German textbook and lessons on ethics for fifth and sixth graders. Jūratė Baranova, who met the 2019 tour group in Vilnius, passed away in early 2021.

Sonja and Antanas Last Meeting (Chapter 39): The final interaction between Sonja and Antanas happened in a slightly different way than I depicted. I changed it so their final meeting happened, then she was captured by the Gestapo and taken to the Šiauliai ghetto. She never returned back to his house. The final interaction and her emotional state were clearly documented in her testimony.

Berl and Sonja in Šiauliai Ghetto (Chapter 39): Berl-David and Sonja indeed met in the Šiauliai ghetto in approximately December 1942. I triangulated the dates and events in Berl's memoir with details in Sonja's testimony to arrive at the best estimation of their meeting. In *The Jews of Biržai* I had created a closer relationship between Berl and Sonja than may have existed. When they met in the Šiauliai ghetto, Berl described the meeting as "she fell into my arms sobbing." Their stay in the Šiauliai ghetto only overlapped one year, until the "end of the 1943 peat season" which occurs in the autumn, and then she was transferred to another work camp.

Figure 30. The memorial that identifies the location where the Jews were liberated on a death march from Dachau. Photo by author.

Berl-David Magid in Šiauliai, Stutthof, Kauffering, and Dachau: Berl Magid remained in the Šiauliai ghetto almost three years. After July 1944, he was transported to a concentration camp in Stutthof, Poland. At the beginning of 1945, he was transferred to a concentration camp in Kauffering, Germany, which was a satellite camp of the infamous Dachau concentration camp. In April of 1945, while on a dreadful Dachau Death March, he was liberated by the U.S. Army's 522nd Field Artillery Battalion, in a field near Waakirchen, Germany, ending four years in captivity. The inscription on the monument (figure 30) where he was liberated, translated from German by Jacob Hogan, reads, "Here, in the last days of the war, on May 2nd, 1945, the suffering of thousands of unfortunate people from the concentration camp Dachau was ended. Many died before the liberation."

Yizkor List of Names

This chapter is a reference section to memorialize the Jews of Biržai. Yizkor in Hebrew translates literally to "may God remember." This chapter contains three tables that will help to remember the Jews of Biržai that died during the summer of 1941.

The following tables are included with each section containing a preface to describe the information in the table:

- Table 1: Murdered Biržai Jews between June-August 1941: Buried in the cemetery.
- Table 2: Biržai murder victims on the memorial wall.
- Table 3: Summary of Biržai Jewish families and their record status.

Murdered Biržai Jews buried in the cemetery

Seventeen of the thirty Jews who perished before August 8, 1941, and were buried in the Jewish cemetery are known by name. Table 1 contains the currently known names of Biržai Jewish citizens that were murdered between June 22 and August 8, 1941. These names are on the memorial wall in Biržai.

TABLE 1: MURDERED JEWS BETWEEN JUNE-AUGUST 1941: BURIED IN THE CEMETERY.

Surname	Given Name	Status
APTEKIN	Josefas	On the Memorial Wall (2019)
BEDER	Berelis	On the Memorial Wall (2019)
BEDER	Motelis Yosel	On the Memorial Wall (2019)
BELICKI	Gersonas	On the Memorial Wall (2019)
BERNŠTEIN	Jehuda Leibas	On the Memorial Wall (2019)
FRIDMAN	Ansa Rivke	On the Memorial Wall (2019)
FRIDMAN	Yehudah Leiba	On the Memorial Wall (2019)
HENDLER	Bencionas	On the Memorial Wall (2019)
HENDLER	Moišė Šija	On the Memorial Wall (2019)
KIRŠON	Davidas	On the Memorial Wall (2019)
KIRŠON	Golda	Added to the memorial Wall (2021)
KIRŠON	Mirijam	Added to the memorial Wall (2021)
KIRŠON	Rachelė	On the Memorial Wall (2019)
LEVIN	Abraomas Zalmanas	On the Memorial Wall (2019)
LURJE	Mošė	On the Memorial Wall (2019)
MAS	Icikas	On the Memorial Wall (2019)
ŠERMAN	Hercas	On the Memorial Wall (2019)

Murdered Biržai Jews between June and August 1941

My research has identified 16 persons whose murders took place before the August 8 massacre, which murders relate strongly to the Biržai holocaust tragedy. Yad Vashem testimony from the sister of Motel Vainer, who was born Biržai in 1921 to Zalman and Hene, indicated that he died from the torture of nationalists who caught him during an escape attempt to Russia. Motel's murder could have been in Biržai, but more likely it occurred en route from Biržai to Russia. Motel's name is on the memorial wall. A Yosef Rosin account identified a "local shokhet" as being murdered shortly after the Nazis entered Biržai. Unfortunately, Rosin does not provide a name and, given the large number of shokhets in Biržai at that time, identifying this individual has not been possible. As described in Chapter 31, two Jewish men from Vaškai, Biržai residents Itsik and Berl Fisher, Avram-Leyb's son, Yankl from Anykščiai, Shmuelkeh, Shmuel, the butcher, a gentleman with surname Portnoy, the shingle maker's son, Yoske Moskevich, and six yeshiva students from Białystok were amongst the 30 Jews who departed on a train from Biržai on July 19. The train returned empty two hours later. The 30 Jews were subsequently murdered at a site unknown. It is also not known if their bodies were ever returned to Biržai. A summary of the names:

- Motel Vainer
- A local shokhet
- Two Jewish men from Vaškai
- Itsik and Berl Fisher
- Avram-Leyb's son, Shmuelkeh
- Yankl from Anykščiai
- Shmuel, the butcher
- One of Portnoy brothers
- The shingle maker's son
- Yoske Moskevich
- Six yeshiva students from Białystok

These victims may or may not have been buried in the Jewish cemetery. The exact dates of many of the individual killings are not known.

Jews of Biržai murder victims on the memorial wall

In June 2019, the construction of a memorial was completed, and a dedication ceremony was held at the Astrava Grove inside the Pakamponys Forest, outside of Biržai, Lithuania. The memorial included a wall inscribed with the names of Jewish people that were massacred between June 22 and August 8, 1941. While the count of the murdered is documented with a widely accepted fact to be 2,400, there are only 551 names on the wall as of August 2021.

Sources: The names inscribed on the Biržai Memorial were provided to the architect by Jonathan Dorfan. As of August 2021, and in time for the eightieth anniversary of the massacre, there were a total of 551 names engraved on the memorial wall. The list of victims comes from two primary sources. The first source, which yielded 432 names, is the Yad Vashem *Database of Shoah Victims' Names.* The second source, which yielded 119 unique names, is from testimonials.

A Call to Action: If you know or surmise that any of your relatives were murdered during the holocaust, especially if they were born in Biržai, **please honor their memory and legacy by entering them into** *The Central Database of Shoah Victims' Names* **on the Yad Vashem website** (https://yvng.yadvashem.org/). It only takes a few minutes to enter the information on the form. Future updates to the Biržai memorial wall will include names added to the Yad Vashem database subsequent to July 2021. It would also be appreciated in such cases that the testifier contact Jonathan Dorfan directly at jdorfan@yahoo.com.

The Biržai Memorial Wall List of Names

The data in table 2 includes the surname, given name, and birth year, when known, of the victims that are currently inscribed on the memorial wall. The names are purposefully engraved in Lithuanian, to remind visitors to the wall that these Jewish people were, after all, Lithuanian citizens. Some of the given names are unknown and they are listed as Nežinomas[67]. The list (table 2) of the 551 names that are on the memorial wall as of July 2021 is preceded by a photo (figure 31) of the memorial wall:

---

67   Nežinomas means unknown in Lithuanian.

Figure 31. The memorial wall dedicated in June 2019 in the Astrava Grove in the Pakamponys Forest. Reproduced by permission of Merūnas Jukonis.

TABLE 2: BIRŽAI MURDER VICTIMS ON THE MEMORIAL WALL.

Surname	Given Name	Birth Year
ABEL	Izraelis	
ABRAMOVIČ	Chaja Riva	1921
ABRAMOVIČ	Ita	1926
ABRAMOVIČ	Mošė	1885
ABRAMOVIČ	Rachelė	1918
ABRAMOVIČ	Raina	1916
ALZUCKI	Bela	1931
ALZUCKI	Davidas	1939
APTAKIN	Nežinomas	
BAS	Aronas	1914
BAS	Gita	1914
BAS	Jehuda	1916
BAS	Pautilas	1864
BAS	Taubė Reizė	1875

Surname	Given Name	Birth Year
BEDER	Berelis	
BEDER	Chackelis	1929
BEDER	Chana Sora	1899
BEDER	Motelis	1922
BELICKI	Nežinomas	
BERNŠTEIN	Jehuda Leibas	
BERNŠTEIN	Liba Šeina	
BERŠON	Rubenas	
BEZEMACHER	Chaimas	
BEZEMACHER	Fania	
BICK	Nechama	1899
BICK	Zalmanas	1902
BIRGER	Elijus	1933
BIRGER	Lina	1902
BIRGER	Mordechajus	1910
BIRGER	Mošė	1931
BOKŠTEIN	Šlomas	
BOROCHOV	Šalomas	
BRIL	Nežinomas	1915
BRIL	Nežinomas	1937
CADIKOVIČ	Pese	1889
CADIKOVIČ	Šmuelis	
CHAIT	Avadija	1900
CHAIT	Baruchas	1934
CHAIT	Baruchas	
CHAIT	Bela Bihla	1870
CHAIT	Berylas	
CHAIT	Bluma Rivka	1905
CHAIT	Davidas	
CHAIT	Dovidas	
CHAIT	Feigė	1871
CHAIT	Gitelė	1899
CHAIT	Hinda	
CHAIT	Hodelė	
CHAIT	Jechielis	

Surname	Given Name	Birth Year
CHAIT	Jenta Freida	
CHAIT	Jocheveta	
CHAIT	Jocheveta	
CHAIT	Leiba	1865
CHAIT	Leizeris Abelis	1908
CHAIT	Mejeris	
CHAIT	Merė Mindelė	1903
CHAIT	Michaelis Davidas	1894
CHAIT	Mošė	1910
CHAIT	Mošė Leibas	
CHAIT	Nachimas	1930
CHAIT	Pinchas	
CHAIT	Raisa Braina	
CHAIT	Šimšonas	1898
DAVIDSON	Chaja	
DAVIDSON	Zacharijus	
DORFAN	Mendelis	1863
DORFAN	Mirijam	1867
EVIN	Avramas Leiba	
EVIN	Bačeva	
EVIN	Chaja Uriazon	
EVIN	Chana Liba	
EVIN	Golda Lėja	
EVIN	Sara	
EZRACHOVIČ	Bencionas	1901
EZRACHOVIČ	Idelė	1901
EZRACHOVIČ	Aronas	1880
EZRACHOVIČ	Jenta	1882
FAKTOR	Chana	
FAKTOR	Donas Beras	
FAKTOR	Eta	
FERBER	Arzikas	1918
FERBER	Avraomas Šlomas	1876
FERBER	Batia Rachelė	1916
FERBER	Sara Lėja	1914

Surname	Given Name	Birth Year
FERBER	Šmuelis	1920
FERBER	Vita Eida	1875
FERD	Ita	
FIN	Zundelis	1916
FRIDLENDER	Chaimas	1894
FRIDLENDER	Henia	1926
FRIDLENDER	Mina	1900
FRIDLENDER	Mirijam	1928
FRIDLENDER	Mošė	1930
FRIDLENDER	Reizė Sara	1931
FRIDLENDER	Tirca	1896
FRIDMAN	Asna	1880
FRIDMAN	Leibas	1878
GAVARTIN	Beila Chana	
GAVARTIN	Bencionas	
GEN	Chana	
GEN	Mendelis	
GEN	Šmuelis	
GER	Geršas	
GER	Israelis	1905
GER	Joelis	1883
GER	Joelis	
GER	Josifas	
GER	Kreina	
GER	Leibas Mošė	1925
GER	Liza	
GER	Mirijam	
GER	Šeina Dvora	1878
GERŠONOVIČ	Henė Mirijam	
GESELEVIČ	Etelė	1882
GESELEVIČ	Leibas	1880
GESELEVIČ	Motelis	1908
GIRES	Chaimas	1922
GIRES	Cipora Feiga	1920
GIRES	Izaokas	1919

Surname	Given Name	Birth Year
GIRES	Leizeris	1900
GIRES	Lėja	1921
GIRES	Malka	1902
GLĖZER	Berelė	
GLĖZER	Faivelis	1922
GLĖZER	Feiga Lėja	
GLĖZER	Geršonas	1903
GLĖZER	Moišė	
GLĖZER	Pešė	1905
GLĖZER	Rafaelis	1924
GUD	Bencionas	1886
GUD	Chulcė	
GUD	Libe	
GUD	Mošė Zivas	
GUD	Šimonas	1881
HAIT	Gita	
HAIT	Indale	
HAIT	Joselis	
HAIT	Mošė	
HAIT	Riva	
HAIT	Rocha	
HAIT	Zelikas	
HARIS	Rachelė	1910
HENDLER	Aba Reuvenas	
HENDLER	Asnat	
HENDLER	Bencionas	
HENDLER	Estera Breina	
HENDLER	Moišė Šija	
HENDLER	Sara	1923
HENDLER	Šmuelis	1920
HIRŠOVIČ	Chaja Estera	1905
ICGAL	Berlas	1898
ICGAL	Jerachmielis	1924
ICGAL	Keila	1900
ICGAL	Reizelė	1921

Surname	Given Name	Birth Year
JAKOVLEV	Rachelė	
JANKELEVIČ	Hinda	
JAŠINAVKAR	Zeidilas	
JUZENT	Musia	
KAC	Aba Reuvenas	
KAC	Basia	1932
KAC	Benjaminas Elizieris	1895
KAC	Chana Bacha	
KAC	Cipė Merė	1889
KAC	Dovidas	
KAC	Elka	
KAC	Israelis Jerachmielis	1922
KAC	Leizeris	1928
KAC	Meiras	
KAC	Mina	1929
KAC	Mirijam	
KAC	Mošė	1892
KAC	Perel Roza	1877
KAC	Rachelė	
KAC	Rivka	
KAC	Ruchla Lėja	
KAC	Šalomas Zivas	1875
KAC	Vulfas Šalomas	1924
KAC	Zelikas	
KAIT	Feigė	1875
KAIT	Libė Pesė	1877
KAIT	Nairas Bokas	1870
KAIT	Rivka	
KAIT	Sorė	1885
KAIT	Šorė	1865
KAMRAZ	Bilas	
KASMAN	Aronas	1900
KASMAN	Chaimas	1929
KASMAN	Henia	1900
KASMAN	Liba	1923

Surname	Given Name	Birth Year
KERBEL	Achbaras Šija	
KERBEL	Hana	
KERN	Blima	1913
KILIUS	Aizikas Abelis	
KILIUS	Nežinomas	1920
KILIUS	Slova	1885
KIRŠON	Davidas	1894
KIRŠON	Golda	
KIRŠON	Mirijam	
KIRŠON	Rachelė	1900
KIVOVIC	Freida	1916
KIVOVIC	Icchakas	1897
KIVOVIC	Sara	1901
KOBEL	Bela	1914
KOLODIČKI	Beila	1930
KOLODIČKI	Ela	1932
KOLODIČKI	Genė	1925
KOLODIČKI	Nežinomas	1935
KOLODIČKI	Sara	1903
KOLODIČKI	Selda	1928
KOPLEVIČ	Abraomas	1932
KOPLEVIČ	Aronas	1924
KOPLEVIČ	Chana	1900
KOPLEVIČ	Hiršas Jankelis	1900
KOPLEVIČ	Rachelė	1928
KOROČINSK	Berkas Zaidelis Dovas	1909
KRAVIC	Aba Jehuda	
KRAVIC	Rachelė Feiga	
KRECHMAR	Michaelis Miša	1870
KRECHMAR	Šore Dveira	1902
KRECHMAR	Sulė Lėja	1895
KRECMER	Beila Rivka	1897
KRECMER	Beilca	1916
KRECMER	Davidas Geršonas	1893
KRECMER	Gindlė	1892

Surname	Given Name	Birth Year
KRECMER	Haimas	1863
KRECMER	Hana Genė	1870
KRECMER	Hiršas Mejeris	1915
KRECMER	Israelis Geršonas	1892
KRECMER	Israelis Leiba	1885
KRECMER	Jehielis Michaelis	1860
KRECMER	Levas Leiba	1900
KRECMER	Libė Gnendel	1889
KRECMER	Meiras Idlė	1905
KRECMER	Mošė	1895
KRECMER	Rivka	1899
KRECMER	Sara Feigė	1875
KRECMER	Sara Lėja	1877
KRECMER	Šmuelis Ruvenas	1886
KRECMER	Tesa Dina	1880
LEVIN	Abraomas	1889
LEVIN	Elijas	
LEVIN	Golda	1886
LEVIN	Israelis	1917
LEVIN	Mendelis	1912
LEVIN	Rivka	1910
LEVIN	Sara	1890
LEVIN	Zorachas	1885
LEVIT	Moisėjus	1888
LEVITAN	Chaja	1899
LEVITAN	Golda	1934
LEVITAN	Leibas	1932
LIFŠIC	Abraomas	
LIFŠIC	Abraomas Leiba	1928
LIFŠIC	Chaja Etelė	1870
LIFŠIC	Josefas	
LIFŠIC	Leibas Arielis Elizieris	1866
LIFŠIC	Lėja	
LIFŠIC	Zalmanas	
LIFŠIC	Zuzana	1906

Surname	Given Name	Birth Year
LIMAN	Breina	1880
LIMAN	Chaimas	1890
LIMAN	Davidas	
LIMAN	Etelė	
LIMAN	Marija	1923
LIMAN	Meiras	1910
LIMAN	Mendelis	1895
LIMAN	Musia	1914
LIMAN	Nežinomas	
LIMAN	Nežinomas	1912
LIMAN	Nežinomas	1910
LIMAN	Nežinomas	
LIMAN	Pinchas	1927
LIPŠIC	Devora	
LIPŠIC	Icchakas	1927
LIPŠIC	Ida	
LIPŠIC	Mina	
LIPŠIC	Mošė	
LIPŠIC	Reizelė	
LIPŠIC	Šimšonas	1888
LUBIN	Asnata Mina	
LUBIN	Estera Rachelė	
LUBIN	Jakira	
LUBIN	Mordechajus	
LURJE	Aronas Jakovas	
LURJE	Bencionas	
LURJE	Chasia	
LURJE	Cvi	
LURJE	Elizieris	1870
LURJE	Freida	
LURJE	Guta	1909
LURJE	Liza	1907
LURJE	Meiras	1921
LURJE	Mina Rivka	
LURJE	Mošė	1900

Surname	Given Name	Birth Year
LURJE	Sara	1874
LURJE	Sara	
LURJE	Tama	1876
LURJE	Taubė	
MAGID	Aba Mošė	1878
MAGID	Meckė Mirijam	1915
MAGID	Perelis	1926
MAGID	Pnina	1917
MAGID	Šeina Rivka	1882
MAGID	Zelda	1920
MAS	Icikas	
MAS	Sara	
MAS	Velvelis	
MEIROVIČ	Bilha	
MEIROVIČ	Cheinda	
MEIROVIČ	Hinda	1895
MEIROVIČ	Jakovas	1896
MEIROVIČ	Mirijam	
MEIROVIČ	Šlomas	
MELAMED	Dveira	1876
MELAMED	Icchakas	1925
MELAMED	Jehuda	
MELAMED	Leizeris	1914
MELAMED	Mirijam	1925
MELAMED	Movsha Girsh	1932
MELAMED	Paja Nankin	1895
MELAMED	Rivka	1922
MELAMED	Rivka	
MELAMED	Rivka Eta	1911
MELAMED	Zelda Lėja	1913
MELAMED	Peisakh Ruven	1895
MELER	Josefas	
MILNER	Cirke	
MINDLIN	Elija Seikas	1892
MINDLIN	Leibas	1924

Surname	Given Name	Birth Year
MINDLIN	Lėja	1924
MINDLIN	Michaelis	1919
MINDLIN	Rivka	1922
MINDLIN	Slova Chasia	1886
MOFŠOVIČ	Jafa Šeina	1906
MOFŠOVIČ	Perelė	
MORAL	Rachelė	1924
MOREIN	Asna Gidelė	1910
MOREIN	Davidas	1900
MOREIN	Elijas	1905
MOREIN	Izraelis	1905
MOREIN	Perė	1880
MOREIN	Zalas	1880
MORIL	Gitelė	1926
MORIL	Rasia	
MORIL	Šeina	
MORIL	Simcha	
MORIL	Taibalė	1928
MOROZ	Bunia	
MOROZ	Feigelė	
MOROZ	Freida	
MOROZ	Libale	1927
MOROZ	Nechama	1925
MOROZ	Ruvenas	
MOROZ	Šimonas Meiras	
MOVŠ	Benjaminas	
NAHAMOVIČ	Elijahu	
NAHAMOVIČ	Hindė	
NAHAMOVIČ	Šlomo	
NOVESED	Šeina Rivka	
NOVOSED	Manucha	
NOVOSED	Reuvenas	
NUDELMAN	Baruchas Ašeris	
ORLOVSKY	Beilė	1889
ORLOVSKY	Nežinomas	

Surname	Given Name	Birth Year
ORMAN	Liebe	
ORMAN	Meiše Ilija	1922
ORMAN	Šmuelis	
PAS	Hiršas	
PASVALECKI	Chenė Perla	
PASVALECKI	Mošė Israelis	
PEN	Beila Sorė	1930
PEN	Golda	
PEN	Šeina Golda	1894
PESACHOVIČ	Berlas	1869
PESACHOVIČ	Tonia	1871
PFENIG	Sara	1924
POSVOLECKI	Šlovė Tirca	
POSVOLECKI	Šolomas Davidas	1902
RABIN	Estera	1914
RABIN	Gita	1916
RABIN	Josefas	
RABIN	Moša	1918
RABIN	Ševa	1885
RACEMOR	Aba	
RACEMOR	Chana	
RACEMOR	Charna Feiga	1921
RACEMOR	Henia	1927
RACEMOR	Jakobas	
RACEMOR	Nežinomas	
RACEMOR	Nežinomas	
RACEMOR	Sara	1924
RACEMOR	Sara Gitelė	1907
RACEMOR	Zeligas	1931
REBĖ	Peresas	
RIF	Danielis	
RIGMANT	Chaimas	
RIGMANT	Hiršas	1917
RIGMANT	Nežinomas	
RIGMANT	Rivka	1919

Surname	Given Name	Birth Year
ROKHMAN	Rivka	1910
ROZENKOVIČ	Dvora	1913
ROZENKOVIČ	Izraelis	1920
ROZENKOVIČ	Jentė	1884
ROZENKOVIČ	Perelė Lėja	1923
ROZINKOVIČ	Mendelis	
RUBIN	Berlas	1915
RUBIN	Chasia	1909
RUBIN	Mendelis	1883
RUBIN	Reizė	1886
SANDLER	Bačeva	1880
SANDLER	Dobkė	1904
SANDLER	Frieda	1902
SANDLER	Genė Merel	1897
SANDLER	Geršonas Šalomas	
SANDLER	Hiršelis	
SANDLER	Israelis	1880
SANDLER	Mana	1908
SANDLER	Mošė	1895
SANDLER	Nežinomas	
ŠAPIRA	Liba	1878
ŠAPIRA	Mošė	1876
SEGAL	Baša	
SEGAL	Berkė	
SEGAL	Davidas	
SEGAL	Frumkė	
SEGAL	Lėja Gitelė	1900
SEGAL	Manė	
SEGAL	Meiras	
SEGAL	Riselė	
SEGAL	Solomonas	
SEGAL	Tevkė	
ŠEK	Zundelis	
SENCIPER	Chana Bela	1900
ŠERMAN	Basia	

Surname	Given Name	Birth Year
ŠERMAN	Beinis	1880
ŠERMAN	Hercas	
ŠERMAN	Jakovas	1927
ŠERMAN	Rachelė	1920
ŠERMAN	Taubė Jonas	1930
SIEV	Rachelė	1901
SIRALSKA	Jocheveda	
SIRALSKA	Hena	
SLUZITEL	Chaja Sara	1891
SLUZITEL	Hinde	1916
SLUZITEL	Hiršas	1889
SMILGA	Berlas	
SMILGA	Estera	
SMILGA	Feiga	1924
SMILGA	Joškė	
SMILGA	Rachelė	1935
ŠNEIDER	Elchananas	1902
ŠNEIDER	Lėja	1868
ŠOCHEN	Bačeva	1924
ŠOCHEN	Chana Lėja	1900
ŠOCHEN	Danielis	1928
ŠOCHEN	Lėja	
ŠOCHEN	Nežinomas	
ŠOCHEN	Nežinomas	
ŠOCHEN	Šimonas	1920
ŠOCHEN	Šlomas	1885
SOCHET	Chaja Rivka	1880
SPORATSKI	Hana	1898
ŠREDERIS	Elazaras	1906
ŠREIBERG	Mošė	1885
SROLOVIČ	Etelė	1905
ŠTEIN	Chaimas Jakobas	1911
ŠTERN	Chana	1880
SUBOTNIK	Pesia	
SUGALSKI	Henia	1912

Surname	Given Name	Birth Year
SUGALSKI	Jocheveda	1880
ŠULMAN	Jerachmielis	
ŠUSTER	Ada	1916
ŠUSTER	Estera Bracha	
ŠUSTER	Lėja	1918
ŠUSTER	Meiras	
ŠUSTER	Mere	1893
ŠUSTER	Mošė	
ŠUSTER	Šimšonas	
TABAKIN	Alteris	
TABAKIN	Chaimas	
TABAKIN	Cheina	1912
TABAKIN	China	
TABAKIN	Cyla	
TABAKIN	Joselis	1886
TABAKIN	Leizeris Velve	
TABAKIN	Liochelis Abelis	1913
TABAKIN	Sara	1924
TABAKIN	Šeina Kreinda	1885
TABAKIN	Šimenas Arije	1912
TABAKIN	Šmarijahu	
TABAKIN	Šmerelis	1886
TABAKIN	Šmuelis	
TABAKIN	Šmuelis Michaelis	1914
TABAKIN	Tuvija	1888
TABAKIN	Vulfas	1918
TRIFSKIN	Nachumas	
VAINER	Arija	1895
VAINER	Cadokas	1880
VAINER	Cipora	
VAINER	Etelė Mirijam	1910
VAINER	Hesė	1916
VAINER	Heslė	1920
VAINER	Ita	
VAINER	Jakovas	

Surname	Given Name	Birth Year
VAINER	Leiba Šolemas	1923
VAINER	Lėja	1895
VAINER	Motelis	1921
VAINER	Nežinomas	
VAINER	Rachelė	
VESTERMAN	Benjaminas	1935
VESTERMAN	Borisas	1902
VESTERMAN	Rachelė	1905
VIN	Baruchas	1924
VIN	Beras Zundelis	
VIN	Chana	1921
VIN	Elijas	
VIN	Rochka	1925
VIN	Sema Lėja	1896
VINER	Sulamita	
VINIK	Mordechajus	1875
ZAK	Cadikas	
ZAK	Elijas	1893
ZAK	Hinkė	1922
ZAK	Hiršas Zvi	
ZAK	Izaokas	1920
ZAK	Lėja	
ZAK	Rivka	1924
ZAK	Rivka	
ZAK	Roza Šošana	1920
ZAK	Sara	1923
ZAK	Tauba	1896
ZAKS	Motelis	1903
ZELBOVIČ	Chasa	1930
ZELBOVIČ	Hene Glika	1893
ZELBOVIČ	Leiba	1895
ZELBOVIČ	Mendelis	1891
ZELBOVIČ	Myra	1925
ZELBOVIČ	Sora Judes	1922
ZELIKOVIČ	Jechielis Michaelis	

Surname	Given Name	Birth Year
ZELIKOVIČ	Juna	1916
ZELIKOVIČ	Reuvenas	1937
ZELINGER	Janku	1886
ZONDOLOVIČ	Gita	1885
ZONDOLOVIČ	Šnoiras	1885
ZUNDELOVIČ	Chana	1911
ZUNDELOVIČ	Estera	1927
ZUNDELOVIČ	Lipkė	1896
ZUNDELOVIČ	Mendelis	1896
ZUNDELOVIČ	Rivka	1885
ZUNDELOVIČ	Šneiras	1896
ZUNDELOVIČ	Zvi	1871

Observations from Abel and Glenda Levitt on the 2019 Biržai Tour and the Holocaust Memorial Dedication

As a descendant of Biržai, one has a strange sense of belonging, of attachment, and of bitterness, anger, and deep resentment. We fell that Jews, including Glenda's family in Biržai and Jews in all towns, cities, and villages, with very few exceptions, including Abel's family in Plungyan, were brutally murdered not only by the Nazis but by the willing participation of Lithuanians. We have a deep sense of connection to Biržai. We walked the ground they walked, we breathed the air they breathed, we gazed at the sky that they gazed at, and our heads pound at the thought of what they went through. We are haunted by the knowledge that man is capable of being the evilest of the animal kingdom.

We also know that we are privileged to have found wonderful Lithuanians. We have been able to carry out our remembrance projects in partnership with the Headmaster, teachers, and students of the high school in collaboration with the staff of the museum, and with active support with the Mayor and members of his committee. It must be noted that it was two Biržaims, Vidmantas and Merunas

Jukonis, the father and son team, our irreplaceable partners, who made every aspect of our memorial tour possible.

Figure 32. Abel and Glenda Levitt (far right) with members of the Valintėlis family at the Biržai Memorial dedication in June 2019. Reproduced by permission of Abel and Glenda Levitt.

We felt a deep sense of satisfaction at the local participation of surrounding schools attending our talks. A deep sense of admiration for the students and teachers who participated in our program at the museum. We felt a deep sense of admiration for the performances and addresses at the high school, satisfaction that at last there is an acknowledgment of the history of the Lithuanian citizens of their town, who were murdered because they were Jews.

We felt an overwhelming sense of relevance and sadness at the Friday evening service and dinner. Powerful that we were there, to have a Friday evening service and traditional Shabbat dinner for us to share and for the local citizens to see and experience. They were able to see who we are, celebrating and perpetuating our heritage, while thinking of life of the Jews so cruelly extinguished in August 1941.

We felt an overwhelming sense of satisfaction at the tree planting ceremony to honor the Savers of the Jews. It took some persistence to convince our contacts at the museum, but once convinced, they did an amazing job of research, planning, and organization.

We think that the highlights of joy and wonder throughout our time spent in Biržai was that two of our children, plus two of our grandchildren arriving from Israel, were able to join us at the tree planting ceremony. They were able to witness Savers and Jewish descendants, including children planting trees, school children carrying the yellow flowers, the mass of us together with local Biržaim and visitors walking the same path our ancestors walked to forest at Pakamponys.

We watched with pride as the children placed the yellow flowers to form a large Magen David. The vision that we dreamt for Biržai unfolded right in front of us, and it was overwhelmingly emotional to hear the outstanding Biržai school choir singing two exquisitely moving songs in perfect Hebrew. As we watched and listened to the choir sing hauntingly beautiful songs in impeccable Hebrew, standing on the steps of the mass grave of the 2,400 murdered, 900 of which were children, we were overwhelmed by a soaring complexity of emotion. There we were, together with some members of our family and with our group of fifty Biržai descendants, who are after all survivors, only because our ancestors left Biržai. At that moment, we felt pride, pride that here we were, Israelis standing in the Pakamponys Forest and we were at last giving names to the few and honoring the spirit of the unknown with our symbol, the Magen David.

About Abel and Glenda Levitt

Abel and Glenda Levitt made aliyah from Cape Town, South Africa, in 1979 with their four children, ages five to fifteen. Today, they have four married children living in Israel and thirteen grandchildren, the oldest aged twenty-six and the youngest six.

They received the Medal of Honor "Lithuanian Diplomacy Star" on June 4th, 2019 at the Embassy of the Republic of Lithuania in the State of Israel. The award was presented to them by the Lithuanian Ambassador in Israel, Edminas Bagdonas, on behalf of the Minister of Foreign Affairs of Lithuania, Linas Linkevičius. This award was presented to them in recognition of their work in commemoration of historical memory.

The Jewish community of Cape Town presented them with a certificate acknowledging their work in Lithuania to memorialize the Litvak history of South African Jewry to promote knowledge of the Holocaust and to rebuild reconciliation and partnerships with Lithuanians. This was presented to them during their visit to Biržai in June 2019 by Ben Rabinowitz.

They also each received the "Plungės Rajono Savivaldybė" medal, the inscription translated to Plungė District Municipality, for their work in Plungyan.

Summary of families and their record status

After realizing that there is a gap of 1,849 names that are missing from the memorial wall, a research initiative began in early 2020. Table 3 is a summary listing by family surname.

The Intent: Create a list of Jewish people born after 1860 who had a connection to Biržai until Aug 1941. With such a list, descendants of these families can conduct their own genealogical research.

What It Is Not: The research goal was not to add additional names to the memorial wall, although it is my hope that it may become the reader's goal. The Biržai Memorial wall committee considers additions from both Yad Vashem records and other testimonials.

The list of Jews of Biržai family names is not:

- To be interpreted as making any conclusive statements about the verification of holocaust victims.

- To provide any analysis, decision making, or interpretation of the data.

- To imply population totals that would indicate the number of Jews living in Biržai during 1941.

- Has not gone through detailed quality assurance checks by a third party, nor has it been verified, validated, or cross referenced.

Sources: A list of surnames (table 3) was culled from the following sources:

- Biržai Memorial Wall list (table 2)

- Details from Yad Vashem *Shoah Database* as they pertain to Biržai

- Lists of Biržai phone book entries between 1928–1940 and Biržai Jewish-owned properties from 1937 provided by the Biržai Region Museum Sėla

- Stories and testimonies that were collected from various websites including Eilat Gordin Levitan and Kehilalinks on Jewishgen.org

- A database export of Biržai residents deported to Russia in June 1941 from www.lietuviaisibire.lt

- Verbal and electronic communication of stories from people meeting during the June 2019 tour of Biržai and the memorial dedication

- Testimonials from Biržai Jewish, Righteous gentiles and Lithuanian survivors

- Berl Magid's memoir, *What I Have To Tell: Pages From a Life*

- Additional books, articles, and private family trees. See bibliography for a complete listing.

Using the list of surnames initially generated from the above sources, the All Lithuanian Database (ALD) from JewishGen.org was searched for available data for each family. ALD provides data available from the following Lithuanian sources:

- Internal passports
- Marriages and divorce records
- Birth records
- Death records
- Revisions lists (census)
- Evacuation lists
- Tax and voter lists

Record Status: In addition to the family surname and a total number of people born and associated with Biržai between 1860 and 1941, the final step was to provide a column in the list to assist the reader in their genealogical research. The column named **record status** contains a value based on the existence or absence of certain records in the data:

- Lived: data exists for people that were evacuated, immigrated to another location, provided survivor testimony, memoirs, or from other sources.

- Died Biržai: data exists for people that died after the German occupation in June 1941 yet before the massacre at Astrava on August 8, 1941 (table 1), or documentation exists for people that died in the Astrava massacre on August 8, 1941 (table 2). Both groups are labeled as Died Biržai.

- Died Elsewhere: data exists for people that were Biržai natives or lived in Biržai, but were killed in other towns in Lithuania, Latvia, Poland, or other locations.

- Missing: for people where there is an absence of data, the outcome is unknown, therefore the data is Missing.

Notes About Data: The data was centralized by the author from various sources. The reader will observe many anomalies in the data; they are detailed below. The author presents the data "as is" from the sources.

- While the list of surnames is extensive, it by no means covers all surnames of Biržai families.

- There are two entries for married women: one associated with their maiden name, and a second entry where they are counted with their married family. This was done to assist with searching, yet admittedly led to an increase in the totals. In particular, it inflates the count of known persons murdered at Astrava (now 551) by about 160 persons. There are approximately 800 married women in the list.

- There are possible duplicate records in cases where there is not enough unique information to differentiate, consolidate it into one record, and then remove the duplicate.

- There are inconsistencies due to differing sources providing conflicting data.

- Some records may have transposed first and last names due to data inconsistencies or translation errors.

- There are conflicting entries based upon different birth years, differing parents, or conflicting spouses.

- There are problems due to translations from different languages: Hebrew, Yiddish, Lithuanian, and Russian into English.

- If a death record existed for a person prior to 1941, that person was excluded from the list, however that data would be included in the online searchable database.

The list below (table 3) summarizes the totals and record status details for each family surname.

The searchable database is hosted on the website **http://www.menschenit.com**. This database provides all of the individual records with much more supportive data. As of the publication date of this book, there are over 6,600 names in the database that spans over 650 unique family surnames.

It is possible that values in the record status have been misassigned and other discrepancies exist within the database. In order to improve the quality of the data, there will be a form on the website to gather suggested updates and a process to contact the author.

TABLE 3: SUMMARY OF BIRŽAI JEWISH FAMILIES AND THEIR RECORD STATUS

Surname	Grand Total	Lived	Died Biržai	Died Elsewhere	Missing
ABEL	2	0	1	0	1
ABELZON	5	0	0	0	5
ABRAM	12	3	5	0	4
ACHBER	23	0	0	0	23
AIZENMAN	4	0	0	0	4
ALOI	4	0	0	0	4
ALSFEIN	8	0	1	0	7
ALZUTSKI	6	0	2	0	4
ANISHESHEKI	1	0	0	0	1
ANTSEL	36	0	0	0	36

Surname	Grand Total	Lived	Died Biržai	Died Elsewhere	Missing
ANTSISKI	3	0	0	0	3
APTEKIN	4	0	1	0	3
ARBOR	1	0	0	0	1
ARIMOVICH	3	0	0	0	3
ARMIST	5	0	0	0	5
ARNEST	1	0	0	0	1
ARONOV	20	0	0	0	20
ARSH	4	1	0	1	2
ATLAS	9	0	0	0	9
BABIN	34	0	0	0	34
BAGRANSKI	2	2	0	0	0
BAKHVSTER	3	0	0	0	3
BAKISHOK	4	0	0	0	4
BALISOK	16	0	0	0	16
BALONO	3	0	0	0	3
BAND	21	0	0	0	21
BANK	3	0	0	0	3
BARBAN	6	0	0	0	6
BAS	29	1	5	0	23
BAT	1	0	1	0	0
BAUER	34	0	0	0	34
BEDEK	2	0	0	0	2
BEDER	9	1	4	0	4
BEGUN	2	0	0	0	2
BEINER	4	0	0	0	4
BEK	1	0	0	0	1
BEKER	15	4	1	0	10

Surname	Grand Total	Lived	Died Biržai	Died Elsewhere	Missing
BELENKIY	2	0	0	0	2
BELICKI	4	0	2	0	2
BENCELOVICIUS	10	9	0	0	1
BENDER	1	0	0	1	0
BER	12	0	1	0	11
BERD	2	0	0	0	2
BERELIOVICH	3	0	0	0	3
BERGAUZ	3	0	0	0	3
BERGEL	24	1	1	0	22
BERKAIL	7	0	0	0	7
BERKOV	1	0	0	0	1
BERMAN	13	0	0	1	12
BERNSHTEIN	4	0	2	0	2
BESNITSKI	1	0	0	0	1
BEZMANOVICH	4	0	0	0	4
BEZMENMACHER	8	0	2	0	6
BIK	9	0	3	0	6
BINN	1	0	0	0	1
BIRGER	9	0	4	0	5
BIRKAN	3	0	0	0	3
BLANK	1	0	0	0	1
BLEKHER	1	0	0	0	1
BLIDEN	1	0	0	0	1
BLOKH	4	1	0	0	3
BLUMBERG	2	0	0	0	2
BOKHER	24	1	0	0	23
BOKSTEIN	3	0	1	0	2

Surname	Grand Total	Lived	Died Biržai	Died Elsewhere	Missing
BOLIN	1	0	0	0	1
BONER	4	0	1	0	3
BOROCHOVITZ	2	0	1	0	1
BORODOVK	3	0	0	0	3
BORUKHOVICH	4	0	0	0	4
BOYER	5	0	0	0	5
BRAND	1	0	0	0	1
BRAUDE	2	0	0	0	2
BRAVO	1	0	0	0	1
BRAYNDL	1	0	0	0	1
BREGER	1	0	0	1	0
BRENER	11	0	0	0	11
BRETSCH	2	0	0	0	2
BRIL	18	0	2	1	15
BRINT	1	0	1	0	0
BRONER	1	0	0	0	1
BRUKHOV	7	0	0	0	7
BUDOW	1	1	0	0	0
BUKETS	7	0	0	0	7
BUKSHTEIN	1	0	0	1	0
BURLAND	2	0	0	0	2
BUSRACHEV	2	0	0	0	2
CADIKOVICH	35	4	3	0	28
CANTOR	4	0	0	0	4
CHAN	1	0	0	0	1
CHEREP	4	0	0	0	4
CHESLER	1	0	1	0	0

Surname	Grand Total	Lived	Died Biržai	Died Elsewhere	Missing
CHIMERMAN	1	0	0	0	1
CHODOS	4	0	0	0	4
CHOSID	11	0	0	3	8
CIGARAITE	1	0	0	0	1
COHEN	1	0	0	0	1
DAICH	1	0	0	0	1
DANISHEVSKI	4	0	0	0	4
DAVIDOV	11	0	0	0	11
DAVIDOVICH	11	0	1	0	10
DAVIDSON	7	3	2	0	2
DAVIMES	1	0	0	0	1
DIBOBES	25	0	0	0	25
DIMANT	4	0	0	0	4
DIRMEIG	13	0	0	0	13
DORFAN	17	0	2	0	15
DRAZNE	2	0	0	0	2
DRUMLEVICH	6	0	0	0	6
DUNSKI	3	0	0	0	3
DVEROVICH	6	0	1	0	5
EDELMAN	9	0	0	0	9
EIDELSHTEIN	2	0	0	0	2
ELIASON	2	0	0	0	2
ELKIND	2	0	0	0	2
EMANUEL	10	0	0	0	10
EPSTEIN	4	0	0	0	4
EREZ	1	0	0	0	1
ESTERMAN	3	0	0	0	3

Surname	Grand Total	Lived	Died Biržai	Died Elsewhere	Missing
ETING	5	0	0	0	5
EVIN	37	6	8	1	22
EZRAHOVICH	21	0	6	0	15
EZROKH	2	0	0	0	2
FAIN	9	0	0	1	8
FAINBLIUM	1	0	0	0	1
FAIVUSH	1	0	1	0	0
FAKTOR	9	0	3	0	6
FARBER	18	0	0	0	18
FATS	3	0	0	0	3
FEINZILBER	1	0	0	0	1
FELDSHER	4	0	0	0	4
FELER	2	0	0	0	2
FENDEL	2	0	0	0	2
FENIG	1	0	1	0	0
FERBER	10	4	4	0	2
FERD	15	1	2	0	12
FERD FERBER	2	0	2	0	0
FIDLER	1	0	0	0	1
FIN	17	3	1	0	13
FINKELSHTEIN	4	0	0	0	4
FIRMAN	1	0	0	0	1
FIRST	10	0	1	0	9
FISHER	6	0	2	0	4
FISHMAN	4	0	0	0	4
FLAKS	35	1	0	0	34
FLOKH	2	0	0	0	2

Surname	Grand Total	Lived	Died Biržai	Died Elsewhere	Missing
FOSS	4	0	0	0	4
FRAGIF	1	0	0	0	1
FRAIS	1	0	0	0	1
FRANKEL	4	1	0	0	3
FREID	3	0	0	0	3
FREIDAITE	1	0	0	0	1
FRID	1	0	0	0	1
FRIDBERG	2	0	0	0	2
FRIDLENDER	21	2	8	0	11
FRIDMAN	39	11	3	0	25
FRIEDLANDER	1	0	1	0	0
FROIMAN	2	0	0	0	2
FUR	1	0	0	0	1
FURMAN	42	0	0	0	42
GAK	4	0	0	0	4
GALIN	11	0	0	1	10
GALSMAN	1	0	0	0	1
GANDZ	1	0	0	0	1
GARBER	1	0	0	0	1
GARNBLIUM	1	0	0	0	1
GAVARTIN	3	0	2	1	0
GEL	12	0	0	0	12
GELLER	2	0	0	0	2
GELVAN	5	0	0	0	5
GEN	6	0	3	0	3
GENDEL	1	0	0	0	1
GENDLER	66	23	8	0	35

Surname	Grand Total	Lived	Died Biržai	Died Elsewhere	Missing
GER	46	4	10	1	31
GERLACH	1	0	0	0	1
GERMANISHEK	9	0	0	0	9
GERSHON	1	0	0	0	1
GERSHONOVITZ	6	1	2	0	3
GERSHOV	1	0	0	0	1
GERTSFELD	1	0	0	0	1
GESELEVICH	40	2	3	1	34
GINZBURG	4	0	0	0	4
GIRES	8	0	8	0	0
GIRNUN	6	0	0	0	6
GIRSH	10	0	0	0	10
GLEZER	112	6	7	1	98
GLIKMAN	23	0	1	1	21
GOK	2	0	0	0	2
GOLDBERG	10	0	0	0	10
GOLEMBOK	4	0	0	0	4
GOLIES	1	0	0	0	1
GOLSHMID	10	0	0	0	10
GOLTS	3	0	0	0	3
GOLUB	1	1	0	0	0
GORDON	30	0	2	1	27
GREISER	12	0	0	0	12
GRENETS	38	0	0	0	38
GRENSHTAL	1	0	0	0	1
GRIES	1	0	0	0	1
GRIN	7	0	0	1	6

Surname	Grand Total	Lived	Died Biržai	Died Elsewhere	Missing
GRINBERG	5	0	0	0	5
GRINBLAT	4	0	0	0	4
GRINGON	1	0	0	0	1
GUD	10	1	5	0	4
GURVITZ	6	0	0	3	3
GUTMAN	9	3	0	0	6
HARIS	1	0	1	0	0
HAVARTIN	3	0	0	0	3
HENKIN	1	0	0	0	1
HERMAN	1	1	0	0	0
HIRSCHOVICH	2	0	1	0	1
HOFENBERG	1	0	0	0	1
HOHIM	1	0	0	0	1
IAKOBSON	7	0	1	0	6
IAVNO	2	0	0	0	2
IAVOIS	7	0	0	0	7
ICGAL	4	0	4	0	0
IDELZAK	6	0	0	0	6
IKHILAK	2	0	0	0	2
ILMAN	17	0	0	0	17
IOKHELSON	2	0	0	0	2
IOKHVED	1	0	0	0	1
IOSELOVICH	5	0	0	0	5
ISAEV	2	0	0	0	2
ITMAN	4	0	0	0	4
ITSIKOVICH	7	1	0	0	6
IUDELEVICH	3	0	1	0	2

Surname	Grand Total	Lived	Died Biržai	Died Elsewhere	Missing
IZAKSON	10	0	0	0	10
JAKOVLEV	5	0	2	0	3
JANKELOVICH	17	2	1	1	13
JASINAVKAR	1	0	1	0	0
JEGERMAN	1	0	0	0	1
JOFFE	30	1	0	3	26
JONAS	1	0	0	0	1
JOSELOVICH	2	0	0	0	2
JUDELEVICH	1	0	0	0	1
KAB	3	0	0	0	3
KABELUN	31	0	0	0	31
KAC	78	0	21	6	51
KACEV	40	0	0	1	39
KADER	14	0	1	0	13
KAGAN	7	0	0	0	7
KAHN	2	0	0	1	1
KALMANOVICH	3	0	0	0	3
KALVARIA	2	0	0	0	2
KAMRAZ	7	0	1	0	6
KAN	2	0	0	0	2
KANNEL	7	4	0	0	3
KANTOR	11	0	0	0	11
KAPLAN	11	2	0	0	9
KARAIMSKI	6	0	0	0	6
KARE	1	0	0	0	1
KARLIN	37	0	0	1	36
KARPOV	2	0	0	0	2

Surname	Grand Total	Lived	Died Biržai	Died Elsewhere	Missing
KARTUN	6	1	0	0	5
KASFER	15	0	0	0	15
KASMAN	20	0	5	0	15
KAZHDAN	1	0	0	0	1
KERBL	14	2	2	0	10
KERN	2	0	1	0	1
KESEL	19	1	0	0	18
KHAIMOVICH	3	0	1	0	2
KHAIT	174	4	44	4	122
KHARMATS	1	0	0	0	1
KHAZON	15	0	0	0	15
KHEIVITS	2	0	0	0	2
KHENKIN	6	0	1	0	5
KHOLOV	2	0	0	0	2
KHRAPUN	3	0	1	0	2
KIL	12	0	4	2	6
KINVINSKIY	2	0	0	0	2
KIRSHON	9	1	4	0	4
KIRSHT	3	0	0	0	3
KIRSHTEIN	3	0	0	0	3
KIRZHNER	1	0	0	0	1
KISSIN	4	1	0	0	3
KIVOVICH	6	0	3	0	3
KLAF	1	0	0	0	1
KLEADMAN	2	0	0	0	2
KLEIN	2	0	0	0	2
KLEINSHTEIN	8	0	0	3	5

Surname	Grand Total	Lived	Died Biržai	Died Elsewhere	Missing
KLITSNER	73	0	0	0	73
KOBEL	2	0	1	0	1
KOBLENTZ	4	2	0	0	2
KOCEN	2	0	0	0	2
KOLODICKI	8	0	6	1	1
KONKOROVICH	3	0	1	0	2
KOPEL	3	0	1	0	2
KOPLEVICH	5	0	5	0	0
KOROCINSK	1	0	1	0	0
KORS	1	0	0	0	1
KORSAKISOK	9	0	1	0	8
KOSTIN	14	0	0	0	14
KOTLER	17	0	0	0	17
KOTSIN	11	0	0	0	11
KOVALSK	4	0	0	0	4
KOVENSKA	6	0	0	0	6
KRAKINOV	2	0	0	0	2
KRAVIC	1	0	1	0	0
KRAVITZ	2	0	2	0	0
KRECHMER	84	3	23	9	49
KREICHER	7	0	0	0	7
KREINER	2	0	0	0	2
KREITSER	1	0	0	0	1
KREMER	31	0	1	0	30
KRIKSHT	22	3	0	0	19
KRINIK	1	0	0	0	1
KRINTSMAN	2	0	0	0	2

Surname	Grand Total	Lived	Died Biržai	Died Elsewhere	Missing
KRONZON	1	0	0	0	1
KROVETS	1	0	0	0	1
KRUT	2	0	0	0	2
KUBELSON	1	0	0	0	1
KUBILIUN	3	0	0	0	3
KUPE	26	0	0	0	26
KUPER	4	0	0	0	4
KUPO	1	0	0	0	1
KUPORSHTEN	3	0	0	0	3
KURMAN	5	0	0	1	4
KURZAN	4	0	0	0	4
KUSNER	2	0	0	0	2
LACK	1	1	0	0	0
LAND	3	0	0	0	3
LANES	7	0	0	0	7
LAPE	13	0	0	0	13
LEIBOV	5	0	0	0	5
LEITES	3	0	0	0	3
LEIZEROVICH	2	0	0	0	2
LERMAN	1	0	0	0	1
LEV	3	0	0	0	3
LEVIN	52	4	8	0	40
LEVINSHTEIN	29	3	1	0	25
LEVINSON	1	0	0	0	1
LEVIT	17	0	1	0	16
LEVITAN	7	1	3	0	3
LIBERMAN	9	0	2	0	7

Surname	Grand Total	Lived	Died Biržai	Died Elsewhere	Missing
LIKHB	1	0	0	0	1
LIMAN	27	2	16	2	7
LINTUN	3	0	0	0	3
LINTUP	11	1	0	0	10
LIPSHITS	75	8	20	0	47
LIUN	14	0	0	0	14
LOPERT	6	0	0	0	6
LUBIN	5	0	4	0	1
LURIA	46	0	21	0	25
MACHTENBERG	3	3	0	0	0
MAGARAM	1	0	0	0	1
MAGID	10	4	5	0	1
MAHSS	3	0	0	0	3
MAIERER	4	0	0	0	4
MAIMANT	4	0	0	0	4
MAIS	2	0	0	0	2
MALER	29	1	1	0	27
MALIAR	6	0	0	0	6
MALK	5	0	0	1	4
MAN	40	0	1	0	39
MANDEL	13	0	0	0	13
MAS	18	0	3	0	15
MATISON	10	1	0	3	6
MATZ	1	1	0	0	0
MAUSH	2	0	0	0	2
MEIEROVICH	34	0	7	0	27
MEIERZON	2	0	0	0	2

Surname	Grand Total	Lived	Died Biržai	Died Elsewhere	Missing
MEILEKH	4	0	0	0	4
MELAMED	88	1	12	0	75
MELNIK	2	0	0	0	2
MENDEL	4	0	0	0	4
MERE	26	0	0	0	26
MERKEL	1	0	0	0	1
MGLINSKIY	4	0	0	0	4
MICHELSON	12	0	1	0	11
MIGDOLISOK	2	0	0	0	2
MIKHALOVICH	1	0	0	0	1
MIKHELOV	1	0	0	0	1
MILINKE	2	0	0	0	2
MILMAN	1	0	0	0	1
MILNER	30	0	3	0	27
MILUN	2	0	0	0	2
MINDLIN	7	0	6	0	1
MIRVIS	7	1	0	0	6
MITEL	3	0	0	2	1
MIULLER	2	0	0	0	2
MIZERIKH	2	0	0	0	2
MON	2	0	0	0	2
MORDKHELOVICH	24	0	0	2	22
MOREIN	32	0	6	0	26
MORGIL	8	0	1	0	7
MORIL	13	1	5	0	7
MORKHEL	1	0	0	0	1
MOROZ	40	0	8	1	31

Surname	Grand Total	Lived	Died Biržai	Died Elsewhere	Missing
MORSH	4	0	0	0	4
MOSKATISHSKOI	7	0	0	0	7
MOVSH	4	0	1	0	3
MOVSHOVICH	27	4	2	1	20
MULER	12	0	0	0	12
MUNITS	1	0	0	0	1
MUZIKANT	1	0	0	0	1
NAINKIN	55	0	1	0	54
NASHATIR	2	0	0	0	2
NATELIOVNA	1	0	0	0	1
NEKAN	1	0	0	0	1
NEKRICH	4	4	0	0	0
NIDEL	5	0	0	0	5
NOKHIMOVICH	26	0	3	0	23
NOR	11	0	0	1	10
NOTER	5	0	0	0	5
NOVOSEDZ	42	0	4	0	38
NUDEL	4	1	0	0	3
NUDELMAN	1	0	1	0	0
OGINTS	11	0	0	0	11
ONI	39	0	0	0	39
OPENGEIM	7	0	1	0	6
OPERT	4	0	0	0	4
ORELIOVICH	20	0	0	0	20
OREMAN	2	0	0	0	2
ORLAUSK	2	0	2	0	0
ORLIN	4	0	0	2	2

Surname	Grand Total	Lived	Died Biržai	Died Elsewhere	Missing
ORMAN	13	0	3	0	10
OSHR	30	2	1	1	26
OSTROV	17	0	0	0	17
PALEC	1	0	0	0	1
PANOVK	4	0	0	0	4
PAS	2	0	1	0	1
PASKVOLETSKI	54	2	4	1	47
PEER	21	8	1	0	12
PEISACHOVICH	14	1	0	0	13
PEISAKHZON	1	0	0	0	1
PELOVICH	3	0	0	0	3
PEN	8	0	3	4	1
PERECH	2	0	0	0	2
PEREL	12	1	0	0	11
PERELSON	19	0	0	0	19
PERETS	15	1	0	0	14
PERMAN	13	0	0	0	13
PERR	1	0	0	0	1
PESAKHOVICH	3	0	3	0	0
PFENIG	1	0	1	0	0
PIAN	1	0	0	0	1
PIK	3	0	0	0	3
PIKSER	1	0	0	0	1
PIKSHTEIN	1	0	0	0	1
PILNIK	1	0	0	0	1
PILVINSKY	5	0	1	0	4
PINKHASOVICH	5	0	1	0	4

Surname	Grand Total	Lived	Died Biržai	Died Elsewhere	Missing
PINTUSHEVICH	2	0	0	0	2
PLAIN	3	0	1	0	2
POGRUND	7	0	0	0	7
POLIAK	2	0	0	0	2
PORTNOY	14	1	1	0	12
POZEL	4	0	1	0	3
PREIS	7	1	0	0	6
PRICHIANSKY	2	0	0	0	2
PROPIS	16	0	0	3	13
RABIN	20	0	5	0	15
RABINOVICH	19	0	0	0	19
RACEMOR	27	0	12	0	15
RAF	24	0	1	0	23
RAHOVICH	1	0	0	0	1
RAKOVSOCHIK	9	0	0	0	9
RAPEIKA	31	0	0	0	31
RATERT	2	0	0	0	2
RATSEMOR	2	0	0	0	2
RAVI	1	0	0	0	1
RAZMARIN	1	0	0	0	1
REBE	23	0	1	0	22
REGDESH	1	0	0	0	1
REIKIN	2	0	0	0	2
REZNIK	1	0	0	0	1
REZNIKOVICH	3	0	0	0	3
RIBAK	1	0	0	1	0
RIF	1	0	1	0	0

Surname	Grand Total	Lived	Died Biržai	Died Elsewhere	Missing
RIGMANT	23	0	5	0	18
RIMER	4	0	0	0	4
RIVKOVICH	1	0	0	0	1
RIZ	1	0	0	0	1
ROBOTNIK	1	0	0	0	1
RODE	8	1	0	0	7
ROFE	10	0	0	0	10
ROGOV	3	0	0	0	3
ROKHKIND	4	0	0	0	4
ROKHMAN	8	0	1	0	7
ROLNIK	1	1	0	0	0
ROM	3	0	0	0	3
ROZENKOVICH	11	2	5	0	4
ROZMARIN	19	0	0	0	19
ROZOMFING	6	0	0	0	6
RUBIN	47	0	4	0	43
RUDIK	2	0	0	0	2
RUSSIN	5	0	0	0	5
RUVEN	5	0	0	0	5
RYBACK	1	0	0	0	1
SADLER	1	0	0	0	1
SAFRANOVICIUS	1	1	0	0	0
SALIT	2	0	0	0	2
SAMUEL	1	0	0	0	1
SANDLER	156	4	10	0	142
SARFAS	1	1	0	0	0
SCHLOMOWITSCH	1	0	1	0	0

Surname	Grand Total	Lived	Died Biržai	Died Elsewhere	Missing
SEGAL	66	0	12	0	54
SEGALIN	3	0	0	0	3
SENCIPER	1	0	1	0	0
SHABELIOV	2	0	0	0	2
SHADOVICH	5	2	0	0	3
SHAKHAR	16	0	0	1	15
SHALAT	12	0	0	0	12
SHALKOVSKI	2	0	0	0	2
SHAN	2	0	0	0	2
SHANDLER	1	0	0	0	1
SHAPIRO	47	2	2	1	42
SHAPOCHNIK	1	0	1	0	0
SHEINER	1	0	0	0	1
SHEK	15	2	1	0	12
SHELKOVSKI	2	0	0	0	2
SHEMER	19	0	0	0	19
SHENDLER	21	0	0	0	21
SHENKER	31	2	0	0	29
SHEPSEHLEVICH	8	0	0	0	8
SHER	22	0	0	0	22
SHERAN	1	0	1	0	0
SHERMAN	61	3	5	0	53
SHERMAT	2	0	0	0	2
SHEVSHELEVICH	1	0	0	0	1
SHINDLER	2	0	0	0	2
SHMIDT	2	0	0	0	2
SHMILG	29	0	5	1	23

Surname	Grand Total	Lived	Died Biržai	Died Elsewhere	Missing
SHMOLER	1	0	0	0	1
SHNEIDER	50	0	2	0	48
SHOCHAT	51	5	3	4	39
SHOFER	26	0	0	0	26
SHOKHEN	42	2	8	0	32
SHON	4	0	0	0	4
SHPEVATSKI	4	0	0	0	4
SHPITS	4	0	0	0	4
SHREBERG	6	0	1	0	5
SHREDER	1	0	0	0	1
SHTEIN	38	0	0	0	38
SHTERN	1	0	0	0	1
SHUGALSKIY	6	0	2	0	4
SHULMAN	8	1	0	0	7
SHUR	8	0	0	0	8
SHUSTER	137	14	8	1	114
SHVARTS	4	0	1	0	3
SHVIL	1	0	1	0	0
SIEV	1	0	1	0	0
SIMONOVICH	8	0	0	0	8
SIRALSKA	4	0	2	0	2
SKAIST	2	0	0	0	2
SKREBESHKIN	7	0	0	0	7
SLEP	1	0	1	0	0
SLUZHITEL	26	1	3	2	20
SMILG	2	0	0	0	2
SMOLETS	23	0	0	0	23

Surname	Grand Total	Lived	Died Biržai	Died Elsewhere	Missing
SOBEL	7	0	0	0	7
SOKHER	1	0	0	0	1
SORREL	2	0	1	0	1
SPEVATSKI	3	0	0	0	3
SPORATSKI	1	0	1	0	0
SRAGO	26	0	0	0	26
SRAIBERG	2	0	0	0	2
ŠREIBERG	1	0	1	0	0
SROLOVICH	4	0	0	0	4
SROLOWITZ	1	0	1	0	0
STARP	5	0	0	0	5
STEIMAN	1	1	0	0	0
STEIN	1	0	1	0	0
STERN	1	0	1	0	0
STRAUKH	1	0	0	0	1
SUBOCH	1	0	0	0	1
SUBOTNIK	1	0	1	0	0
SUGALSKI	3	0	2	1	0
SULMAN	1	0	1	0	0
SUTSKEVER	1	0	0	0	1
SVIL	2	0	0	0	2
TABACHNICK	1	1	0	0	0
TABACK	59	0	0	0	59
TABAKIN	108	1	18	1	88
TABAN	5	0	0	0	5
TAC	3	0	1	0	2
TANELOVICH	2	0	0	0	2

Surname	Grand Total	Lived	Died Biržai	Died Elsewhere	Missing
TARSHIS	5	0	0	0	5
TARUSKI	4	0	0	0	4
TATS	1	0	0	0	1
TAUB	14	0	0	0	14
TAUCK	6	0	0	0	6
TAUROG	4	0	0	0	4
TEIMAN	4	0	0	0	4
TEPER	5	0	0	0	5
TIKOCKIY	2	0	0	0	2
TINFAVICIUS	1	0	0	0	1
TITKAN	5	0	0	0	5
TKACH	4	0	0	0	4
TODRES	1	0	0	0	1
TOIK	22	0	0	0	22
TORT	3	0	1	0	2
TRAPID	1	0	0	0	1
TRAUB	25	0	0	0	25
TSALYOVICH	16	1	0	0	15
TSIBUL	6	0	0	0	6
TSINERMAN	6	0	0	0	6
TSON	2	0	0	0	2
TSYBER	1	0	0	0	1
TUKH	1	0	0	0	1
TUMULEVICH	2	0	0	0	2
TURETSKI	1	0	0	0	1
ULMAN	6	0	3	0	3
UNKNOWN	1	0	1	0	0

Surname	Grand Total	Lived	Died Biržai	Died Elsewhere	Missing
URIASHZON	13	0	1	0	12
VAINER	196	2	21	1	172
VAINSTEIN	1	0	0	0	1
VAMEL	2	0	0	0	2
VASERMAN	10	1	0	0	9
VASHKI	2	0	2	0	0
VEGER	3	0	0	0	3
VEILBERG	2	0	0	0	2
VERZHBOVSK	4	0	0	0	4
VESTERMAN	8	0	3	0	5
VIDMAN	7	0	0	0	7
VIN	23	1	6	0	16
VINIK	27	0	0	1	26
VISHKIN	4	0	0	0	4
VOINOVICH	1	0	0	0	1
VOLNIK	4	0	0	0	4
VOLODSKA	1	0	1	0	0
VOLOVICH	3	0	0	0	3
VULF	2	0	0	0	2
VULFOVICH	5	0	0	0	5
WASSERMAN	3	0	0	1	2
WERCHOL	1	1	0	0	0
WOLK	1	0	0	0	1
YAKEVEN	1	0	0	0	1
YAKHILEVSK	2	0	0	0	2
YAKOBSOHN	29	0	0	0	29
YANKELOVICH	12	0	0	0	12

Surname	Grand Total	Lived	Died Biržai	Died Elsewhere	Missing
YANKELSON	3	0	0	0	3
YOKIM	1	0	0	0	1
YOSELOVICH	4	0	1	0	3
YUDELEVICH	9	0	0	0	9
ZAGORSKI	14	0	0	0	14
ZAK	45	0	15	2	28
ZALMANOVICH	6	0	0	0	6
ZANDEL	5	0	0	0	5
ZEBINSKI	1	0	0	0	1
ZEIMELSK	3	0	0	0	3
ZELBOVICH	19	1	6	0	12
ZELEZNICK	4	0	0	0	4
ZELIKOVICH	6	0	1	2	3
ZELINGER	1	0	1	0	0
ZELMANOVICH	6	0	0	0	6
ZILBERBLAT	1	1	0	0	0
ZILBERG	8	1	0	0	7
ZINGER	57	0	0	0	57
ZIVETS	3	0	0	0	3
ZUNDELEVICH	37	1	8	1	27
ZYS	4	0	0	0	4
ZZ BROTHERS FROM VAŠKAI	2	0	0	0	2
ZZ OTHERS FROM THE BIRZAI AREA	21	0	21	0	0
ZZ THE BUTCHER	1	0	1	0	0
ZZ WINE SELLER	1	0	0	0	1

Surname	Grand Total	Lived	Died Biržai	Died Elsewhere	Missing
ZZ YESHIVA STUDENTS FROM BIAŁYSTOK	6	0	6	0	0
Totals	6606	247	697	100	5562

Notes:

1. The total number of names, 6,606, in the list does not imply population totals that would indicate the number of Jews living in Biržai during 1941. The population in 1941 is generally believed to be at or below 3000.

2. The total for the column Died in Birzai, 697, is inflated by the presence of about 160 married women who are entered with two families: once with their married name and, if known, also with their maiden name.

End Notes

Additional History of Biržai

The Prince of the House of Radzivill wanted to foster economic development, so he invited various Jews to relocate to Biržai. He promised them protection from their neighbors. Prince Radzivill was a trustworthy protector for the Jews in Biržai. Christopher II Radzivill, said in 1607, "In case of violence, Christians must protect the Jews as well as themselves, for local Jews are members of the city." Various documents from 1662 and 1683 mention Jews settling there and receiving the rights of settlement. Prince Radzivill had a castle built, surrounded by a moat for protection, near a serene lake.

The Karaite settlement, which predated rabbinical Jews[68] in the Biržai area, was present and mentioned in documents from 1625. The Karaites lived on two streets in Biržai. They had their own synagogue and cemetery. In the eighteenth century the Karaite settlement ended, and their synagogue was turned over to the rabbinical Jews. The Jewish community of Biržai enjoyed a robust prayer life. They maintained three prayer houses, two study houses, and a synagogue.

Some of the well-known rabbis who lived and worshiped in Biržai included:

- Yehuda Leib Bernshtein
- Elhanan-Bunem Wasserman (Head of the Yeshiva)

---

68 Karaite Judaism adheres only to the written Torah, the five books of Moses, while Rabbinic Judaism includes oral interpretations not included in the Torah.

- Pinkhus Lintup
- Benjamin Movsh

A 1686 edict helped to describe the coexistence of Christians and Jews. Some highlights included the desire to create an atmosphere of peaceful coexistence and mutual assistance, equal working conditions for all artisans of the city, and allowing Jews to have a separate bath. The rights of self-rule bestowed upon Biržai had great meaning for the city. The city grew quickly, and guilds and trades expanded. The city of Biržai became an important and strategic point on the northern border of the Grand Duchy of Lithuania (GDL). Biržai prospered from the time it received their Magdeburg rights[69] until the middle of the 17th century.

The Jewish population in Biržai was as follows:

- 1760s: it was 1,040
- 1847: it had risen to 1,685
- 1897: it was up to 2,510
- 1935: approximately 4,945

During World War I, the Jewish population was expelled to Russian territories and their Biržai homes destroyed. Part of the Jewish community returned after the War. During World War I, the Germans laid a narrow train track which connected the town with Šiauliai, which later helped the town develop. In the years that Lithuania was independent, 1918 to 1940, the city began to expand and hundreds of new homes were built. By 1934, 257 brick homes and 362 new wooden homes had been erected. Twenty-eight new streets were opened, the city had 9,000 residents and had become an administrative center of the district.

---

69 Magdeburg rights were a set of town privileges which guaranteed the degree of internal autonomy within cities and villages granted by the local ruler.

A 1935 German map of the Baltic countries indicating the Jewish population by district, including Biržai, can be found on the United States Holocaust Memorial Museum website: https://encyclopedia. ushmm.org/content/en/document/german-map-of-the-baltic-countries. According to the map, the Jewish population in Biržai, or Birsen in German, was 4,945. This number is most likely inclusive of the Biržai district, as most scholarly estimates put the Jewish population in Biržai immediately prior to WWII at or below 3,000.

Description of Businesses in Biržai

A 1931 government survey showed that there were then 99 businesses in Biržai, of which 77 (78%) were owned by Jews. Of those businesses, 80 were artisans including 63 Jews (79%) that were organized in the "Union of Jewish Artisans." Regarding more professional careers, there were 2 Jewish doctors (out of a total of 3), 2 Jewish lawyers (also 2 non–Jewish), and 2 Jewish engineers (as well as 1 non–Jewish).

By 1940, Jewish families had various ways to make a living as business owners, trades, and professionals. Below is a sampling of some professions and names of Jews in those professions:

- Jewish tailors: Forty, including sisters Cherne and Eta Leya Nankin, Khaya Rozmarin, sisters Ita Ienta and Hana Bokhur, Ginda Brukhov (nee Davidovitch), and Yenta Vinick. Esther Mine Levin and Khaim Portnoy survived.

- Butchers: Twenty-two including Abraham Leiba Evin, who was a butcher, rabbi, and shokhet (slaughterer following Jewish law), Leiba Zelbovich, Samuel Zundelvich, Yudel Gordon, Leizer Glezer, and Shmuel Hillel Rubin Ha Cohen.

- Schoolteachers: Eighteen including Leia Ferd (nee Shpits), Beile Liman (nee Kamraz), David Kesel, and Rivka Pilvinsky (nee Srolovich).

- Shoemakers: Six including Shaia Mones Geselovich, Moishe and Chase Gnendel Malk (nee Reb), Shmuel Itsik Reznikovich, and Gersh Zak.

- Dentists: Ten including Hena Raize Shapira (nee Eting), Rokhe Etel Kantor, and Moise Gendler.

- Doctors: Nine including Josefas Aptekin, Freida Eting, Avram Zalman Levin, Eliyahu Levin, and Chaim Gershonovicius.

- Lawyers: Three including Zvee Bagranski, David Katz, and David Kirshon.

- There was even an organ grinder named Girsh Markus Foss.

Many of the Jewish businesses were run from the home. The Jewish houses were small and wooden, and they were built in a line along the same street. A distinctive feature was that the front doors overlooked the street. The entrance to the Jewish house was always directly from the street because the Jews were doing business from their homes and they did not want it to be difficult for a buyer to enter. The buyer could only go into one room, where the Jewish owner invited them.

Additional Information on Jewish Family Locations

In Chapter 1 there is a map of the shtetl streets where many of the Jews of Biržai lived. The following table lists the Jewish families that lived there, including their house number and year they lived on the street where that data was available, can be found at the rear of the book. Some of the street names have changed:

- Rinkos, formerly J. Janonio
- Zemaites, formerly Apaščios
- Zemoji, formerly Rabino Lintupio

TABLE 4. THE JEWISH RESIDENTS OF THE SHTETL.

NUM	SURNAME	YEAR	NUM	SURNAME	YEAR
Basanaviciaus			Dagilio		
4	RAPEIKA	1938	1	JEGERMAN	1940
4	NIDEL	1937	1	GALIN	1937
4a	NAINKIN	1937	1	PANOVK	1937
4a-4	EVIN	1937	3-5	FRIDLENDER	1937
7	SMILG	1939	3-5	GLEZER	1937
8	KAC	1940	3-5	KRECHMER	1937
8	ZELBOVICH	1936	6	KHAIT	1920
8	ZELEZNICK	1936	7	TSODIKOVICH	1935
8	FUR		7	ALSFEIN	
9	JUDELEVICH	1937	8	BOKHER	1937
14	BER	1940	8	TSODIKOVICH	1935
16	PILVINSKY	1937	10	CADIKOVICH	1937
18	RACEMOR	1937	10	TSODIKOVICH	1937
19	ROZENKOVICH	1937	11	DIRMEIG	1920
20	LIPSHITS	1937	11	GLEZER	1920
21	RACEMOR	1937	12	SHOFER	1937
22	KHAIT	1937	12	VINIK	1937
22	VAINER	1937	13	BAS	1927
22	ZINGER	1937	14	KRETCHMER	1924
25	BERNSHTEIN	1940	15	SHIMANOVICH	1927
40	BECKER	1937	19	SHKOLNER	
42	VIN	1937		PREIS	1938
44	KAC	1937		EPSTEIN	1937
	BRAND	1937		GRINBLAT	1937
	DAVIDOV	1937		JOFFE	1937
	ETING	1937		MAS	1937
	FIN	1937		MAS	1937
	LIPSHITS	1937		PRICHIANSKY	1937
	OSHR	1937		SHOKHEN	1937
	POSVOLETSKY	1937		ZUSMAN	1927
	SEGAL	1937	Karaimų		
	SHAPIRO	1937	3-5	BERGEL	1937

NUM	SURNAME	YEAR
3-5	SANDLERIO	1937
4	NAHAMOVICH	1941
5	GENDLER	1940
6	MEIEROVICH	1940
6	VIDMAN	1937
8	PERETS	1937
9	LEVINSHTEIN	1938
10	LEVIN	1937
11-13	FERD	1937
11-13	FERD FERBER	1937
11-13	GESELEVICH	1937
11-13	KACEV	1937
11-13	KREMER	1937
11-13	LEVITAN	1937
11-13	VAINER	1937
12	NAINKIN	1937
12-15	SHEPSEHLEVICH	1937
16	SEGAL	1920
18	SEGAL	1922
26	NAINKIN	1940
Pasvalio		
1	KAC	1931
6	LIPSHITS	1922
19	MOREIN	1920
29	KAC	
31	GESELEVICH	1931
35	KHAIT	1933
35	POSVOLETSKY	1926
38	KRECHMER	1935
44	SHERMAN	1933
49	RAF	1931
	FINKELSHTEIN	1940
	DIAMANTAS	
Rinkos		
1	BELICKI	1940

NUM	SURNAME	YEAR
1	GERSHONOVITZ	1940
1	SHERMAN	1937
2	MALER	1938
2	GURVITZ	1937
3	KHAIT	1940
3	EVIN	1937
4	GLEZER	1937
4	SANDLERIS	1937
4	SHNEIDER	1937
4	ZAK	1936
4	MELAMED	1928
5	RABIN	1940
5	SHUSTER	1937
5	GLIKMAN	1928
6	ZELBOVICH	1937
6	TABAKIN	1928
6	KHAIT	
6	SHAN	
7	BEKER	1940
7	SHUSTER	1933
7	KRIKSHT	
11	SHUSTER	1920
12	LEVIN	1929
12	SHUSTER	1920
13	PANOVK	
13	SHUSTER	1920
14	FURMAN	1938
14	SHUSTER	1930
15	GLEZER	1940
15	SHUSTER	1920
16	SHUSTER	1920
17	PEISACHOVICH	1920
17	SHUSTER	1920
18	ZAK	1940
20	VAINER	1938

NUM	SURNAME	YEAR
21	RAFKIN	
22	GELVAN	1924
23	RIGMANT	1937
	ABEL	1937
	BLUMBERG	1937
	DORFAN	1937
	GRINBLAT	1937
	HENKIN	1937
	LAPE	1937
	LEVIN	1937
	MAS	1937
	MICHELSON	1937
	ORMAN	1937
	POSVOLETSKY	1937
	RABINOVICH	1937
	RUBIN	1937
	TABAKIN	1937
	VIN	1937
	DAVIDSON	1935
	KRETCHMER	1925
Tilto		
4	GOLTS	1935
5	BEGUN	1921
5	LIPSHITS	1921
5	PEER	1921
8	KAC	1928
10	TABAKIN	1920
16	SHTEIN	1922
17	ETING	1928
22	OSHR	1921
24	LIBERMAN	1937
27	ROZENKOVICH	1928
38	VIN	1937
Vilniaus		
1-3	LURIA	1937

NUM	SURNAME	YEAR
1-3	MELAMED	1937
1-3	MILNER	1937
3	MELAMED	1941
3	KOTSIN	1920
4	BERKAIL	1937
4	KIRSHON	1937
4	PERE	1937
4	REB	1937
5	MEIEROVICH	1937
5	MORIL	1937
5	ORMAN	1937
5	SHNEIDER	1937
5	VAINSTEIN	1937
5	FERD	
6	LEVIN	1905
6	BERKAIL	1937
6	REB	1936
8	RAPEIKA	1940
10-12	LEVIT	1937
10-12	MEILACH	1937
10-12	ZELBOVICH	1937
11	BIRKAN	1937
11	KHAIT	1937
11	REB	1937
14	BRIL	1937
15	GER	1937
15	KOTLER	1937
17	LEVIN	1937
17	PIAN	1920
18	KHAIT	1921
18	SHOCHAT	
19	JANKELOVICH	1937
20	GARBER	1940
21	BOROCHOVITZ	1937
21	YAKOBSOHN	1931

NUM	SURNAME	YEAR
22	SHEK	1937
22	MICHELSON	1922
23	BOKHER	1937
24	BRIL	1928
27	MAGID	1937
27	RAZMARIN	1937
28	GEL	1938
29	KANNEL	1932
32	RAZMARIN	1940
32	KHAIT	1928
33	SHOCHAT	1939
34	POSVOLETSKY	1937
34	RUBIN	1924
35	YANKELOVICH	1939
41	BOKHER	1924
43	YAKHILEVSK	1940
52	MELAMED	1919
	BRUKHOV	1931
	VEINSTEIN	1921
	BOKHER	1920
	TAUB	1920
	GLEZER	1927
	KHAIT	1926
	GER	1921
	ORLOVIOCH	1919
	BOKHER	
	POSVOLETSKY	
	SHNEIDER	
Vytauto		
1	KAC	1931
1	LURIA	
3	GRENITS	1927
3	DRUMLEVICH	1926
6	CHODOS	1940
8	FRIDMAN	1933

NUM	SURNAME	YEAR
9	SANDLER	1937
9-11	MAROZ	1937
10	DAVIDOV	1940
10	LIMAN	1940
10	MENDEL	1921
11	MAS	1937
11	VIN	1937
11	MOROZ	1934
12	SANDLER	1937
13	MAS	1940
13	LIPSHITS	1937
13	NOVOSEDZ	1937
14	GENDLER	1940
17	SANDLER	1934
17 & 19	RAKOVSHCHIK	1937
18	SHEK	1939
18	ZELBOVICH	1933
19	LURIA	1940
19	IAKOBSON	1920
19	RAKOVSHCHIK	1920
20	GENDLER	1933
20	RAKOVSHCHIK	1920
21	BEDER	1940
21	GENDLER	1940
22	EZRACHOVICH	1939
22	RAKOVSHCHIK	1920
22	ZUNDELEVICH	1920
22	EDELMAN	
22	SHPEVATSKI	
22	SHVIL	
23	LIPSHITS	1940
27	FRIDMAN	1940
27	MAS	1940
27	POSVOLETSKY	1937
28	NAINKIN	1939

NUM	SURNAME	YEAR
29	GENDLER	1925
30	TINFAVIČIUS	1940
31	ORLAUSK	1937
34	LEVIN	1940
35	POSVOLETSKY	1928
41	ORLOVICH	1933
42	KLITSNER	1925
44	APTEKIN	1887
55	SMILG	1922
64	KISSIN	1940
68	SEGAL	1938
	JONAS	1939
	LIMAN	1923
	MELAMED	1939
	NAINKIN	1939
	SEGAL	1934
Zemaites		
1	VAINER	1937
2	SANDLER	1940
2-4	KRECHMER	1937
2-4	SADLERIS	1937
4-6	SMILG	1937
7	SANDLER	
10	KRECHMER	1940
13	SHUSTER	1934
14	FLAKSAS	1937
16	KRECHMER	
17	BERGEL	
17	MINDLIN	1933
17	BERGEL	
21	GENDLER	1933
	BERGEL	1937
	GERLACH	1937
	KHAIT	1937
	ŠUSTERIAI	1937

NUM	SURNAME	YEAR
Zemoji		
2	GLEZER	1937
4	EVIN	1937
4	VASERMAN	1937
6	KANTOR	1934
6 or 7	JOFFE	1925
6 or 7	KREMER	1925
8	BALISOK	1937
8	GOLDBERG	1937
8	KOVENSKA	1937
9-11	MATISON	1937
9-11	MAUSH	1937
12	FAKTOR	1920
13	BAS	1937
13	OGINTS	1937
15	MORDKHELOVICH	1937
15	SANDLER	1937
19	LINTUP	

Additional Information on Russian Deportations

In Chapters 16-17, this story focuses on the surprise deportations of Jews and Lithuanians by the Russians. The following table[70] lists the 29 Jews of the 343 people deported June 14-15, 1941. The data (table 5) includes information on their family surname, given name, birth year, and deportation location. Any fields that are empty is due to missing data from the documentation.

Note: The website http://www.menschenit.com will contain a complete list of the all the individual records.

---

70   Data retrieved from http://www.lietuviaisibire.lt/lt/represuotieji/
     region:Qmlyxb7Fsw==/year:MTk0MQ==.

TABLE 5: DEPORTATIONS TO RUSSIA IN JUNE 1941.

Surname	Given Name	Birth	Destination
BEKERIENĖ	Ida	1895	Tomsko
BEKERIS	Chaimas	1880	Tomsko
BEKERIS	Icikas Chaimas	1927	Tomsko
BEKERYTĖ	Geta	1924	Tomsko
FRIDMAN	Pesia	1902	Tomsko
FRIDMANAS	Elijas	1892	Krasnoyarsk
FRIDMANAS	Levas	1927	Tomsko
FRIDMANAS	Motlas	1929	Tomsko
FRIDMANAS	Zalmanas	1932	Tomsko
GENDLERIS	Elchononas	1923	Tomsko
GENDLERIS	Lėja	1889	Tomsko
GENDLERIS	Mauša	1886	Krasnoyarsk
GENDLERIS	Natanas	1918	Tomsko
LIPŠICAITĖ	Cerna	1927	Krasnoyarsk
LIPŠICAS	Chackus	1885	Krasnoyarsk
LIPŠICAS	Davidas	1930	Krasnoyarsk
LIPŠICAS	Johamas	1929	Krasnoyarsk
LIPŠICIENĖ	Roza	1890	Krasnoyarsk
MOVŠOVIČ	Chana	1927	
MOVŠOVIČ	Perla	1928	
MOVŠOVIČ	Šeina	1901	
MOVŠOVIČIUS	Izraelis	1893	
NEKRIČ	Chaja	1935	
NEKRIČ	Menucha Emilė	1914	
NEKRIČ	Šušana	1939	
NEKRIČAS	Leiba	1906	
NUDELIS	Hiršas Aronas	1920	
ŠAFRANOVIČIUS	Simcha	1924	Irkutsko
ŠARFAS	Abramas Chaimas	1913	

Bibliography

1. 15min. 2013. "Vienintelį Po Žudynių Gyvą Likusį Biržų Žydą Tėvams per Karą Padėjusios Slėpti Elvyra Čižauskienė Ir Regina Kežienė: „Būtina Kalbėti Ne Tik Apie Žydų Žudikus, Bet Ir Apie Jų Gelbėtojus" | 15min.Lt." 15min.Lt. 15min. August 19, 2013. https://www.15min.lt/naujiena/aktualu/istorija/vieninteli-po-zudyniu-gyva-likusi-birzu-zyda-tevams-per-kara-padejusios-slepti-elvyra-cizauskiene-ir-regina-keziene-butina-kalbeti-ne-tik-apie-zydu-zudikus-bet-ir-apie-ju-gelbetojus-582-362238.

2. admin. 2019. "Personal Story in Moral Holocaust Education - Biržų Žydų Istorijos Ir Kultūros Draugija." Biržų Žydų Istorijos Ir Kultūros Draugija. June 12, 2019. https://www.birzaijewish.lt/en/be-kategorijos-en/personal-story-in-moral-holocaust-education/.

3. Arad, Yitzhak. 1976. *The "Final Solution" in Lithuania in the Light of German Documentation*.

4. "Asisbiz Junkers Ju 87B2 Stuka 2.SG2 (T6+JK) Barbarossa 1941-0B." n.d. Asisbiz. Accessed November 3, 2020. https://www.asisbiz.com/il2/Ju-87/StG2.1/pages/Junkers-Ju-87B2-Stuka-2.SG2-(T6+JK)-Barbarossa-1941-0B.html.

5. "Betar." n.d. Jewish Virtual Library. Accessed November 28, 2020. https://www.jewishvirtuallibrary.org/betar.

6. "Bien." n.d. JewishGen KehilaLinks. Accessed February 16 3, 2020. https://kehilalinks.jewishgen.org/birzai/Bien.html.

7. "Birzh 1." n.d. JewishGen KehilaLinks. Accessed October 8, 2020. https://kehilalinks.jewishgen.org/birzai/Birzh_1.html.

8. Chen, C. Peter. n.d. "Battle of Coral Sea | World War II Database." WW2DB. Accessed August 3, 2020. https://ww2db.com/battle_spec.php?battle_id=16.

9. Cohen-Mushlin, Aliza, Sergey Kravtsov, Vladimir Levin, Giedrė Mickūnaitė, and Jurgita Šiaučiūnaitė-Verbickienė. 2010. *Synagogues in Lithuania A-M*. VDA leidykla.

10. Dean, Martin, and Mel Hecker. 2012. *The United States Holocaust Memorial Museum Encyclopedia of Camps and Ghettos, 1933-1945*.

11. Dickmann, Ch, and Saulius Sužiedėlis. 2006. *The Persecution and Mass Murder of Lithuanian Jews during Summer and Fall of 1941*.

12. Frieden, Menachem Mendel. *A Jewish Life on Three Continents: The Memoir of Menachem Mendel Frieden*. Translated by Lee Shai Weissbach. Stanford University Press, 2013.

13. "Get out of Dodge - Idioms by The Free Dictionary." n.d. TheFreeDictionary. Com. Accessed November 11, 2020. https://idioms.thefreedictionary.com/get+out+of+Dodge.

14. "Ghetto/Vilkaviskis/01." n.d. Museum of Family History. Accessed November 25 2020. http://www.museumoffamilyhistory.com/ce/ghetto/vilkaviskis-01.htm.

15. "Hashomer Hatzair." n.d. Jewish Virtual Library. Accessed November 28, 2020. https://www.jewishvirtuallibrary.org/hashomer-hatzair.

16. History.com Editors. "Great Purge." HISTORY. A&E Television Networks. July 7, 2020. https://www.history.com/topics/russia/great-purge.

17. History.com Editors. "London Is Devastated by German Air Raid." HISTORY. A&E Television Networks. December 21, 2020. https://www.history.com/this-day-in-history/worst-air-raid-on-london.

18. "Jewish Resettlement and Ghettos." 2012. The Holocaust. http://facebook.com/alphahistory. July 19, 2012. https://alphahistory.com/holocaust/jewish-resettlement-ghettos/.

19. "JewishGen Lithuania Database." n.d. JewishGen - The Home of Jewish Genealogy. Accessed October 16, 2021. https://www.jewishgen.org/databases/Lithuania/.

20. "Jews of Lithuania." n.d. Haruth Leichter's Resource Page. Accessed August 16, 2020. http://www.haruth.com/jw/JewsLithuania.html.

21. "Juedischer Friedhof Biržai." n.d. Biržai. Accessed July 3, 2020. http://www.birzai.de/ziele/juden/juedischer-friedhof-birzai.html.

22. Leivers, Dorothy. 2009. *Road to Victory*.

23. "Lithuania Publishes List with 190 233 Lithuanians Deported by Soviet Union - Baltic News Network - News from Latvia, Lithuania, Estonia." 2020. Baltic News Network - News from Latvia, Lithuania, Estonia. https://www.facebook.com/BNN-News-137027629677971. June 2, 2020. https://bnn-news.com/lithuania-publishes-list-with-190-233-lithuanians-deported-by-soviet-union-213965.

24. "Lithuanian Citizenship for Persons Who Emigrated from Lithuania to South Africa, and for Their Descendants." n.d. Migration Law Center. Accessed June 22, 2020. https://www.migration.lt/lithuanian-citizenship-for-persons-who-emigrated-from-lithuania-to-south-africa-and-for-their-descendants.

25. Magid, Berl-David. בערל־דוד מאגיד. 1992. *What I Have To Tell: Pages From a Life*.

26. Mishina, Ekaterina. 2015. "The Secret Protocol That Changed the World - Institute of Modern Russia." Institute of Modern Russia. June 10, 2015. https://imrussia.org/en/law/2275-the-secret-protocol-that-changed-the-world.

27. "'Not Ordinary but Never Strangers - Biržai Jews' - Birzu Muziejus Sela." n.d. Titulinis - Birzu Muziejus Sela. Accessed October 16, 2021. https://www.birzumuziejus.lt/zydai.

28. "Occupation of the Sudetenland – The Holocaust Explained: Designed for Schools." n.d. The Holocaust Explained: Designed for Schools.

Accessed October 3, 2021. https://www.theholocaustexplained.org/
life-in-nazi-occupied-europe/foreign-policy-and-the-road-to-war/
occupation-of-the-sudetenland.

29. "Online Journal - Online Journal - The Expulsion of the Jews from
Lithuania in the Spring of 1915." n.d. LitvakSIG Lithuanian-
Jewish Special Interest Group. Accessed August 13, 2020. https://
www.litvaksig.org/information-and-tools/online-journal/
expulsion-of-the-jews-from-lithuania-in-the-spring-of-1915-the.

30. "Oral History Interview with Algimantas Gureckas - Collections Search
- United States Holocaust Memorial Museum." n.d. Collections Search -
United States Holocaust Memorial Museum. Accessed September 15, 2021.
https://collections.ushmm.org/search/catalog/irn42272.

31. "Oral History Interview with Jonas Mekas - Collections Search - United
States Holocaust Memorial Museum." n.d. Collections Search - United
States Holocaust Memorial Museum. Accessed October 15, 2021. https://
collections.ushmm.org/search/catalog/irn619022.

32. "Oral History Interview with Regina Drevinskienė - Collections Search
- United States Holocaust Memorial Museum." n.d. Collections Search
- United States Holocaust Memorial Museum. Accessed June 23, 2021.
https://collections.ushmm.org/search/catalog/irn518274.

33. "Oral History Interview with Teodoras Valotka - Collections Search -
United States Holocaust Memorial Museum." n.d. Collections Search
- United States Holocaust Memorial Museum. Accessed October 3, 2021.
https://collections.ushmm.org/search/catalog/irn45240.

34. "Preserving Our Litvak Heritage - Volume I (Pages 26-51)." n.d. JewishGen
- The Home of Jewish Genealogy. Accessed April 29, 2021. https://www.
jewishgen.org/Yizkor/lithuania4/lit4_026.html.

35. "Rabbi Pinchas HaKohen Lintup." n.d. Jewish Virtual Library.
Accessed November 28, 2020. https://www.jewishvirtuallibrary.org/
rabbi-pinchas-hakohen-lintup.

36. "Radio Speech by Molotov 22-06-1941 - TracesOfWar.Com." n.d. TracesOfWar.Com. Accessed October 8, 2020. https://www.tracesofwar. com/articles/4627/Radio-speech-by-Molotov-22-06-1941.htm.

37. Raimonda Ragauskienė. 2018. "Self-Rule in GDL Biržai - EN.DELFI." DELFI. DELFI. January 23, 2018. https://en.delfi.lt/history/ self-rule-in-gdl-birzai.d?id=76976927.

38. "Represuotieji - Lietuviai Sibire." n.d. Lietuvos Gyventojų Tremtys Ir Kalinimas Sovietų Sąjungoje. Accessed October 3, 2021. http://www.lietuvi-aisibire.lt/lt/represuotieji/region:Qmlyxb7Fsw==/year:MTk0MQ==.

39. "Revisionist Zionism." n.d. Jewish Virtual Library. Accessed October 3, 2021. https://www.jewishvirtuallibrary.org/revisionist-zionism.

40. Sudarsky, Mendel, and C. Leikowicz. 1951. *Lite/Mendel Sudarsky (et.al.) Editor, Vol. 1; Leikowicz, C., Editor.*

41. "The History Place - World War II in Europe Timeline: August 19, 1934 - Adolf Hitler Becomes Fuehrer of Germany." n.d. The History Place. Accessed October 3, 2021. https://www.historyplace.com/worldwar2/timeline/becomes.htm.

42. "The History Place - World War II in Europe Timeline: June 1933 - Nazis Open Dachau." n.d. The History Place. Accessed November 28 2020. https://www.historyplace.com/worldwar2/timeline/dach-early.htm.

43. "The History Place - World War II in Europe Timeline: September 15, 1935 - The Nuremberg Race Laws." n.d. The History Place. Accessed October 3, 2021. https://www.historyplace.com/worldwar2/timeline/nurem-laws.htm.

44. "The Jager Report." n.d. FCIT | Florida Center for Instructional Technology. Accessed October 3, 2021. https://fcit.usf.edu/holocaust/resource/docu-ment/DocJager.htm.

45. "The Nuremberg Race Laws | Holocaust Encyclopedia." n.d. Holocaust Encyclopedia | United States Holocaust Memorial Museum. Accessed September 28, 2020. https://encyclopedia.ushmm.org/content/en/article/ the-nuremberg-race-laws.

46. "The Untold Stories. The Murder Sites of the Jews in the Occupied Territories of the Former USSR." n.d. Accessed January 14, 2020. https://www.yadvashem.org/untoldstories/database/writtenAccounts. asp?cid=987&site_id=1376.

47. "Timeline Lithuania 1930-2012." n.d. Timelines of History: Online Directory of Historical Timelines. Accessed May 30, 2020. https://timelines. ws/countries/LITH_B.HTML.

48. "Tzedakah 101 | My Jewish Learning." n.d. My Jewish Learning. Accessed October 5, 2020. https://www.myjewishlearning.com/article/tzedakah-101/.

49. Vanagaitė, Rūta, and Efraim Zuroff. 2020. *Our People*. Rowman & Littlefield.

50. "We Shall Fight on the Beaches - International Churchill Society." 1940. International Churchill Society. June 4, 1940. https://winstonchurchill.org/ resources/speeches/1940-the-finest-hour/we-shall-fight-on-the-beaches/.

51. "Welcome to the Biržai Site." n.d. Eilat Gordin Levitan. Accessed October 1, 2021. http://www.eilatgordinlevitan.com/birz/birz.html.

52. Wikimedia Foundation, Inc. "Afrika Korps." Wikipedia, the Free Encyclopedia. December 15, 2002. https://en.wikipedia.org/wiki/Afrika_Korps.

53. Wikimedia Foundation, Inc. "Eau de Vie." Wikipedia, the Free Encyclopedia. February 18, 2005. https://en.wikipedia.org/wiki/Eau_de_vie.

54. Wikimedia Foundation, Inc. "Fifth Column." Wikipedia, the Free Encyclopedia. September 24, 2002. https://en.wikipedia.org/wiki/ Fifth_column.

55. Wikimedia Foundation, Inc. "History of Lithuania." Wikipedia, the Free Encyclopedia. 2 November 2021, at 16:10 (UTC). https://en.wikipedia.org/ wiki/History_of_Lithuania#Independence_(1918%E2%80%931940).

56. Wikimedia Foundation, Inc. "International Red Aid." Wikipedia, the Free Encyclopedia. June 20, 2005. https://en.wikipedia.org/wiki/ International_Red_Aid.

57. Wikimedia Foundation, Inc. "June Deportation." Wikipedia, the Free Encyclopedia. June 16, 2007. https://en.wikipedia.org/wiki/June_deportation.

58. Wikimedia Foundation, Inc. "June Uprising in Lithuania." Wikipedia, the Free Encyclopedia. May 13, 2005. https://en.wikipedia.org/wiki/June_Uprising_in_Lithuania.

59. Wikimedia Foundation, Inc. "Kaunas Pogrom." Wikipedia, the Free Encyclopedia. May 29, 2007. https://en.wikipedia.org/wiki/Kaunas_pogrom.

60. Wikimedia Foundation, Inc. "Kazan Ethnic Communities." Wikipedia, the Free Encyclopedia. August 13, 2009. https://en.wikipedia.org/wiki/Kazan_ethnic_communities#Jews_of_Kazan.

61. Wikimedia Foundation, Inc. "Kippah." Wikipedia, the Free Encyclopedia. November 28, 2003. https://en.wikipedia.org/wiki/Kippah.

62. Wikimedia Foundation, Inc. "Klaipėda." Wikipedia, the Free Encyclopedia. December 19, 2002. https://en.wikipedia.org/wiki/Klaip%C4%97da.

63. Wikimedia Foundation, Inc. "Klezmorim." Wikipedia, the Free Encyclopedia. February 25, 2004. https://en.wikipedia.org/wiki/Klezmorim.

64. Wikimedia Foundation, Inc. "Magdeburg Rights." Wikipedia, the Free Encyclopedia. February 25, 2003. https://en.wikipedia.org/wiki/Magdeburg_rights.

65. Wikimedia Foundation, Inc. "Munich Agreement." Wikipedia, the Free Encyclopedia. December 18, 2002. https://en.wikipedia.org/wiki/Munich_Agreement.

66. Wikimedia Foundation, Inc. "Operation Barbarossa." Wikipedia, the Free Encyclopedia. 1 November 2021, at 21:31 (UTC). https://en.wikipedia.org/wiki/Operation_Barbarossa.

67. Wikimedia Foundation, Inc. "Pioneer Movement." Wikipedia, the Free Encyclopedia. June 11, 2002. https://en.wikipedia.org/wiki/Pioneer_movement.

68. Wikimedia Foundation, Inc. "Resettlement to the East." Wikipedia, the Free Encyclopedia, Inc. May 29, 2020. https://en.wikipedia.org/wiki/Resettlement_to_the_East.

69. Wikimedia Foundation, Inc. "Schutzmannschaft." Wikipedia, the Free Encyclopedia. March 20, 2006. https://en.wikipedia.org/wiki/Schutzmannschaft.

70. Wikimedia Foundation, Inc. "Schutzstaffel." Wikipedia, the Free Encyclopedia. 29 September 2021, at 10:30 (UTC). https://en.wikipedia.org/wiki/Schutzstaffel.

71. Wikimedia Foundation, Inc. "Shidduch." Wikipedia, the Free Encyclopedia. March 27, 2004. https://en.wikipedia.org/wiki/Shidduch.

72. Wikimedia Foundation, Inc. "Soviet Deportations from Lithuania." Wikipedia, the Free Encyclopedia. April 19, 2014. https://en.wikipedia.org/wiki/Soviet_deportations_from_Lithuania.

73. Wikimedia Foundation, Inc. "Soviet Occupation of the Baltic States (1940)." Wikipedia, the Free Encyclopedia. May 3, 2010. https://en.wikipedia.org/wiki/Soviet_occupation_of_the_Baltic_states_(1940).

74. Wikimedia Foundation, Inc. "Stahlhelm." Wikipedia, the Free Encyclopedia. July 28, 2004. https://en.wikipedia.org/wiki/Stahlhelm.

75. Winston, Rabbi Pinchas. n.d. "God Is In Control • Torah.Org." Torah.Org. https://www.facebook.com/torah.org/. Accessed April 3, 2020. https://torah.org/torah-portion/perceptions-5774-behar.

76. "Yad Vashem Documents Archive." n.d. Yad Vashem Documents Archive. Accessed October 11, 2021. https://documents.yadvashem.org/index.html?language=en&search=global&strSearch=sheine%20sonia%20beder&GridItemId=3552470.

77. "YIVO | Gordonia." n.d. The YIVO Encyclopedia of Jews in Eastern Europe. Accessed August 14, 2020. https://yivoencyclopedia.org/article.aspx/Gordonia.

78. "YIVO | Misnagdim." n.d. The YIVO Encyclopedia of Jews in Eastern Europe. Accessed August 31, 2020. https://yivoencyclopedia.org/article. aspx/Misnagdim.

79. Zollman, Joellyn. n.d. "What Were Shtetls? | My Jewish Learning." My Jewish Learning. Accessed February 16, 2020. https://www.myjewishlearning.com/article/shtetl-in-jewish-history-and-memory/.

Index

M

N

O

About the Author

Michael R Bien at the memorial wall in Biržai, June 2019.

Michael has been exploring his family genealogy since 2004 when he discovered his connection to Biržai Lithuania. Biržai became a focal point for him as he traced his relatives back five generations. He has dedicated many hours researching, letter writing, DNA testing, translating Yiddish and Russian documents to English, cold calling people, and trips to libraries to review microfiche.

He visited Biržai in 2019 as part of the memorial dedication. He spent time walking the streets of the shtetl, seeing the town and meeting people, and experiencing the community of his relatives. He delivered a lecture about the importance of education in Jewish life to the Biržai high school students and tour participants.

Michael is also a graduate of The Pennsylvania Status University with a Master of Engineering degree. He lives in Pennsylvania, USA with his wife and children.